WE'RE NOT WORTHY

WE'RE NOT WORTHY

JASON KLAMM

foreword by DAVID WAIN

COVER ILLUSTRATION: Adam Koford
LAYOUT: Arkadii Pankevich
ENDPAPER DESIGN/AUTHOR PHOTO: John Fig

Illustration credits appear in the back of the book.

LIBRARY OF CONGRESS CONTROL NUMBER: 2023934715

LC record available at https://lccn.loc.gov/2023934715

ISBNs: 9781948221269 (hardbound), 9781948221276 (ebook)

1984 Publishing logo is © and ™ of 1984 Publishing, LLC.

Printed and bound in PRC.

1984 PUBLISHING
Cleveland, Ohio / USA
1984Publishing.com
info@1984publishing.com

Contact the author at sketchcomedybook@stolendress.com

FIRST EDITION
9 8 7 6 5 4 3 2 1

For Lily, Katie and Kayden.

CONTENTS

FOREWORD

Growing up in Cleveland, Ohio in the '70s and '80s, I didn't drink or do drugs or have a lot of girlfriends, but I did watch a lot of movies and TV with my friends. And my heart always gravitated to (what I later learned was called) SKETCH COMEDY: *Saturday Night Live*, Steve Martin, *Monty Python*, Mel Brooks, *SCTV*, *The Muppet Show*, Carol Burnett. It was the time of the very first VCRs, so I watched this stuff over and over again, ingesting it into my bloodstream.

When I got to NYU in late '80s, I was lucky enough to meet ten other friends who were also turned on by this peculiar art form of sketch: the challenge of trying any idea and taking it as far as it can go, each self-contained piece having to establish a world, characters and a premise in a matter of seconds, while telling a complete story in a few minutes or (sometimes much) less.

This was a time when the genre was in a relatively fallow period on American TV. The most exciting non-narrative comedy was in the form of a talk show that was also at the same time spoofing the very idea of doing a talk show: *Late Night with David Letterman*. I loved his notion doing the thing while simultaneously commenting on it.

Our group at NYU started creating our own sketches. We grew as collaborators, learning—and influencing—each other's rhythms and tastes. Over the next few years, a lucky chain of events resulted in our troupe (now called The State) having our own show on MTV.

At the same time The State was forming, other (often overlapping) clusters of like-minded sketch fans were finding each other in New York, LA, Toronto, Chicago and elsewhere. All these groups experimented with different styles, together giving rise to the explosion of '90s sketch comedy TV shows that Jason Klamm has so lovingly chronicled in this book.

Some of these shows began as sketch groups who developed their voice on the live stage before moving to TV (*Kids in the Hall, The Bert Fershners, Upright Citizens Brigade, The State*); others were built around specific performers (Dana Carvey, Ben Stiller, Tracy Ullman, *Mr. Show*); or spoofed another TV genre (*Viva Variety, Not Necessarily the News*); while others made early attempts at diversifying the largely white genre (*In Living Color, House of Buggin', MADtv*) and went to head-to-head with *SNL*, which, arguably, remained the reigning king.

These shows were the launching pad for so many future stars, and they also set the stage for the next wave of TV sketch innovators like Lonely Island, *Little Britain*, Chapelle, *Comedy Bang! Bang!*, Tim Robinson, *Portlandia, Key & Peele*, and so many others.

Jason delves into the minds of the creators, writers, and performers who brought these iconic shows to life, giving us a window into how it all went down. Enjoy!

— *David Wain*

PROLOGUE

I wrote my first joke when I was eight. It was terribly inappropriate, if topical. I became obsessed with how jokes worked, and I soon discovered sketch comedy. Eventually, sketch would become one of my life's great passions. I produced a few sketch comedy albums, created sketch pilots for TV, and for over a decade, I hosted a podcast about comedy records called *Comedy on Vinyl*, as an excuse to talk about Weird Al and sketch comedy, even though most of my guests picked the same three albums to talk about over the course of it, and those were usually stand-up records.

Like a lot of comedians, I've rewritten my own history with comedy over and over again as I remember more and more things from my childhood. It has happened more in researching this book than at any other time in my life; every time I interviewed someone, I'd remember an earlier instance that broke my little comedy brain. My introduction to meta comedy was *The State*—scratch that, it was *In Living Color*—nope, it was actually *Mathnet*, a kids' show that taught you math by way of a *Dragnet* pastiche. This happened with this book's namesake, too: the movie *Wayne's World*.

"We're not worthy" was already a quote from the "Wayne's World" sketches on *SNL*, but in the 1993 movie, it happens after Wayne Campbell (Mike Myers) and Garth Algar (Dana Carvey) use their backstage passes to hang out with Alice Cooper and the band, post-concert. It is preceded by what remains one of my favorite scenes in any comedy film, in which Alice Cooper, playing himself, waxes historical on the city of Milwaukee, where the concert has just happened. His guitarist, Pete, tells Wayne and Garth about how it's the only major American city in history to have elected three socialist mayors. Eventually, the boys are invited to stay, and when the realization that they're suddenly being welcomed in dawns on them, they both kneel and bow in reverence, repeating the phrase, along with "We're scum! We suck!" Alice then invites them to kiss his ring.

I memorized this film as a kid. I can still quote a good chunk of the first twenty minutes or so of the film, because my best friends, Dan Gomiller, Mike Shaver and I would all watch the film on repeat; I wore out my VHS copy. This was partially to memorize it even more (if that's a thing), thinking my friends would be impressed, rather than concerned for me. *Wayne's World* defined a chunk of my childhood for this very silly reason, so it's natural that I'd rewritten my love of the "Wayne's World" sketches, too.

In my head, since my greatest childhood comedy idol was Phil Hartman, I was surely watching *Saturday Night Live* as early as I could remember, waiting impatiently for my favorite characters, Wayne and Garth, to make it to the big screen. Then I remembered something critical: My parents actually got our *Wayne's World* VHS from McDonald's. Yes, the eatery. It was, apparently, only $5.99 when one purchased any large sandwich, so they brought it home and— whether I had liked Wayne and Garth beforehand or not—I fell in love with what would end up being *Saturday Night Live's* biggest and most unrepeatable box office success. I know for sure I waited with bated breath for *Wayne's World 2* to arrive on pay-per-view later that same year, feeling the same way most of the other paying audiences had (not great).

Sometime later, on May 26, 2011, I was backstage—or what passed for one—at a bar in Los Angeles. Molly Malone's, a small place on Fairfax, had a great performance space set apart from the rest of the bar, where, on a typical night, you'd find musicians, or maybe a comedy podcast setting up to perform. Tonight, though, the audience was expecting *Wayne's World*, only there was no projector and there wouldn't be a Myers or a Carvey in sight. In fact, yours truly would be portraying Garth Algar and my friend Allen Rueckert would be playing Wayne Campbell.

Memorizing would not be an issue that night, as I felt I was born to re-play Wayne; in a show where both the audience and the cast are getting progressively drunker, it turns out you just keep the scripts in your hands anyway. This was "A Drinking Game," where we did a costumed stage reading of a different movie like this each month, and I was finally getting the chance to act out the film I'd seen more than any other.

By the end of the night, one very drunk, overly-kind person said to me, "if you closed your eyes, you'd swear it was Dana Carvey," and any potential bitterness over not being Wayne was out the window. The kindness kept coming for everyone in the group, all of them professional actors, except myself at the time. There were moments of taking it all in graciously, and other moments of pure heaven, living in the moment that I'd recreated one of my favorite films, and feeling as though I, myself, was not worthy of this praise or this bliss.

This is a very small, very specific, very self-centered example of what 1990s North American sketch comedy has meant to one person on this planet. The ripple that has been felt by comedians, comedy lovers and even casual audiences has never stopped. In nearly every show I got to research for this book, I found at least one name I was familiar with, whether it was a household name or not, and in most, there was a plethora of them. While I couldn't devote a single chapter to every one of these fifty-plus shows, that's an impressive hit rate. Others, of course, like *In Living Color*, *Mr. Show with Bob and David* and *The State* are so crammed with brilliant comedy performers that, today, you can't avoid the names who came out of those shows. Importantly, the number of influential comedians who watched these shows and are creating brilliant sketch now is also impressive.

Ironically, given the book's title, the one show I was least-tempted to write about was *Saturday Night Live*. It is the American Civil War of comedy: It's been written about so much that there's nothing, in terms of the show's history, that hasn't been covered to death. This is where the book's format comes in. It isn't an oral history, though that is where I begin to retell the history of many of these shows. When I interviewed these 150 people, I tried to find the seed of something new that would get me to the core of what that show was about. Sometimes, this was doing my best Nardwuar impression and throwing out some unusual fact from ancient news coverage of the interviewee; other times, it was a simple observation, but each time I got an untold story, or an angle I'd never heard before, it ended up here in this book.

As someone who grew up worshipping sketch comedy as the art form above all others, this book is telling the history of '90s sketch comedy through that lens. Approachable-seeming (read: often cheap-looking) sketch comedy in the '90s made many people my age want to make sketch ourselves. DIY sketch was nothing new, but the home video revolution led slowly and inevitably to the digital age, with seemingly endless self-publishing platforms at creators' fingers. It was a massive sea change, all at least somewhat predicated upon the idea that "anyone can make comedy."

On top of this, the actual comedy being produced on TV in the '90s was ground-breaking, if only because network TV was starting to loosen their grip when it came to censorship. This led, as it does, to the kind of experimentation that can cause both beautiful social satire at best, and screaming dreck at worst. Networks were also trying this new thing called hiring and casting people who look like the rest of the world, which by nature started to change what could be talked about on television, and just as importantly, who was talking about it. Sketch comedy had never been this diverse, this fast, and the impact that group of writers, actors and directors subsequently had on the TV and film world is unmatched, especially compared to the two prior decades in which *Saturday Night Live* was the strongest contender.

Famous names, cheap cameras and the burgeoning internet wouldn't combine to equal a sketch revolution all on their own, though. There's something about the tone and atmosphere of '90s sketch comedy that goes back to The Second City theater and its predecessor, The Compass, the latter of which was founded on the ideals of bringing theater to everyone, making it approachable, and sometimes involving the audience. You are supposed to feel like you're part of it. We can argue all day about the good and bad of everyone having a shot at the big time, but this approach is more about having a shot at the baseline of just getting to do it, with success and fame being at best a possibility. Truth be told, the existing studio pipeline was designed to shit out stuff that we then accept as the best the comedy world has to offer, *because it's on TV*. The internet has proven that idea to be false, and sketch shows have changed as a result.

What follows is the history of maybe the most prolific decade of sketch comedy yet. It just preceded widely-available high speed internet, and a precipitous drop in the number of sketch TV shows on the air. Drawing first from interviews, as well as press contemporaneous to these shows, these histories show the human side of making the best sketch shows of the era, which include some shows you may not have heard of.

Starting with the interviews is the reverse of how this thing is normally done, but since many of the shows I endeavored to cover have never been written about before, I felt it made the most sense to start from a single story, and work outward. As one does, I fact-checked dates and verifiable facts when they came up, but the core of these stories is about the experience, especially when that experience was funny.

Stories about dramatic tension behind the scenes of a comedy show, while sometimes interesting, don't make for funny overall.[1] Go watch *Studio 60 on the Sunset Strip* if you don't believe me. Here are several funny (and otherwise) stories about the making of funny shows filled with sketches, along with some facts that, I hope, aren't too boring or old. Also, if you're hardcore about someone saying *sketch* and never *skit*, like I used to be, take note: Many of the big comedy names I interviewed used those two words interchangeably. We'll all be fine.

— *Jason Klamm*

---

[1] An alternative name for *Hee Haw*, if I recall correctly.

Friday Night Frolic:
The Birth of Sketch Comedy on TV

The first fully-formed sketch show on TV wasn't. Fully formed, that is. No TV show was entirely populated by comedy sketches in those days. What you had instead—and what still puts butts in seats today—was variety. Where now you might find a big or up-and-coming pop music group thrown in with your sketch, in the '40s and '50s you'd get a mix of acts designed to meet the general public palate. Some music, dance, sketch, and uncategorizable light entertainments such as plate spinners were all the basics you needed for a variety show then, and in the earliest days of television, there was no need to change that.

By the late '40s, when American TV was just starting to take shape, vaudeville was just a style of entertainment. You couldn't go see a vaudeville show in 1947, but you could see vaudeville acts and vaudeville-inspired performers and performances, only they were doing their comedy either in clubs or, in some cases, Broadway revues. These took many different formats, but they were primarily a mix of sketches and music, often featuring writers and performers who would eventually go on to take over Broadway, television and movies. *New Faces of 1952*, for example, is a rollicking revue featuring Eartha Kitt, Paul Lynde, and a young Melvin Brooks (the soundtrack is an album worth listening to for the history alone).

In early 1948, The National Broadcasting Company and the short-lived DuMont Network—rival networks, it's worth noting—announced that they would be collaborating, both premiering the same program, called *Friday Night Frolic*, on January 28th. Described in the *New York Daily News* as "The first full scale Broadway-type musical revue on television," *Friday Night Frolic* was to be fronted by Sid Caesar, along with his eventual *Your Show of Shows* counterpart, Imogene Coca. By the night that it aired it would have a new title, *The Admiral Broadway Revue* (sponsored by Admiral, a TV manufacturer), and would include the tried-and-true combination of Broadway-style dances, songs and sketches—the kind of stuff you could usually only get if you lived in a big metropolitan area.

Finally, television was bringing popular entertainment back to the populace, and the fewer than a million people who owned a TV at the time were spared the $7 admission fee. All they had to do for that deal was spend the equivalent of $6,200 in 2023 money to do it (TVs were expensive). By the early '50s, TV prices would drop because the cost of the technology went down, although too late for Admiral. The demand for TV sets as a result of the viewership of *Broadway Revue* was purportedly so high, that Admiral had to eventually cancel the show after only nineteen episodes, spending their money instead on manufacturing more televisions.

The premiere episode of *The Admiral Broadway Revue* is a whirlwind, as far as shows of the day were concerned. It's hard to cast your mind back to a time before everything you're used to was even conceived of, but if you just imagine that all you'd ever had was radio and suddenly—BAM—here comes a movie in your living room, your head would probably have been spinning. Sid Caesar's opening monologue, "A Date in Manhattan," is a period piece, such as it is, set in 1939, when things were just so much cheaper and simpler. It's unapologetically urban, but more importantly, it's *metropolitan*. He makes it relatable and weird and fast, spouting vocal sound effects like a proto-Michael Winslow. Caesar burns through what a date was like in 1939, singing a short song with the chorus, "I've got five dollars and it's burnin' a hole in my pocket!" Cheesecake costs ten cents in 1939, but *now* in 1949, it's a damn dollar, and the waiter is always French because Sid needs you to hear him do an accent.

As Caesar told it, he grew up around every possible accent and dialect in his parents' restaurant, and he learned to mimic them, often to the patrons' faces. He was an accent nerd, in today's parlance, and it paid off huge. His gibberish versions of any and all languages were impressionistic—giving us a touch of something familiar, yet not, at the same time.

As the series continued, the country would be treated to sketches much like what you'd find in that loaded first episode, like "Nonentities in the News," where normies (in this case, actors playing them) get interviewed "on the street," something that would become a staple of late-night shows later on; a sketch about a Tarzan-like character; and maybe the standout sketch of the whole thing, where Imogene Coca performs a huge ballet spoof that starts with her emerging from the water, and spitting that water all over the stage. The lack of composure with which she imbues her characters is a thing to behold.

One of the more fascinating parts of watching this seemingly barebones production (despite its $15,000/episode budget, or around $185,000/per in 2023 money) is seeing sketch comedy on video shot fairly statically. The cameras this early in the TV industry were heavy and not built for a lot of (if any) movement. Some of the sketches just play like something Sid Caesar might try out at a friend's party for laughs, like the bits Carl Reiner and Mel Brooks did that eventually evolved into their "The 2000-Year-Old Man" routine. Static shots or not, Caesar's movie parody (in episode one, performed as a monologue) would end up evolving into one of the more memorable features of the follow up to *The Admiral Broadway Revue,* entitled *Your Show of Shows.*

Your Show of Shows

A year after the Admiral show premiered, NBC debuted *Your Show of Shows*, again starring Sid Caesar, Imogene Coca, and a supporting cast made up of Carl Reiner, Howard Morris, and James Starbuck. The show would end up as the standard-bearer for TV variety and sketch comedy for decades. Sid Caesar had started, like many of his contemporaries, performing comedy at resorts in the Catskills. His live show's producer, Max Liebman, decided to move into television after realizing that a wholly-new, live stage show each Saturday night up in the mountains was probably good training for a live television show.

Your Show of Shows was, of course, known for its variety players, too—not just the comics. Some of the singers and dancers, for instance, might put on a single-scene song and dance number. These could reasonably be called "sketches," in the sense of a brief scene, just not in the way a comedy dork today might think about it. Many of these performers would get in on the sketch action, too, like singer Bill Hayes.

"When you learn a new song and staging, memorize it in a day or two—it's a challenge," Hayes recalls. He emphasizes that live TV meant *live TV* and that there was no messing about—timing was everything, in every sense of the word. No one was improvising, or ad-libbing, as they'd have called it then. Making sure I understand the discipline this took, Hayes reminds me, "All the sketches were memorized to the second."

If things didn't go according to that plan—if you went over time, for instance—they cut right to commercial, mid-stream. "We were under orders from NBC to stop the show at precisely 10:29," Hayes says. "One time we had a very, internationally famous violinist, he was scheduled to go last. We learned the hard way not to put a guest star at the end." Of course, the violinist kept playing, until someone ran up to him to explain that he was no longer on the air.

For such a brief run on TV, a huge number of influential names would end up coming out of *Your Show of Shows*, though not some of the names you may have heard. Carl Reiner, Mel Brooks, and Neil Simon are perhaps the most famous names of the group. Not included in this group are two other names often associated wrongly with *Your Show of Shows*; Larry Gelbart worked on *The Sid Caesar Show* and *Caesar's Hour*, while Woody Allen worked only on the former. *Your Show of Shows* brought vaudeville into our living rooms, just in time for it to have a slow death.

Laugh-In

In 1967, Peter Bergman (eventually of comedy troupe The Firesign Theatre) invented the love-in, where hippies got together to practice peace and love in Elysian Park in Los Angeles, inspiring innumerable imitators. The following year, two veteran club comics, Dan Rowan and Dick Martin, starred in *Rowan and Martin's Laugh-In*, signaling perhaps the fastest selling-out of counterculture ideals in the history of The United States.

The first episode opens with a mock protest and some near-psychedelia, before reminding us that two guys in tuxedoes are the hosts of this show. "A Laugh-In is a frame of mind," Dan Rowan tells the audience, adding that the point of the show is to enjoy some laughs to "forget about the other ins." Rowan explains the concept of flower power to co-host Dick Martin, who plays the goofball who doesn't quite get it, in their team-up. They aren't exactly square, in the parlance of their day, but they are still nowhere near the hippies you might expect to host it.

Created by former aspiring actor George Schlatter, *Laugh-In* was the result of a tiny attention span, according to Schlatter himself. "*Laugh-In* was an accident," Schlatter says. "It was my own minimal attention span. And I wanted to do a show that was just about jokes." NBC was last in the ratings after *Gunsmoke* and *The Lucy Show*, so Schlatter proposed something wildly different; rapid-fire, joke-after-joke comedy. "NBC saw it and they said, 'We can't air that, it doesn't make sense.' And I said, 'Well, we ran it for kids and they understood it, and they're brighter than you are.'" Schlatter then came up with the idea of having two square-seeming hosts who could be middle-of-the-road enough to appeal to everyone.

Laugh-In is memorable just as much for its frenetic energy as it is its catchphrase, "sock it to me" (most notably spoken by that nutjob peacenik, Richard Nixon). Sketches might sometimes just be a gathering of people in costume, as set up for a "character" to break a fourth wall and throw a one-liner to the camera, usually set in a cocktail party. Sometimes there were sudden cutaways to side characters like Arte Johnson's Wolfgang, often referred to as a "German soldier," (though he's clearly a Nazi) who looks into the camera to say the line "very interesting," often with some playful (for a Nazi) twist on it.

A lot of the relatively story-light, on-location pieces and the interstitials feel like *Python*'s would later on, in aesthetics alone. The show plays with editing a lot, hence the fast pace and lack of focus, in some ways also kinda-sorta proto-MTV—clearly geared toward bringing in a younger audience. It's the kind of non sequitur stuff kids ten years ago might have called "random."

It may be Rowan and Martin's show, but the standouts are the character performers, perhaps best exemplified by Ruth Buzzi. Her commitment to a character in the pilot who has been set up with Dick Martin on a date, and then beautifully brings the house down with a song about birds is the stand-out piece in the pilot. If you're all about jokes per minute, *Laugh-In* still reigns supreme, possibly because of its unusual editing process. "The editing that we had done on *Laugh-In* was a new technique," Schlatter says. "We would shoot it on videotape, transfer the videotape to film, which had edge numbers, and we would edit the film, and then spliced the videotape to match what we had done on film."

You can't call *Laugh-In* daring, as much as you can groundbreaking, in terms of visuals, editing and the fact that it cast more women and people of color than was typical at the time. The show featured folks like Lily Tomlin and Flip Wilson, as well as future movie stars like Goldie Hawn, who was a dancer at the time, and whose screwing up of her test lines endeared her to Schlatter. The show was also staffed by writers like future *SNL* creator Lorne Michaels and his comedy partner, Hart Pomerantz. *Laugh-In* had a huge impact on pop culture, which continued on through *Saturday Night Live.* Even with a not-so-stellar diversity ratio, and certainly not ideal parts (many of the women were only hired as dancers), it was a step in the right direction. The show would end up running for six seasons, with an attempted revival in 1977 that ran only six episodes, and which counts among its one notable star a young Robin Williams.

Hee Haw

Middle America has a history of being talked down to, but by 1969, it was time to do that to the south. As he tells the story, eventual kingmaker producer Bernie Brillstein looked on his desk at 3 AM one morning and noticed scripts for a bunch of country-fried sitcoms of the time like *Green Acres* and *Beverly Hillbillies,* and a script for *Laugh-In.* He claims he'd been told several times that "a frog can't host a show," every time he tried to sell a prime-time show for *The Muppets,* so he was desperate to sell something. He then asked his wife what sound a donkey makes, and history was, more or less, born.

Hee Haw (set in the thankfully fictional Kornfield Kounty) is decidedly more musical of a show than *Laugh-In,* cutting either to full musical numbers by country stars of the day or to Roy Clark and Buck Owens quite literally picking and grinning, telling jokes between strums. At first, *Hee Haw* looks like it wants to have *Laugh-In's* frenetic pace, but instead it's clear they're filling out the gaps between music and jokes, with literal footage of people laughing at nothing.

Sometimes they cut to the cornfield and people hop out of it, telling jokes to one another, a segment modeled right after *Laugh-In*'s joke wall, a psychedelic panel of windows where the same thing happens, only with hipper music. *Hee Haw* technically lasted through the early '90s, making it the only hold-out of the vaudeville-style variety show with any staying power past the '70s.

The Carol Burnett Show

There was, perhaps, no show in the '60s and '70s that embodied the spirit of pop culture parody and pastiche more than *The Carol Burnett Show*. Carol Burnett grew up loving films, so it was natural she'd want to put herself inside some of her favorites, with a comic twist.

"When I was a little girl, my grandmother and I used to save our pennies, and go see movies," Burnett says. "I'm with my best friend in the neighborhood. After we'd see a movie, we go back to our neighborhood, and act out what we saw. So that's how I learned to do the Tarzan yell, and stuff like that." It was a natural progression for her and, after high school, she joined the relatively new group The Stumptown Players. This was her first foray into sketch comedy, putting on shows written by the resident Stumptown writers.

"I was the baby. The rest of them were all graduate students, and I was a freshman. When they asked me to come and be a part of that group, I felt like I'd won an Oscar." It wasn't just a group that put on revues; this was an entertainment boot camp. "We worked very hard. We not only performed, but we made costumes, we built the scenery. I had to learn all of that." Do-it-yourself theater has been around forever, and that homemade aesthetic still shows up in shows today—often on purpose.

It wouldn't be long before Burnett's hard work paid off, and she found herself playing the new girlfriend of Buddy Hackett's lead role in the short-lived sitcom *Stanley*. Even before the show was canceled, though, she was working on a nightclub act and preparing to appear on TV's biggest program, *The Ed Sullivan Show*. That appearance, in which she sang a comic love song satirically aimed at then Secretary of State John Foster Dulles (purportedly the human equivalent of a wet paper bag) put her on the map, even if it took another decade before she'd find herself pretending to be movie stars again.

"When I got my show, I could really be Betty Grable, I could be Rita Hayworth. I'd have a wig and lighting, costumes and everything. So I was in heaven." Parody, especially in the hands of her contemporaries like Stan Freberg (noted despiser and parodist of rock n' roll music) could lean toward the outright mean-spirited, so when *The Carol Burnett Show* did a send up of a movie, it was usually out of pure love. "I'd say, can we do a take-off on *Mildred Pierce*? [The writers] would watch the movie, but I didn't have to. I knew it so well."

When she parodied *Mildred Pierce*, a Joan Crawford black-and-white noir film told mostly in flashback, it became *Mildred Fierce*. It looked good (even though Burnett made her version in color) and took its time to pull jokes out of a well-known film of the day. "Joan Crawford called me and she was funny, she said, 'I loved it. You gave it more effing production than Jack Warner.'" This—only a week after she'd performed her most iconic take on an icon, wearing a curtain and curtain rod in a *Gone with the Wind* parody entitled "Went with the Wind." *The Carol Burnett Show* lasted eleven seasons, with a pretty regular core cast of Vicki Lawrence, Harvey Korman, and Tim Conway.

The Smothers Brothers Comedy Hour

Just as the revolution was about to be televised, the Smothers Brothers were canceled. Brothers Tommy and Dick Smothers had respectively played the buffoon and the straight man for years, but when the time came to speak their minds with their new platform, they pushed the limits of what could be said on television, including bringing on performers like Pete Seeger, who had been blacklisted from the airwaves for being a communist, and David Steinberg, whose satirical religious sermons were a definite source of controversy for a sketch show ever teetering on the edge of cancellation.

While Steinberg believes you can blame him for the cancellation, it was a slow burn. The show started out as a lightly-subversive variety show in 1967, in the thick of The Vietnam War. The light subversiveness quickly made its way from subtext to text, though, the show employing some ham-handedness to reach its core audience strictly for satirical purposes. Subtle satire disguises itself too easily as pap, so they pulled out the big comedy guns, hitting targets like LBJ, the war, gun rights and pot.

This was no small accomplishment, either. There were only three networks on TV at the time, and CBS, home of *The Smothers Brothers Comedy Hour*, brought down the censorship hammer consistently, especially if the targets of satire were too close to home. During the Nixon years, especially, CBS was particularly worried about rumors that the Nixon administration not only could, but was seriously interested in, taking away CBS's broadcast license. Tommy, the more left-leaning of the two brothers in real life, was the one taking the censorship most to heart, and the one hitting back most frequently.

The fact that the show lasted as long as it did seems surprising, though Saul Ilson, co-head writer of *The Smothers Brothers Comedy Hour*, points out that rather than pulling viewers from ratings behemoth *Bonanza*, *The Smothers Brothers* stayed above water in an unexpected way. "We built our own audience of the college kids, and a younger audience, the audience that the advertisers really liked." Ilson had been traveling back and forth between Hollywood and his native Canada to write variety shows for years before *The Smothers Brothers* came along. It started out as your typical variety show, but that changed through the influence of shows like the satirical news program *That Was the Week That Was,* Tommy Smothers' desire to say something with comedy, and the mere fact that the times were changing. "We just thought the subject matters were contemporary. There were things we could talk about. We'd talk a little bit about the Vietnam War. But the truth of the matter is, it just started to grow, and it became the style of our show. And at that time, nobody was doing it."

One of the big reasons people weren't talking about this stuff on comedy programs—other than the idea that comedy should always be light and fluffy—is that no one wanted to be on President Johnson's bad side. "We had Jim Backus playing President Johnson, and we had Nanette Fabray playing Lady Bird," Ilson recalls. "The premise of the sketch is that the President of the United States discovered that the Russians were ten years ahead of us in barbecue sauce. So he called a cabinet meeting and he went crazy." The real-life Johnson kids were purported *Smothers Brothers* fans, and told daddy what they'd seen on TV that night. Johnson then called up William Paley, the president of CBS, and told him, "Get those son-of-a-bitches off my back!"

In the middle of the show's run, Richard Nixon became president, which became its own source of frustration. Soon enough, staff of the *Smothers Brothers* show were on Nixon's Enemies List, alongside such noble cohorts as Paul Newman and DJ Norman Wain (father to David Wain of *The State*). Still, they continued to make the kind of comedy the younger generation wanted, though to do it they often had to sneak things by the censors. "Sometimes when we wrote a script, we put in a red herring," Ilson says. "I remember once we put in a joke in a sketch where Dickie says to Tommy, 'You know, Tommy, I just discovered something that you're not going to believe . . . Ronald Reagan is a known heterosexual.'" The censors immediately said it couldn't go on air, so after a feigned fight, the writers got their actual desired joke in the show. Tommy's back and forth with the censors was a game that he would end up losing, in the long run, despite playing games with his own staff during the regular operation of the show.

Lorenzo Music, eventually best known as the voice of Carlton the Doorman on the sitcom *Rhoda*, and later the voice of *Garfield*, was a writer on *The Smothers Brothers Comedy Hour*. When his contract option was up to be renewed, Tommy invited the whole family to his house, around Christmastime. "My parents were visiting," remembers his wife, Henrietta. "I had to bring my parents and my newborn baby to this house, where a whole bunch of single guys and Tommy were hanging around on a Sunday, drinking and shooting pool." Tommy invited Lorenzo to go play a game. They were away for a while, and when they returned, it was quite clear that Lorenzo had won.

"He came out and we made nice for a minute and he said, 'I think maybe we should go.' Later on, he told me that what it had really come down to was that if he could beat Tommy at pool, Tommy would renew his contract." What Henrietta describes as a "miracle," may be indicative of the kind of mind CBS was up against. This could also explain why, against all odds, it took CBS so long to nail *Comedy Hour* on a technicality of a late-delivered episode, and cancel them, even with that unaired episode in the can.

The Smothers Brothers would eventually sue CBS over breach of contract, since everyone agreed that any first amendment claim would cause the case to be thrown out (individually, we have freedom of speech, but if we're on someone's platform, the owner of that platform doesn't have to grant us any such freedom). It made more sense to win publicly against this media behemoth. After eight weeks, Tom and Dick Smothers won their case.

In the end, *The Smothers Brothers Comedy Hour* stands as a case-study of what censorship *almost* is, and certainly might have been behind the scenes, given the pressure placed on executives from the highest office in the land. Being canceled, winning their case, and being remembered for political commentary made way for even more satire to not only have a place on national TV, but for it to finally have some teeth.

Monty Python's Flying Circus

While this book's subject matter means I can do no more than flirt with British TV sketch comedy, we are talking about the '90s, the first decade when kids who were first exposed to *Monty Python's Flying Circus* (some of them in real time, if they lived in Canada, or near the border) were making their own TV sketch programs. While the word *irreverence* gets thrown around a lot in reference to sketch comedy, *Python* did bring a form of irreverence to North American TVs that we just weren't used to. They were inspired by The Goons (the best-known members this side of the pond being Peter Sellers and maybe Spike Milligan), and, in kind, they inspired a bunch of young comedy-lovers to laugh at British references they couldn't begin to get.

You can't underestimate the fact that *Monty Python's Flying Circus*, while cutting-edge in terms of satire in the UK, over here really just looked like a bunch of English guys pretending to be much-too-English. The accents, the voices, the childlike energy and all the literary and historical references you could one day bother to actually look up all combined to make an entire generation re-think what they knew about comedy. It confused us into liking it.

Exposure on PBS led to an increase in popularity for the group, after two hellish, laughless appearances on *The Tonight Show* and *The Midnight Special*. Eventually, the group starting touring, making more movies, and, in some cases, appearing on *Saturday Night Live*. Eric Idle would eventually give his Beatles parody group, The Rutles, their US premiere on *SNL* in its third season.

Monty Python's influence over future American comedians is almost unrivaled, perhaps mostly due to its sheer disregard to the sketch form, or at least its ability to play with the idea of disregarding the sketch form. The idea of one sketch flowing into another, or being interrupted and not having a "proper ending" wasn't exactly new, but it was unconventional in 1969, when the show premiered. Give a comedian rules and they'll try to flout them (they're mostly contrarians); give a comedian a complete lack of rules, on the other hand, and suddenly they'll try to figure out how every element of this golden anarchy actually works.

Second City Television

In 1973, Bernie Sahlins brought The Second City theater company to Toronto. It is no overstatement to say that the cast this location attracted (many of whom also made up a huge portion of the first Toronto production of *Godspell,* along with Victor Garber and Paul Shaffer) would, along with the cast of *The National Lampoon Radio Hour*, end up changing the face of comedy, through *Saturday Night Live* and an absolute takeover of early-'80s comedy cinema. Along with Gilda Radner and John Candy, you'd find the likes of Dan Aykroyd, Andrea Martin, Eugene Levy, Joe Flaherty, and Brian Doyle-Murray at Second City Toronto. Eventually, Catherine O'Hara and Martin Short would join the group.

Dave Thomas (who joined *Godspell* a year in, when much of the original cast had moved on) was spending his time working in advertising while his friends were all performing at Second City Toronto. "Eugene calls me and he says, 'There's a cast change in Second City. They're opening a show in Pasadena. If you can get down here right away, and audition, you might get in.'" Thomas flew to Pasadena to give his dream a shot, and for the next two years, he was in the cast of Second City Toronto. This meant that he would be there when discussions started happening about how to bring Second City—the cast and the name—to television.

"They decided to do *SCTV* because Lorne (Michaels) had come up in 1975 and started pilfering cast from Second City for *SNL*." The now-legendary first cast of *Saturday Night Live* was loaded with Second City people from both the Toronto (Gilda Radner and Dan Aykroyd) and Chicago (John Belushi) chapters. The gap was noticeable, but it was time to make something bigger happen. Bernie Sahlins, who had co-founded the original Second City with Paul Sills and Howard Alk in 1959, was spearheading the whole idea.

"It seemed like a stupid idea to some of us," Thomas recalls. "'There already is a sketch comedy show on and it's really successful.'" Competition, so they felt, would be impossible without the money to make it happen. When it did—seemingly against the odds— start production, *Second City Television* began with a budget of CA$7,000 (CA$35,000 in 2023), or about a tenth of what your typical sketch pilot costs. They would bring in Harold Ramis as head writer, and they settled on the idea that their sketch show was set in a low-end TV station in the fictional town of Melonville. "Harold rightly assumed that the charm of this little station is its cheapness." When you know you're going to see the DIY seams, you might as well make them a part of the show.

Many of the cast wanted better props and makeup and sets, but making do with what they had gave the show a specific charm. It's the kind of charm that makes the performances really stand out. You can't hide beneath a sheen that isn't there. The show would go on to create late-night horror movie host Count Floyd (Flaherty), red-headed sexpot comedian Dusty Towne (O'Hara), The Shmenge Brothers (Candy and Levy), Bob and Doug McKenzie (Rick Moranis and Dave Thomas), Ed Grimley (Martin Short), and the very horny station manager, Edith Prickley (Andrea Martin), to name only a few. They were only on in forty-eight markets, but they had a show.

After two seasons, the show was on the ropes, when financing dropped out, and the cast scattered to the wind, mostly to LA, auditioning on the cachet *SCTV* had provided them. When the show was about to come back, the producers were desperate, offering up producer titles to everyone involved to entice them to return. They even offered to shoot Eugene Levy and Andrea Martin's bits for season three all in one chunk so they could go right back to auditioning in LA. They were now shooting in Edmonton, thousands of miles away from Toronto, to complicate things further. As it happened, though, Brandon Tartikoff at NBC decided to air *SCTV* on some NBC affiliates, bumping their number of markets to nearly 400. Now people could really see them, finding them on the same network as *Saturday Night Live*.

The money didn't exactly pour in, but they *did* have some. The props, sets, hair and makeup began to look better. This was also when Bob and Doug McKenzie would be created as a middle finger to CanCon (Canadian Content regulations), which required that a certain percentage of material of all programs be explicitly Canadian. The two caricature Canadians ended up being the most well-known characters in the show's run and the only ones to get their own movie, *Strange Brew* (as well as the comedy album *The Great White North*, a perfect piece of meta-comedy album art).

The show ended after eight seasons, in 1984. Through that time, it went from Canadian broadcast TV, to Canadian and US broadcast TV, to cable, and from thirty minutes long, to ninety minutes, then down to forty-five. For such a mess of a production, the characters, the setting and the show's aesthetic undoubtedly influenced the '90s sketch comedians who favored strong, memorable performances over that more easily-sold sheen.

The Richard Pryor Show

"They will free my mother if the show is good," Richard Pryor deadpanned to a reporter in 1977. "She's currently down in the basement at NBC." The journalist was attempting to interview Richard and his producer, Burt Sugarman, about *The Richard Pryor Special?*, a prototype for what would become one of the best-loved, if short-lived, sketch series of the twentieth century.

The special originally opened with Pryor saying he wouldn't have to compromise to appear on network TV, and that "I've given up absolutely nothing," only to have the camera to pull out to reveal he now has a Ken doll's lack of genitalia. The network nixed this idea, so the as-aired show opens on a slave ship, the slave driver played by a growling John Belushi, brandishing a whip and looking for a slave for a particular job. One slave jumps ship, so Belushi settles onto Pryor. "You're going to NBC! You're going to do your own special!" Belushi yells. Pryor objects, but it's too late: He's on his way to prime time. The rest of the show is framed around Pryor, backstage, running into characters as he simply tries to get to his show.

The first full sketch of the show is Pryor as a sequined televangelist who needs to get "that white people money" and does so by announcing that the day's donations will go to the Back to Africa Fund. Suddenly, every phone in the place rings. "Works every time," he says with pride. A few sketches later, we're met with a visualized version of Langston Hughes' "Harlem Sweeties," featuring black women of varying skin tones, ending with the simple, elegant statement: "We're all beautiful." It's a comedy special with an agenda of humanizing people who didn't frequently get to TV's center stage, and doing it in as many ways as possible. The show takes some comedic risks for a variety show, acknowledging its audacity near the end, when Pryor is approached by two kids.

They ask if there's anything for kids in the show, to which he tells them there will be "clowns, seltzer bottles, pies in the face . . ." Nothing he suggests satisfies them. One of them speaks up and says "You have a unique vehicle, Mr. Pryor, and we think you should use it as a forum for meaningful expression." After a children's musical piece about how history ignores people of color and a sketch about his fictional militant writers' room, it still ends with him getting a pie in the face.

The special did well enough that it spawned a sketch show later that year, which walks the same line and toys with longer-than-typical sketches. It's arguable that *The Richard Pryor Show* does more with its time than many other shows of the era. In its unconscionably short run of only four episodes, it manages to use sketch to say things that, in other shows, might amount to a throwaway joke or a cheesy platitude.

With an absolutely loaded cast featuring Pryor, Paul Mooney, Marsha Warfield, Tim Reid, Edie McClurg, John Witherspoon, and even Robin Williams, this show deserved more, though we're lucky to have what we have. It's a solid mix of concept/single joke pieces and heavily pointed satire. On one hand, Pryor plays a gunslinger who can't get his gun out of his holster, showing the world what a brilliant physical comedian he was. On the other hand, there's his sketch about playing the country's first black president at a press briefing. He plays the politics game as well as anyone before him, delivering perfect bullshit answers that imply he knows what he's talking about—for instance calling the neutron bomb "a neo-pacifist weapon." As the black journalists from Jet (Warfield) and Ebony (Reid) get more straightforward answers about increasing black visibility in the FBI and in football, his honesty starts to come through. The next journalist to introduce himself gets met with a "Yeah, what?" from Pryor's fortieth president, who then shortly tells him to "sit down." When asked if he'll continue dating a lot of white women, he responds, "As long as I can keep it up!"

Stand-up Marsha Warfield was cast after knowing Pryor from the comedy clubs. She stood out by being funny, and the only comic not to beg for a spot before Pryor, to avoid being a perceived let-down to the audience. She co-stars with Pryor in of the best-known sketches from the show, a silent comedy piece where the two of them are sat at two tables opposite one another in a restaurant. "There was no script," Warfield says. "It said 'Richard and a beautiful woman sit across from each other in a restaurant and seduce each other with food.'" Warfield had no previous sketch experience at all. To make things more difficult, there was no rehearsal. "Richard got married that morning and didn't tell anyone." Props placed plates of all manner of suggestive and not-so-suggestive food in front of each of them, and they rolled cameras.

"I had never considered myself beautiful. I had never done a sketch, no improv, nothing. So I had no idea what the heck I was going to do. And they said 'Okay, you're first.' I said, 'Fi- what?'" The two proceed to sexily eat some non-sexy food in a beautiful piece of silent comedy that crescendos in a make-out session on the floor of the restaurant that is ended by a water hose from the back of the house. "We did one take and one pick-up." That first take included one other piece that didn't make it to air: when Warfield decided to butter her cob of corn, but with her hand.

Pryor would later say that *The Richard Pryor* show was only intended to be four episodes long, while journalistic accounts from the time variously attributed this short run to cancelation, a mutual decision, and dwindling public interest. His show was, after all, programmed into NBC's "family hour," with some claiming that his challenging material was too much for that slot. Pryor's own attitude about the whole thing couldn't have helped, as Warfield saw it. "ABC had taken over the top spot in the network race . . . Richard's show was on NBC. When I saw him in the hallway [on that first day], he had on an 'ABC: We're Number One' t shirt. And I said, 'This is not going to go according to script.'"

The show did finish in the bottom ten of the Nielsen ratings that fourth week, and on the following one it was—for whatever reason— no longer on the air. One reporter, Mike Hughes, of the *Lansing State*

Journal, then pointed out that there were "only three variety shows left" in TV, wondering "what killed variety shows?" He posited an explanation that implicated the variety of pop music on TV, more competition from sitcoms, and "stupidity," which amounted to uneven sketches in shows like Pryor's. Oh, Mike. Uneven sketches are part of the deal.

Not the '80s

You'll notice in this preamble to the '90s that there's very little sketch listed that crosses over into the '80s. This is partially because a few of the shows covered in this book actually did start in the '80s and others, like *Fridays* and *The Smothers Brothers* revival, were important historically, but don't have any overall impact on the '90s, at least in the same way the '70s did. This is strictly mathematical, of course, and based on the fact that the only people I spoke with who brought up *Fridays* were people who had worked on it. The reason *The Muppet Show* isn't included is because I would've just written about that. It's too big of a show, and puppetry encompasses a totally different art form than simply acting in your own body.

In the following discussions of important, or at least interesting, sketch shows, there were inevitable discussions of the many improv and sketch theater companies that formed a pipeline straight to the big time (usually *Saturday Night Live*). This book also covers those groups, since without groups like iO, The Groundlings, and The Second City, not only would we never have had many of the *SNL* casts we've grown to love, but the '80s wouldn't have been the decade of comedy it was. Also, Canada. Canada did a lot of that.

As timeless as some comedy can be—even the right historical piece, if you have the context, can be brilliant—there's always going to be stuff that doesn't hold up. I'm talking about everything from minor problems like dated references, to everything else—rape jokes, gay jokes, misogyny, transphobia, black face, brown face, Asian face—you name it, most shows have done it. It's the kind of stuff people are often quick to explain away by saying "it was a different time!" That's code for "there were fewer penalties then because fewer of the people affected had any power to say or do anything about it." I don't address a lot of this stuff directly, but not because I think we should get over it—it's all worth learning from—it's just that in most cases you won't be surprised to find it, so I'd rather discuss the stuff that I don't hate. I just won't explain it away; it's okay to say this stuff was always bad.

Another note: improv. Yes, I include a few improv shows in this history because they were a relatively new concept—for TV anyway—just toward the end of the '90s. And although sketch and improv are decidedly different art forms, they are means to the same end: (usually) short, (usually) comedic scenes. Some schools may focus on improv, but everyone is trying to get to a similar place.

Of course, before you had specialized schools teaching improv, or comedy (seriously, this is a very new concept), you had vaudeville, then The Catskills. It was a lot of "experience teaching experience," people picking up the rules of comedy and learning them through osmosis. In terms of TV, we'd all be a lot worse off if Imogene Coca and Sid Caesar had never learned their craft on the stage and then agreed to do *Friday Night Frolic.*

2
Stupid Human Tricks:
Late Night with David Letterman

I n 1996, HBO premiered an original TV movie co-starring Kathy Bates, John Michael Higgins and Daniel Roebuck called *The Late Shift*, a fictionalized account of the behind-the-scenes events that led to David Letterman leaving NBC for CBS, and Jay Leno getting to host *The Tonight Show*. Now, a screenwriter's job is to set the scene, and give you little tastes of the world the characters inhabit, for the sake of context. Naturally, at some point, the screenwriter, George Armitage, had to pick something from *Late Night with David Letterman* to showcase the kind of humor that Dave, et al., were known for.

"I was like, 'this is the bit that they picked?'" *Late Night* writer Joe Furey recalls. The sketch is simple: *Late* Night band leader Paul Shaffer has the hiccups, and Dave tries to cure them in various funny ways. "The one I wrote," Furey says, "was he takes a paper bag and puts it over Paul's head . . . and then he takes out a baseball bat and smashes an obvious dummy. I was thrilled that that was what ended up being the one *Letterman* thing they used in that stupid movie." I think I'm safe in assuming this is the one bit of joy that movie brought to anyone who staffed on *Late Night with David Letterman* throughout its eleven-year run.

Starting a book on sketch comedy with Letterman's *Late Night* might seem like a stretch. That is, until you see how reality and written pieces blended so seamlessly that it would be easy to think of it as "another late-night show," when that blending is what makes it the first in a new era of late night. It wasn't always going to be at night, though; in fact, Letterman experimented with the form in his first NBC show, as well.

The David Letterman Show, Letterman's morning program, ran for four months in 1980. It was Dave, being charming with the audience, and actors like Edie McClurg doing bits on stage where they pretended to be behind-the-scenes workers on the program. When *Late Night* premiered in 1982, though, the format was not only less strict, but it buzzed with the energy of "no one's watching, let's wreck some shit." That wrecking, like the light McClurgy bits from the first show, often took the form of sketches, many of which were performed to an often dumbfounded audience. The result was sketch merged with performance art, and it was hard to look away.

The whole of *Late Night with Letterman* may in fact have been performance art. It is frequently talked about as an anti-talk-show, a sandbox where Letterman and his writers could try stuff out because it was late at night and didn't cost that much to produce. The stories of Andy Kaufman's co-interview with his wrestling nemesis Jerry Lawler is the stuff of comedy legend, now, even if the precise amount of planning that went into their seemingly impromptu fight on Dave's stage remains unknown. The line between comedy bit and reality was so blurred, in fact, that writer Joe Furey almost never worked for *Late Night* because of it.

"I was in college and I was living in my sister's apartment," Furey explains. "And my sister had just had a baby and was staying up really late watching *Letterman* and stuff. She said to me one day, 'Hey, you know, last night Dave announced they needed an intern for the show.'" Furey's sister advised him to call up the number that had popped up on the screen that night.

"'They already have somebody. He's just doing it as a joke,'" Furey recalls telling his sister. Mother and sister instincts combined, and she called the *Letterman* offices up for him. A woman named Kathy Michalcik answered.

"Oh, yeah, can you come down today?" Kathy asked. Furey then headed down to 30 Rockefeller Plaza, spoke with the team, and was offered the internship pretty much on the spot, probably because no one else believed it was real, either. Furey's college, SUNY Purchase, didn't care if it was real or not. He needed the credit from his school to keep the internship, but the entire film division said no. Furey then went to the president of the college, who made the credit happen. All of this because of an apparent bit that actually turned out to be real. Joe would continue as a writer on *Late Night* for several years, appearing on camera numerous times, including the time Bill Murray "beat him up" on camera—another moment that made you question the show's reality—if only marginally.

Whether *Late Night* was anti-comedy, or simply the anti-talk-show, it was making waves. This was the show that young college students were up late at night watching because it was very much new. It followed Carson but was nothing like it. It was taking the camera out into the streets and strapping it onto animals, and Dave himself was putting on a Velcro suit and jumping onto a trampoline, barreling toward a Velcro wall. Any bit that had an onscreen title and one of Paul Shaffer's deceptively simple jingles was the icing on that night's cake. It was never 100% clear if Dave wanted you to question what you were seeing, if he hoped you'd fall for it entirely, or if he was just entertaining himself.

Part of the aesthetic that Dave perhaps gifted to—or at least shepherded for—Gen-X culture, was sardonic celebration of the terrible, misguided and disturbing. This wasn't John Waters telling you that his favorite freaks were people, too, but please don't forget they're willing to eat shit off the sidewalk. Instead, Dave and his team took a found objects approach to comedy bits. Not dissimilar to how Dave would treat the people he practically pushed in front of the camera lens, like Calvert DeForest as Larry "Bud" Melman or, eventually on *The Late Show*, Rupert Jee of Hello Deli, any person or thing that didn't typically "belong" on camera was ripe for treatment on a scale of what appeared to be somewhere between genuine love and exploitation.

This extended to written bits, as well, especially any time Chris Elliott was onscreen. His pieces usually tended toward opportunities to play heightened versions of himself, though he would occasionally come on in character, playing Jay Leno, or even playing "Chris Elliott" leading the band while also doing an unaddressed impression of Paul Shaffer. Most famously, perhaps, is "The Guy Under the Seats," who is introduced usually by a noise or an audio scene as Dave tries to continue the show. Eventually we find Chris, under the seats, barbecuing or doing something else out of step with a talk show. In the first such bit, Chris introduces the character *while* in character, calling it an extension of himself, saying he'll be "interrupting the show from time to time." Even the very concept of doing bits and characters had to be given the treatment, even if they'd be staples of that very program.

The magic, it seems, was that while Dave's aesthetic appreciated a good lack of polish, no one was the target of a joke. The joke was the kind of truth that could only come from real people being on TV at a time *just before* there was a camera in every pocket. Awkwardness could be endearing, and Dave's insistence on bringing back the unpolished as regulars made his show the only late-night show that could lay claim to the old city-as-character trope that was more often to be found in the pretentious cinema of the day. *Late Night* didn't make movie stars out of the city dwellers, but it did make celebrities out of them.

The found comedy approach continued with "Dave's Record Collection." What might have been the stronghold of novelty record collection as a hobby, it concentrated, as always, on the weirdest shit the writers could find out in the real world. One writer, Steve Young, ended up taking the segment over when he joined the show in the '90s, and it would end up changing his life significantly, after *The Late Show* went off the air. "I had worked at *Not Necessarily the News* briefly in 1989," Young recalls. "I did end up with a couple of good things in one episode, which happened to win Writers Guild Awards." He was shortly let go, as *Necessarily* was mixing things up, staff-wise, but he soon found himself at The Comedy Channel, one of the predecessors to Comedy Central. There he found himself in a spaghetti factory where everything was being thrown against the wall. There were standouts, like *Mystery Science Theater 3000*, and cult hits like *The Higgins Boys and Gruber*. Steve bounced around the channel, despite not being able to watch anything he might have been working on.

"There was a very sort of uncertain feeling, partly because if you worked on the show in New York City, you could not see what was on the air. It was not on any cable system in New York City . . . you felt like you were sort of pouring comedy into a void and having no idea of whether anyone saw it." Keeping his ear to the ground, Young eventually heard that there was a coming mass exodus of Letterman writers. He took advantage of this, and sent over a writer's packet. Young was hired shortly thereafter, and given an office crammed with record boxes. He would go on to discover among these stupid treasures a number of industrial musicals: Broadway-scale productions using Broadway writers and performers to sell things like plastic and tractors. He'd eventually write a book about his growing obsession, and be the subject of the documentary *Bathtubs Over Broadway*. "Within twenty minutes of my arrival at 30 Rock on that day in spring 1990, something was put in motion, which decades down the road would completely enlarge and transform my life in ways I certainly couldn't have imagined."

Young was only at *Late Night* for a couple of years before Dave cut ties with NBC after being passed over as host of *The Tonight Show*. The first person to truly get boned by *The Tonight Show with Johnny Carson* was Joan Rivers who, in the late '80s, found out through a leaked memo that her name was nowhere on the shortlist for potential replacement hosts, despite being Johnny's go-to guest host. Having guest-hosted over seventy-five times throughout the years, she seemed a shoo-in. Carson had purportedly personally chosen David Letterman for the host spot but, even as the reigning king of late night, Johnny couldn't tip the scales, and NBC chose Jay Leno to host *The Tonight Show*. The feud quickly became the stuff of legend, but Dave and those who could come with him landed not far away, at the Ed Sullivan Theater, and on CBS.

The Late Show with David Letterman

You could make an argument in either direction about what Dave's transfer to CBS meant for the show. Undoubtedly, it was the first time I remember hearing the term "intellectual property," and for years Dave made plenty of hay on the idea that he couldn't use characters or basic concepts that he and his team had created while at NBC. He also got around some of these limitations by simply renaming things. The "Top Ten List" became "The Late Show Top Ten," and "Viewer Mail" became the "CBS Mailbag." Larry "Bud" Melman simply went by his legal name of Calvert DeForest for his appearances on the new show.

The lack of carryover, though, brought Letterman mainstream in a new way. He was creating new stuff for a wider audience—after all, he finally got his 11:30 time slot. The show might have seemed a bit tamer than the original, but people like myself—even as I slowly gravitated toward an absolute obsession with Conan O'Brien's take on *Late Night*—saw this tameness as an attempt to remain subversive while looking even more mainstream with a bigger built-in audience at an earlier hour. Also, Dave was not in his ideal spot: Who could blame a guy for being a little bitter after having a sure thing snatched away from him and, seemingly, sitting back and letting his own show entertain him.

If you were paying attention in 1998 and 1999, you'd have caught at least five obvious examples of Dave doing exactly that. With a straight face, of course, Dave introduced the world to the boy band "Fresh Step," and numbers from the Broadway smash hits *Homecoming, One Small Step,* and *But Boy, Could He Sing.* If you were *really* paying attention of course, you'd have noticed that the boy band he'd just introduced was named after a brand of cat litter.

Jeremy Kushnier, one of four triple-threats cast to play Fresh Step, was in the middle of performing in *Footloose* on Broadway when he got the call from his agent. "'I got an audition for you to be in a boy band.' And I was like, 'Do we need to talk about getting new representation? Doesn't feel like a super good move at this point.'" When his agent explained it was a comedy bit on Letterman, Kushnier wasn't necessarily on board—live comedy wasn't his thing. Which is perfect, since Fresh Step had to take themselves way too seriously to work. The group also included Cory Shafer, Jamie Gustis, Brad Madison and future *Glee* star Matt Morrison, who ended up at *Footloose* after Kushnier put in a word for him and told him to audition.

Fresh Step, even though they didn't sing the actual vocals on air, got top-notch choreography and got to come up with their own looks. "The costumer just sort of like opened the room said, 'Just pick the stupidest stuff you can find and put as much jewelry on as you can find.'" They were the show's only musical act the two nights they appeared, first singing "Ya Gotta Be Fresh," and then "Don't Talk to the Hand, Girl, Talk to the Heart," from the soundtrack to the fake James Van Der Beek / Sarah Michelle Gellar film *Talk to the Hand.* The capper on the whole bit, though, was performing live on MTV's *Total Request Live* with Carson Daly. They staged a single writer in Times Square as the band's fanbase. "I can't believe the funds that are going into this joke that, like, it's something that you would do with your high school buddies." Kushnier recalls loving that Letterman didn't bother to come over and shake the performer's hands, and also thinking—if only briefly—that Fresh Step could step off the screen and become a real boy band. "What if this becomes a thing, like in a Spinal Tap kind of way? Because we all could sing. If they wanted to put us in a studio, it wouldn't be any worse than any other boy band at that point."

The Broadway musicals, too, were complete fabrications, betting on singing and acting chops to sell songs like "Jimmy's Coming Home": One man brandishes a ballpeen hammer menacingly, singing, "Jimmy's comin' home, I'm gonna give him a piece of my mind!" Another man in a newsboy cap follows with, "Jimmy's comin' home, I'm gonna give him a discount on rinds. Rinds, here!" He's at a stand selling the rinds of various foods, like watermelon. Paul Shaffer's musical direction and hiring real musicians and actors to knock these pieces out of the park is a perfect example of using absurdist writing, skilled professionals, a sizable budget and complete indifference to the show's clout to make semi-secret comedy bits. If anything, this was actually a blissful abuse of clout.

Blurring the line between reality and TV further, some bits were never broadcast, because they were never intended for TV. "I was running the monologue from 2004 till the end in 2015," Steve Young remembers. "If I was on call for further surgery on the monologue, I would stand near a window [close to Dave's office} and look out. On the outside window ledge there was an old, hardened, dirty wad of chewing gum that someone had put there, who knows when." A few months of staring at the gum and the sidewalk below passed before he got a creative spark.

"One day I realized, 'Oh, my god, look down there on the street. There's George Clooney getting out of a limo.'" If an SUV pulled up, Steve could be there, and if paparazzi was around, he had an unobstructed high-angle view of whomever was arriving. "There were fans all screaming, you get people signing autographs, you get people waving to the crowd. And I started taking these pictures. After a while, I started Celebrigum.com." In 2011, Steve gave Dave a birthday present: a photo book of his favorite Celebrigum pieces.

Dave fell in love. "'Oh my god, this is fantastic. We have to do an art gallery show of your photos.'" Steve was certain Dave wouldn't actually waste the effort on a bit that wasn't for the show, but that year's holiday party was held at an art gallery. "All funded out of his own pocket, about, I don't know, five dozen of my pictures he had professionally enlarged, printed, mounted and framed." Dave Itzkoff from the *New York Times* came down and did a piece on it (as long as he could interview Letterman).

"If he saw this person is doing something for the weird, fucked up love of it, and it's surprising and unique, the best of his spirit would respond wholeheartedly to that. And he would run with it." Letterman would end up producing *Bathtubs Over Broadway* as well, contributing to a legacy of comedic experimentation and support of those who once made his job possible. Dave retired in 2015, making him the longest-serving host in late-night history, after thirty-three years of inviting his audience into the world of comedy, while letting them know that they had to be prepared to be the joke themselves (or at least a part of it).

3

A Do-It-Yourself Movement: The Compass, The Second City, and The Committee

"Compass, if carried to its logical conclusion, is a sort of 'do it yourself' movement. I'd like to see neighborhoods all over the city form groups like this. It's a search for a community."

—Paul Sills, *Chicago* magazine, Sep. 1955

I n early July 1955, *The Chicago Tribune* ran a brief piece informing the city that something called The Compass would be opening a venue at 1152 E. 55th St. "The idea seems to be improvisational theatre," the piece explains, then toward the end tells us that there will be "debates, folk dancing, lectures . . ." Many things can happen at The Compass, which causes the writer to muse, "which perhaps means encompassing." Arguably, I should be committing to the reality of the bit and *yes, and*-ing here, but boy that's a reach. It was more likely that co-founder David Shepherd was obsessed with compasses because his dad was In the Army, because that's what he told author Janet Coleman in her book *The Compass*. Shepherd almost called his group "The Mirror," because he wanted the audience to see themselves in what they saw on stage.

Perhaps the greatest trick David Shepherd and co-founder Paul Sills had up their sleeves was managing to get people to come to an improvisational show who weren't just their friends and relatives. They'd been experimenting since starting the Playwrights Theatre Club in college, where their best-known production was of *The Caucasian Chalk Circle* (a good name for a majority of improv groups).

Improvisation was still such a new art form, though, that people came to see it for the novelty. The idea had legs, and Sills was groomed to carry on a tradition his mother, Viola Spolin, had started. Spolin founded the Young Actors Company in Los Angeles in 1948, and in 1963 she wrote a groundbreaking book, *Improvisation for the Theater.* She pioneered the idea of theater games, the root of every warm-up game that improv students are now familiar with, like "Zip, Zap, Zop," or "The Mirror Game."

That word *improv,* however, wasn't used at the time. It was strictly *improvisation. Improv* was purportedly first used in 1978, according to Merriam-Webster, though it's not clear where that usage actually came from.

There's one good reason to delineate between the two words: Traditionally, *improvisation* refers to the skillset used for acting as a whole, and *improv* is a slang term strictly for improvised comedy. Or, as Second City director and co-creator of long-form improvisation form "The Harold," Alan Myerson, explains it:

"Let me just preface it by saying that I hate the term *improv.* For me, there's improv and there's improvisation. Improvisation, I think is an art. Improv, I think, is a commercial scam, basically. It's a way of ad-libbing jokes, rather than creating something."

He's not alone in this. What Viola Spolin learned from her teacher, Neva Boyd, and then passed down to her son and their students, was indeed something intended not specifically for comedy; when it was used for comedy, it was still about the acting, not the jokes. Further, the games that would eventually make up the curriculum of any improvisational or improv school were originally developed for social work.

Spolin was raised on games as a kid, and when she was brought to work with Neva Boyd by her sisters, she fit in quickly; Boyd, in all her years, had never met anyone who knew so many games. Boyd was using games to help communicate across all manner of barriers, including verbal. Many of her students were first-generation Americans for whom English was a second language. "She believed that play was extraversive," explains Aretha Sills, improvisation teacher and daughter of Paul. This type of play was intended to get actors out of their own heads, to find a "shared experience," which "helped us easily and happily eliminate some of our social conditioning and fears, and it would drop away and allow us to be in the present time."

Spolin's seminal book came after she began working with The Second City, as she explored the potential of her work to go beyond the bounds of teaching. With a group who can already communicate on a basic level, games and improvisation could become part of training for the theater, and eventually a medium themselves. "That book went on to become the first improvisational theater text that was widely used, and spawned a million little improvisational theaters around the country, and then the world," Sills explains.

Paul Sills took his mother's lessons with him when founding The Compass (and, later, The Second City), and the seemingly simple concept of making it all up using a basic set of rules was, effectively, born. They would end up putting on an improvised play later that year called "The Fuller Brush Man," and an ad for it announced that there would be refreshments. Neither comedy nor strained segues were on the menu, though, at least not explicitly.

Comedy was a natural byproduct of improvisation, but as a pure theater skillset, improvisation is about the moment—finding it, playing it out, revealing it to the audience, truthfully and unabashedly. This is the real reason that some of us are uncomfortable with improv games—mandated (if 100% necessary) sincerity. When Spolin developed these games and techniques to teach disadvantaged kids to cooperate and communicate across multiple barriers, the language she gave them was movement, attention, and living in the moment. Perhaps due to the awkwardness this can create, or the fact that funny faces and situations are relatively universal, these games translate perfectly to comedy. This is why most of the clips you can find of The

Compass performances today are comedic, and why one of the biggest things in comedy within only a few years' time would be Mike Nichols and Elaine May, alums of The Compass.

One other critical element of the pieces performed at The Compass—though not originally part of the plan—was music. "It had never occurred [to] anybody for the pianist to be an integral part of the show, but gradually, this began to happen," recalls Allaudin Mathieu. Mathieu (then known as Bill) was the intermission pianist for The Compass, until he was asked to improvise some French bistro music for a scene that Elaine May and Mike Nichols would be improvising. It was the first time, Mathieu says, that the pianist became part of a scene in such a way. "But I totally forgot about the scene, I was trying to pick out the melody of 'La Vie En Rose.' And onstage, in back of me, I was hearing, 'Garçon, could you play a little softer?' And then, 'Isn't it very noisy in here?' And finally 'Isn't the music very loud in this Bistro?' And I realized, 'Oh, Jesus, there's a scene going on in back of me.'" Mathieu sees this as the beginning of his improv education. "From then on I did my best to help the actors and the scene. I recognized that in this work, everybody's in the service of everybody else."

The Compass would eventually drift around; it ended its reign in Chicago only two years after it started, in 1957, and in 1959, it was at The Crystal Palace in St. Louis. There was soon renewed interest by Paul Sills, as well as Bernie Sahlins (one-time Chief Engineer of the audio recorder manufacturer, Pentron) and former Compass member Howard Alk, in a new cabaret theater experience—something to bring that Compass magic back to Chicago.

The Second City

To tell the story of the name *The Second City* quickly, in the 1950s, a journalist named A.J. Liebling wrote a series of articles in the New *Yorker* which derided Chicago for its current condition (to him, it was in terrible shape), and those pieces were later published in a book called *Chicago: The Second City*. The creators of The Second City theater company—Sills, Sahlins, and Alk—hoped to take the moniker and turn it on its head a bit. Using the same tenets of improvisation as a skillset, they would create sketches that could reliably be performed in repeat showings and would give the audience a taste of live improvisation at the end of the show. Through the years, the likes of Dan Aykroyd, John Belushi, Aidy Bryant, John Candy, Steve Carell, Stephen Colbert, Chris Farley, Tina Fey, Eugene Levy, Tim Meadows, Colin Mochrie, Bill Murray, Mike Myers, Catherine O'Hara, Jordan Peele, Gilda Radner, Harold Ramis, and Ryan Stiles would appear on the various Second City Stages.

Barbara Harris, Eugene Troobnick, Mina Kolb, and Severn Darden were among that first cast, which soon expanded to include Alan Arkin and Paul Sand, as the show increased in popularity. The coffee house cabaret at 1842 North Wells Street in Chicago couldn't hold them all for long, though. Not two years later, in 1961, The Second City sent their original cast to Broadway to open *From the Second City*.

Paul Dooley (*Breaking Away, Sixteen Candles*) remembers reading about The Second City in a magazine before discovering they were coming to New York. He lined up to watch the group perform already classic sketches like "Football Comes to the University of Chicago," and to see a touch of improv on a Broadway stage. "It was a combination of set scenes that were their best scenes, with a couple of open places for 'give us a first line/last line [of the scene to be improvised],' which they were good at," Dooley recalls. "They closed in three months, and it wasn't sold out. I don't think critics knew what to make of it. Theater audiences knew."

Dooley describes the setting as "non-informal," with Broadway stages being a few feet off the ground, with red velvet seats—perhaps not the perfect venue for a group who had been performing on foot-high stages in the Midwest. "In Chicago, you can put your feet on the stage, you can cross your legs and drink a beer and have a cheese-burger." The end of the run meant certain relief for the Chicago-based cast. After three months in a new city and a long stretch without va-cations, things were rough, even as the producers tried to open the show elsewhere, using a few good reviews as their fuel. Eventually, the cast were offered two-week vacations, and the company started auditioning understudies.

"'They're having auditions on Monday, which is dark for us,'" a friend told Dooley. "If you come down here, Sunday night, I'll introduce you to the director. Maybe you'll have a head start and be the first person he talks to." Dooley headed down on Sunday, after their first show of the night, and did indeed meet the director, who asked about his background. Dooley had been doing standup, a lot of sketch comedy, and had performed revues at places like The Tami-ment in the Poconos. Dooley wouldn't need to audition, but he would get to work with the cast to see how he fit in. The director proposed he improvise with the group for their second show of the night.

"I have never improvised, but I played a lot of sketches," Paul explained.

"It'll work out, other people will help you. Just follow them," the director responded. They headed backstage, where the actors were discussing what characters, impressions, and locations they wanted to work with for the improvised set of the next show. Paul Dooley sat back until someone recommended they set a scene in an unem-ployment line.

Dooley decided his crutch would be an Italian dialect, something he assumed would get a laugh, even if he floundered on stage. His scene partner, Alan Arkin, also had a dialect in mind, which normally would mean death for a scene in an era where it would be expected that this particular crutch meant the other actor would be "the straight man." Skilled actors both, they made the scene work despite their instincts that two accents could hamper the scene. When the original Second City cast got their two-week vacation, Paul was invited to be an understudy.

The DIY spirit is all about trust that people can pick up the rules of a game. At worst, the experienced actors around you can fill in the gaps you've made. At best, you become an organic piece of the whole. "When they came back, the management of the club said, 'Well, now that you know what you're doing, you might as well be in the company.' So that's how I got to join Second City."

Toward the mid-'60s, The Second City expanded to include several touring companies. It then diversified into further venues, a TV show, and became the premiere supplier of comedians to *Saturday Night Live*; there was no question that The Second City had become a business. Part of that business was the school, part of it was live theater in Chicago, and the other piece was the touring company.

Meagen Fay joined Second City in the early '80s, and would go on to co-star with Carol Burnett in the 1991 revival of her sketch show. "We grew up just outside Chicago and I had no understanding or interest in Second City," Fay says. Her older brother, Jim Fay, had taken Second City classes and was the household comedy encyclopedia and lover of comedy albums. Fay had been performing in *Servant of Two Masters* and *Love's Labour's Lost* in Chicago when she got a message on her machine from someone named Bernie whose voice she couldn't understand. During a visit from her brother, Bernie called again, and she hung up, as usual. "Bernie Something from the Second Something" immediately flipped a switch for Jim Fay, who told his sister to get in his car immediately.

"So he drives me and he said, 'I will not take you back unless you sign or do whatever that man tells you to do. So you're going to miss your show [this afternoon] . . . whatever he wants, just sign a contract, I'll take you home. And if not, you have to find a bus.'" Jim drove his sister to the Second City, and after trying to talk Sahlins out of it, Fay caved and signed, despite her lack of improv experience. "On my way out of the office, I'm walking down, I'm saying good-bye. And, 'I guess I'll see you in a couple of weeks,' and Del comes out." Del Close, looking his particular disheveled self—taped, broken glasses and all—then removed his jacket. Fay considered offering him a smile and a dollar, but before she could, Del had introduced himself nonverbally. "He was now standing there naked except for his pants down around his ankles and his shoes . . . I grew up with all brothers, so I know what this is. I just don't know why I'm seeing it."

"I just wanted you to see my tracksuit," Close said, making clear the track marks from heroin up and down his body. Fay ran downstairs to her brother, shouting about the naked man upstairs who Sahlins shooed away. Her brother looked at her inquisitively.

"You mean you met Del?" he asked.

Former *SNL* writer Cindy Caponera joined Second City in the '80s. "I was in the touring company with Joel Murray and Chris Barnes," she recalls. "I started out in [the Red Company]. I got moved to the Blue Company. They had all the best gigs—you know, California—and they got on airplanes. Where the Red Company was basically traveling around in a van." By 1987, Cindy was poised to become a mainstage player, which meant people were starting to notice her.

By this point, Joyce Sloane, a producer, had become the mother figure at Second City. At a lunch one day, Joyce took the time to introduce Cindy to the whole Second City group—she was finally going to be the latest mainstage member. "That night, Bernie Sahlins brought Bonnie Hunt up from the touring company to face off with me in an improv battle. So, he gave her my job, basically." The idea of facing off for your position was not part of the Second City playbook. Cindy was bumped down to the e.t.c. company (which plays the smaller stage), where she worked with Steve Carell, along with understudies Stephen Colbert, Paul Dinello and Mitch Rouse (three of the co-creators of sketch show *Exit 57*, where Cindy would later be a writer). She quit not long after.

Second City may have been the standard for improv and sketch in Chicago, but by the '80s and '90s, it was no longer the only game in town. ImprovOlympic (eventually known as iO) started in 1984, and in the next few years places like Annoyance sprung up, taking chances on non-traditional comedy theater with shows like *The Real Live Brady Bunch*, which counted among its cast and crew members future stars Andy Richter and Jane Lynch, and director Joey Soloway.

In LA and New York, these shows and venues would have been called "alternative comedy" or "alt comedy," but in Chicago, it was just part of the ongoing evolution of the form. Because of this, Second City wasn't exactly hip. As Adam McKay recalls, "their shows were very formulaic. They would start with a song, they'd end with a song, they'd do blackouts . . . we just sort of thought that that was kind of the more traditional place, even though we knew there were really funny people there. We just weren't that interested in it." When places like Annoyance were putting on shows like *That Darned Anti-Christ*, it was hard for the middle-of-the-road places to draw in non-traditional voices.

"I really didn't care about getting into Second City, *Saturday Night Live*, any of that," says McKay. "The early version of Upright Citizens Brigade was live, street prank, political comedy. It was pretty *out there*. I was loving it. I mean, it was exactly what I wanted to do." On the side, he was making thirty-five bucks for directing an improv rehearsal, maybe a hundred twenty-five for a class. Second City, on the other hand, paid real money, but they weren't looking outside their circle for new blood. "They were hiring kind of their own people."

David Koechner had traveled to Chicago from a small town in Missouri after plans to maybe go into politics. While there, Koechner checked out Second City. "I had no idea how a person goes about being an actor," Koechner says. "I saw they taught classes. I wrote it down on a matchbook surreptitiously, because I still had that small town in me. Like, I'm writing it down secretly on this matchbook, because I thought someone's going to tap me on the shoulder and go, 'Why are *you* writin' that down?'" He attended The Players Workshop, an improv school affiliated with, but never officially a part of, The Second City. Koechner then eventually moved to Chicago, getting further training at ImprovOlympic (run by Del Close and Charna Halpern) while still keeping an eye on Second City.

"I'd heard that Charna would go through the list of people who are auditioning and put a checkmark by people's names, who she thought should get hired." From what Koechner was told, Joyce Sloan didn't want to be told who to hire, so those checkmarks didn't work out the way Halpern had hoped.

When the new artistic director, Kelly Leonard, came to Second City, things started to change. He kept an eye on the other theaters, with Koechner soon breaking through from iO. The floodgates then opened, and The Second City could now claim as alumni future stars like Amy Poehler, Ian Roberts, and Tina Fey. Even more surprising, long-form improv (improvising an entire show, rather than a short scene or a game), which was a rehearsal staple (though never onstage at The Second City), started to rear its head for actual Second City performances.

This new atmosphere at Second City started to change Chicago's mainstream comedy scene, if such a thing existed, which in turn spread further than anyone could have anticipated. Andrew Moskos, once a representative of Chicago's Citizens for Effective Rapid Transit, took it further than most. "That's where I first saw improv . . . I always respected the operation of Second City, they [had] five stages at its peak, and hundreds of students, and the shows were great." Moskos would eventually found the theater and school Boom Chicago, in Amsterdam. Before that, though, he would be witness to the bellwether of Second City's change to the experimental—Adam McKay's *Piñata Full of Bees*, directed by Tom Gianas and starring McKay, Scott Adsit, Jon Glaser and a host of other future big names in comedy.

Moskos noticed Second City shows changing after that. "It all started getting mixed together, and had energy, more politics, [and was] angrier. And we use that as a bit of a model, like, when we hit an artistic wall, you know, we need to have our *Piñata Full of Bees*." Boom Chicago's alumni list is impressive, on its own, at times home to Jordan Peele, Jason Sudeikis, Amber Ruffin, Nicole Parker, Seth Meyers, Ike Barinholtz, Brendan Hunt and Colton Dunn. As for the Citizens for Effective Rapid Transit? "That is a bogus organization that I invented so I could write op-eds."

Second City Las Vegas

There have been many Second City satellite locations over the years, with their own unique challenges: not every place can have the same old show. Actor Brian Shortall grew up in Chicago, but he didn't learn about Second City until attending Columbia College Chicago and finally catching a few Second City shows. He moved up the ranks to the touring company, before being placed at the Second City location in Las Vegas, replacing Jason Sudeikis as he left for *SNL*. "I did that for a year and a half, did ten shows a week at the Flamingo," Shortall says. He performed in the show written by the cast that had previously included Sudeikis, and then went on to co-write an original show with the group, which they also performed.

For touring companies, the bulk of the show is tried-and-true Second City material, going back sometimes to the beginning of the company's history. Las Vegas, on the other hand, relied on new revues, though the risk of alienating the audience was heightened in this melting pot running over with the impermanent wealthy. "At any given night, you're performing for the family from Ohio, who's next to a guy who just lost ten grand, next to a bachelor party, next to German tourists, next to someone with an escort," Shortall explains, laughing, though with the sort of increasing intensity that tells you how anxiety-inducing this must have been for the Las Vegas cast.

"I'm not exaggerating when I say it's one of the most impossible crowds to unite under the umbrella of 'Hey! Comedy! Try this out, you'll understand this, right?' But that's what I loved about it was the challenge of it." He describes Second City Chicago performances as a "home game," where you'll at least get courtesy claps. Not so in Vegas, where the challenge was to regularly get out of well-dug holes. "It kind of gave you this this ironclad confidence. It didn't matter. You were in charge, you were doing the show. And you were gonna land this plane no matter what."

Second City Toronto

Bernie Sahlins, with financial help from Canadian deli magnate Sam "Shopsy" Shopsowitz, the "hot dog king" of Toronto, brought The Second City to Toronto in 1973. While the wheels wouldn't start turning on the concept that would become *Second City TV* for another three years, articles from around the opening of the theater say this was part of the plan the whole time. The budget, though, could explain why that took a while. "They opened on Adelaide Street, originally, and couldn't get a liquor license, and didn't have air conditioning," Dave Thomas remembers. "And they opened in the summer."

Sahlins sent Joe Flaherty and Brian Doyle-Murray up to Toronto from Chicago to start auditioning their first players for the Canadian theater. This is how Dan Aykroyd, Valri Bromfield, Gilda Radner, and John Candy ended up in the company, though Candy ended up being shipped to Chicago to fill a vacancy there. The first show only ran for a few months before they closed the first location.

The new stage would be at the Fire Hall on Lombard Street, and the new group was, appropriately, on fire. "This cast was pretty deadly," Thomas recalls. "It was Joe Flaherty, John Candy, Gilda Radner, Andrea Martin, Eugene Levy, Dan Aykroyd, and Catherine O'Hara as an understudy. That was even better than [the show] on Adelaide Street." That cast—and Thomas, a member of the audience that particular night—informed comedy for the rest of the next twenty years.

After Martin Short joined the cast, Torontonian Alice Myers saw him perform and told her young son how much he reminded her of Short. "Maybe that's something you should do," she told him. On Mike Myers' last day of high school, he auditioned for Second City Toronto. "My last exam was at twelve o'clock," Myers recalls. "My audition was at three o'clock, and I was hired by five o'clock." He had auditioned once before, but he was too young, unable to perform in places with a liquor license. Instead, his friend, "Black Velvet" songwriter Christopher Ward, got in then. This time, Myers was more than ready, armed with six characters, even if The Second City was kind of his safety school. "I wanted to be in The Kids in the Hall," Myers says.

"We were all thrown out of Second City," remembers Scott Thompson of The Kids in the Hall. "We just were bad. When anyone said there were rules, we were like that Marlon Brando quote [from *Rebel Without A Cause*]: 'What are you rebelling against?'"

He lets me finish the line. "What do you got?"

Deborah Theaker recalls the night that The Kids took over the main stage. "One Monday night, they gave us off, all those guys [filled] in. They got the suggestion of 'nudist colony,' and I guess dropped trou in the audience. I came back the next day, and they were all gone." At this point, Theaker feels that Second City Toronto was afraid of anything dangerous. "It was becoming sort of pedestrian dinner theater. It had gone into a complacency period, because *SCTV* had happened fifteen years before . . . a lot of scenes about, 'Hey, honey, have you got my eggs ready,' and none of us were even middle-aged. But it was almost like we were adopting a very complacent suburban outlook."

Before co-starring in improvised classics like *Best in Show*, Theaker cut her teeth at Second City Toronto. "They called me baby Catherine,"

Theaker remembers. "Because I always looked up to Catherine O'Hara to set the bar for how characters should be done. I've known her since I was nineteen; she was very much a mentor." Growing up watching O'Hara set the standard for what it was to be funny on-screen couldn't possibly have prepared her for the reality of working in live comedy. When Theaker eventually joined Second City Toronto, the dividing line between how women and men were looked upon became grimly obvious.

"At the time, there would be two women in a cast and possibly like six men, [as well as] a male director, a male musical director, a male stage manager," Theaker recalls. Being outnumbered was probably not the surprise. "They used to call one woman 'the window dressing' and one woman 'the talent.' I couldn't believe it." She would get notes about her makeup, while the male actors got up in their street clothes, with no makeup. "I am not a showgirl," she explained. "This is not Vegas. Backstage at Second City Toronto was a sign that read 'Women are always mother, sister, daughter, whore.'" Theaker and fellow Second City member Linda Kash took down the sign and burned it.

"I think at some point, they got confused," Theaker says. "I think maybe they hired me to be window dressing and I wasn't." Even as she took a stand, she still had to lobby with men to get them to participate in scenes with her. She even remembers several performances where she and a frequent scene partner created characters she later recalls seeing pop up on *Saturday Night Live*.

"Dana Anderson and I did performance artists with black turtlenecks, glasses and ski pants, which became 'Sprockets,'" Theaker says. "We did a scene called 'The Get-Eveners,' about a British super spy . . . I also played the villainous Vulva Gigantica," she says, comparing the character to Alotta Fagina in the *Austin Powers* films. "They see somebody else do something and they grab it, or you say something funny, and it ends up somewhere else. Because you don't matter." Theaker would go on to make her mark in comedy, notably in Christopher Guest's improvised films. She credits him with opening comedy up to everyone with the skill to handle it.

The Second City in Toronto was not the place for rebels. It also wasn't just for Canadians, though. While watching the improv landmark film *Waiting for Guffman* as a kid, Derek Waters (creator of *Drunk History*) had a flash of realization that he wanted to make comedy. After graduating high school, he tried out both cities when he realized that his post-high-school career was going to be all comedy. In Chicago, he did check out a Second City show, featuring future *Late Night with Conan O'Brien* performer Kevin Dorff. "I just remember how excited I was to meet that cast afterwards," Waters recalls. Live comedy was more electric than he could've imagined, and he recalls a feeling every performer has had at some time watching a live show: "I want to get up there so bad."

Waters felt like being in Chicago meant you need to have paid your comedy dues already. "I just knew I wasn't ready for Chicago," he recalls. He lived in Toronto for six months, making the most of it before his time ran out—because this was comedy school, he couldn't stay on a student Visa. "I told my parents 'this is my college,'" and he left to pursue his dream. He split his time between The Second City and Keith Johnstone's Theatresports. He then went to Second City in Los Angeles before breaking into TV.

Second City, for the most part, remains true to its old format, because that format makes money and—for the most part—keeps the doors open (even if it has changed hands several times over the years). Since the '90s, thanks to the infusion of subversive performers like David Koechner, Amy Poehler and Adam McKay, experimentation has increasingly found a home there. There have always been alternatives built on taking chances, though, like its earliest offshoot, The Committee.

The Committee

Just as Paul Sills was planning to bring The Second City to Broadway, Alan Myerson was busy directing off Broadway, something he'd practically fallen into. He had been offered a part in a play, or the option to assist the director. "[Assisting] paid $5 more a week. So I took that," Myerson remembers. When the director got sick five days later, Myerson was bumped up to direct. With the help of a friend, Myerson would eventually have coffee with Sills in New York to discuss taking over directing duties from him in Chicago as they built up a new company to replace the original. "For no reason that I can discern, he hired me on the spot . . . I had no background in improvisation at all, except I knew some sort of Stanislavski and improvisational techniques."

The Chicago cast now included Del Close, Anthony Holland, Joan Rivers, Gene Troobnick and Andy Duncan. Myerson's tenure there, though, wasn't long. As he recalls, "Del was very miffed that I was the director and he was not, and he basically engineered a coup." The "coup" worked but, as it turned out, it enabled Sills to return to his home base of Chicago, and Myerson to head back to his in New York City, to direct the original cast.

Eventually, Myerson and Second City performer Irene Riordan would find themselves married, with a dream—if no plans—of opening their own theater. On their Honeymoon in San Francisco, through mutual friends, they were introduced to a psychiatrist and an academic, both of whom suggested they open a theater in the Bay Area. By way of these two new connections, in less than two months they raised $60,000 (nearly $600,000 in 2023 money) to take over The Bocce Ball nightclub. They'd then be removing the bocce ball courts to put in a theater, which they'd call The Committee. Myerson and his growing family moved to San Francisco in August, 1962; The Committee opened April 10, 1963.

Myerson's theater connections in New York and Chicago were plentiful, so he started making calls. One prospect, Myerson's high school friend, was Hamilton Camp, an actor and singer in New York City. Myerson couldn't find him anywhere while he was running workshops to audition actors in New York, and the night before he was set to go back to the West Coast, he found himself stuck in a blizzard. In this complete whiteout, he found himself at Bleaker and MacDougal in the Village. "I heard somebody playing guitar and singing with this angelic voice, which could only be Camp."

He came upon him, eyeing a tip hat full of snow, and told him he'd been looking for him, telling him about his new venture. "Do you want to come?" he asked Camp. "He literally jumped into my arms." He soon saw exactly why, when Camp brought him back to his place— a twenty-five cents-a-night spot in a flophouse, The Mills Hotel (which would eventually become the famous Village Gate club). Camp, his wife, and two children were staying on two mattresses on the floor of the boiler room. The two friends caught up, and Camp played him some music, introducing Myerson to Dylan through, among others, "A Hard Rain's A-Gonna Fall."

On opening night in San Francisco, where not long before people were rolling colored balls around the floor and getting drunk, with friend Dylan's permission, Camp kicked the first Committee show off with that same Dylan song. This was the only piece in the first show that got a bad review.

That premiere effort was workshopped through games and improvising, the same way they would continue for the next eleven years. Like The Second City, The Committee memorized, rather than scripted, their sketches that were developed through improvisation (The Second City's Broadway show only had a "book," or script, after the memorized pieces were eventually transcribed). The first several revues they put on would have standardized beats and some regular improvised pieces, like "Man on the Street," where a screwdriver poses as a microphone and the actors are interviewed as they come on stage, about topics of the day. They'd do some Second City favorites, too, like "First Line/Last Line."

The good reviews for The Committee had the power to bring people into something new for the West Coast, which didn't yet have a Second City or anything like it. Second City always aimed to poke fun at modern American societal foibles; in fact, a lot of writers of the time struggled to find other ways to describe what we now perceive as our general idea of comedy. In a world where comedy could be Shakespeare or vaudeville, you were stuck with hundreds-of-years-old observations about human nature and "what the world is," only the world had already moved on.

Comedy had been a thing of nostalgia, until modern language and changing mores caught up with it. In a Post-Industrial Revolution and post-WWII world, culture was changing at a breakneck speed, so the idea of stand-up, sketch, improv and theater becoming a place where comedy's biggest target was society itself felt new, simply because comedy previously hadn't been able to keep pace. The early '60s was a time when pop culture finally started to catch up, with Dick Gregory, Mort Sahl, Lenny Bruce, and Nichols and May dealing with topical and current issues in their comedy.

In November 1963, President John F. Kennedy was assassinated, prompting the possibly apocryphal opening line of Lenny Bruce's act. The biggest selling album of that year (and at that point, of all time) was *The First Family*, starring comedian Vaughn Meader doing the one thing people knew him for: his JFK impression. Bruce purportedly went on stage the night of the assassination and said something to the effect of "Boy, Vaughn Meader's fucked." That same night, The Committee didn't perform, though they did choose to go on the following night, dealing with the news and horror and shock in their own way, by performing. They started, as always, with "Man on the Street."

From the audience, someone yelled "The Palace of Fine Arts!" and the group went on to poke fun at San Francisco's funding a failed refurbishment of that building. Larry Hankin, who you've seen in several things by now, was last in line, and Scott Beach asked him for his opinion on the troubled refurbishment. "Are you kidding?" Hankin yelled. "The fuckin' president was shot yesterday!" he continued, before going off. Myerson recalls this as a moment of pure improvisation, with Hankin fully immersed in the moment of the scene. It didn't happen for a laugh at anyone's expense, of course, but rather to point out the absurdity of doing a comedy show about current events and ignoring the thing right under everyone's nose.

The Committee drew a certain political mindset and skillset, both of which informed the success of its members. Many of them would go on to be big names in movies and TV, their closest links to TV sketch comedy being Carl Gottlieb and Rob Reiner, who went off to write for *The Smothers Brothers Comedy Hour*. Another was when they gave the stage manager job to a young Gary Austin in the '70s, who would later go on to found the improvised theater group The Groundlings, in LA. Myerson himself would go on to a massive TV directing career, as well as taking occasional work teaching improvisation at San Francisco State. It was here, in the late '60s, that he started experimenting with what the games could become in the hands of his students. This included long-form improvisation, concentrating on full-length productions, rather than shorter, standalone scenes.

Myerson soon shared his teachings with Del Close, who was now running a workshop with the professional actors in The Committee, and The Committee's musical director Allaudin Mathieu, who ran a similar workshop, but for music. "They would start using some of that stuff with the actors. And they would tell me stuff they developed . . . that's what developed into The Harold," Myerson recalls. Mathieu, Myerson and Close invented The Harold together, each using their own perspective. "I tried to musicalize the process," Mathieu says.

"Del tried to make it psychologically true in the moment. And Alan—and all of us—were trying very, very hard to find structure." The name *Harold* came about when Close said "We have to call this thing something," and Mathieu blurted the name out, a reference to George Harrison in *A Hard Day's Night* saying "Arthur," when asked what he called his haircut. "I had the image in my mind of a kind of dull-eyed guy sitting, watching TV with a cigar butt in his mouth and holes in his t-shirt . . . In my mind, it was a way of saying you cannot name the ecstasy of this experience. When it's at its best, you cannot do that. And so let's just call it some inert thing."

The Harold was perhaps the biggest development in the world of improvisation since The Compass started implementing Viola Spolin's teachings. Close would take it to iO and teach an entire new generation the art of long-form improvisation using it, at which point it started to spread and become an accepted improv form. Continuing the tradition of playing with the form, The Upright Citizens Brigade continues The Harold to this day.

The Committee was one of many offshoots of The Second City, itself one of many offshoots of The Compass, but it was arguably the first political improvisation group in the country. This was an extension of the group's active involvement in the world of San Francisco culture and politics that included the anti-Vietnam War and civil rights movements. Myerson still credits Viola Spolin and Paul Sills for the roots of what he did for that decade and in the years that followed. A tool invented for communication between players was slowly expanded to include the audience in the dialogue. Using improvisation for political exploration became a new way of communicating. Short-form improvisation slowly developed into the exploration of something more expansive, resulting in The Harold, now one of the most well-known and widely practiced long-form formats. Paul Sills was searching for a community, and, in a significant way, The Committee was that dream coming to a logical conclusion.

4

Sniglets and Hedgehog Sandwiches: Not Necessarily the News

Two of the biggest names in TV comedy got their start on an HBO sketch/satirical news program called *Not Necessarily the News*. Writers Conan O'Brien and Greg Daniels' first entertainment job was writing for the show's first season. Strangely, this might never have been the case if Douglas Adams hadn't cut English writer John Lloyd out of *The Hitchhiker's Guide to the Galaxy*.

"1978 was a particularly difficult year for me," recalls Lloyd. "My friend Douglas Adams had been commissioned to write this thing called *The Hitchhiker's Guide to the Galaxy*. It was a radio series. He didn't have very high hopes of it. But it was great that he was getting the work." Adams, who would soon rise to prominence as a well-known comedic savant, had been writing with his partner, former classmate Lloyd, for about four years at this point, on many other projects, but Adams had been doing this one on his own. After taking ten months to write the first four episodes of the first series of the *Hitchhiker's* radio show, Adams had hit a wall.

"He ran out of ideas, and I was his best friend," Lloyd remembers. "He said, 'John, I've got sort of stuck, can you help me out? I'm sure there won't be another series, but if there is, we should write it together, because it's really lonely doing this on my own.'" Compared to Adams' average of more than two months per script, the duo banged out episodes five and six in around three weeks. The shows were produced to critical acclaim, reviewed in every national UK paper. Fame and fortune were knocking down their door.

"Suddenly, we hit the big time. And then Douglas sacked me." Emotionally, this was a low point for Lloyd, though he admits this lit a fire under him. He quit his radio producing job and headed to BBC's Light Entertainment division, who were expecting him.

"What kept you?" asked the first BBC executive he met.
"You don't even know who I am," Lloyd responded.

"We've been following what you're doing," the executive said. "We think you're very good. But a producer has to be brave enough to ask, you know, and now here you are." They had six half hours set aside for Lloyd to do whatever he wanted—they even asked him if six was enough. They pitched to him a series that would "poke fun at political correctness," but that wasn't what Lloyd was looking to do.

The one constant among the pitches, though, was that Rowan Atkinson, who had appeared sparsely on TV thus far, should star in it. "Everyone knew he was going to be huge," Lloyd says. As for a writing staff, after producing 500 radio productions over five years, Lloyd had amassed a group of comedy writers he could depend on and set about putting together six shows for the BBC, no pilot needed. "I've begun to think since that it was probably a bit of a scam." Lloyd believes there's a chance that someone in a middle tier position was being asked to make something more dangerous and to prove a point hired a Lloyd, who had no television experience, and his co-producer, Sean Hardie, who had no comedy experience. "Let's watch them crash and burn," he says, imagining the inner monologue of this theoretical executive.

Feeling that the show had to be more "grown up," Lloyd went the circuitous route to cast the show. Instead of working with his friends, who already knew his style, he visited London's West End and The Edinburgh Fringe to scout for names that were available and already relatively famous. The chemistry among this randomly-assembled group was a disaster, and they poured more fuel on the post-crash fire by using up all of their best material in their first of six ordered shows. Lloyd needed some intervention so that no one would ever see this version of the show.

"I think it was the last time I actually knelt by my bed and prayed for a general election to be called. As a result, it was called, thank you god, and the show was canceled." With half a year to rework what they'd started with, they pulled together a younger cast who they already knew, consisting of Atkinson, future *SNL* cast member Pamela Stephenson, Mel Smith, Griff Rhys Jones, and Chris Langham. The show would be cool, grimy and nothing like popular comedy at the time, which could still be found to be flavored to their parents' tastes.

"In *The Two Ronnies,* a phone box on the street was used to make telephone calls. My generation used them as lavatories. They would go in there pissed, use the phone book as some sort of toilet paper, and go in the corner. That's what London was like in that sort of wrecked '70s when we had the worst economy in Europe." The comedy, they knew, should reflect what life felt like in the UK in the '70s, if also endeavoring to do so with some joy. That said, they did want to avoid becoming another Python.

"When I started moving to telly in 1979, the first thing we all said is we're not going to be anything like Monty Python, we have to be completely different. We're not gonna have silly names. We're not going to you know, have men dressed up as women, all that kind of stuff. It's going to be much more down to earth and realistic," Lloyd recalls.

The sketches were shot in a range of styles, and though *Not the Nine O'Clock News* as a title was quite literal, as they were on opposite the news at 9 PM (the title being an homage to Tony Hendra's single-issue satire *Not the New York Times*), it was not strictly a satire of news programs, though there was plenty of that to be found, as well. In one piece, news footage plays of Princess Diana exiting her carriage before the royal wedding, Rowan Atkinson's voice-over dripping with anticipation, before showing disgust at all the wrinkles on her $100,000 wedding gown.

Real news footage often appeared in a manner that *Not Necessarily the News* would end up lifting directly from the show, often cutting political figures' words and actions out of context in conjunction with something much sillier. Many of the stronger sketches—some of which appear on the two *Not the Nine O'Clock News* records from the BBC, including one entitled *Hedgehog Sandwich*—are pure concept sketches. One in particular illustrates the show's goal of avoiding association with Python.

In "General Synod's 'Life of Python,'" a Bishop has directed a film about the life of Jesus Christ, and is stuck debating it with a Python worshiper, who represents a group who see the film as a "thinly-disguised and blasphemous attack on the life of Monty Python." The sketch is a send-up of the then-recent "debate" between Malcolm Muggeridge (a supposed satirist) and the Bishop of Southwark opposing Michael Palin and John Cleese, over whether or not the Python film *The Life of Brian* is blasphemous. In the sketch, the opposition insists that Jesus Christ is a "lampoon of the comic messiah himself," John Cleese—the initials are even the same. The sketch is less than three and a half minutes and is effectively perfect.

Coming to America

"*Not Necessarily the News* came out of that, because a very nice producer called John Moffitt came over from LA and said, 'Hey, John, man you got to come over here and produce this with me because John, you're not gonna believe the girls you're gonna meet and the cars you're gonna drive, man,'" Lloyd says. He responded, "If you really think as a BBC producer I'm going to be lured by cheap offers of automotive and sexual bribes, you're very much mistaken." He claims a visit to LA later made him realize his error, but in the meantime, he did help to get the American version off the ground.

"What me and Shawn Hardie did was cut together a compilation of the best sketches to show what a typical edition [of *Not the Nine O'Clock* News] looked like. We focused largely on American-based sketches, things that would be easy for a network executive to recognize." Today, this would probably be called a "sizzle reel," something quick and poppy to get interest and funding. The tape worked. "I don't think we ever got royalties. I think we probably got a flat fee for doing the edit," Lloyd recalls, without a touch of regret, given his work on the successful *Blackadder* series and the long-running UK quiz show *QI*.

John Moffitt had been producing and directing TV for some time already, including sketch shows, co-producing *The Richard Pryor Show* and executive producing and writing for the series *Fridays*, which helped launch careers like those of Larry David and Larry Charles and featured a notorious guest-starring stint by Andy Kaufman. *Fridays* had just been canceled around the time Moffitt spoke with Lloyd, but the crew had been kept around for whatever the next project would be. ABC had reportedly tried to keep *Fridays* on the schedule, but they could only offer a time slot opposing *Dallas*, the second highest rated show of the year—a death sentence.

Fortunately, HBO then bought *Not Necessarily the News* as its first comedy series. Moffitt brought his crew with him, including future *Mr. Show with Bob and David* director Troy Miller and comedian Rich Hall. Eventually, names like Merrill Markoe, Al Jean, Conan O'Brien, Greg Daniels, Annabelle Gurwitch, Harry Shearer, and future *SNL* and In *Living Color* star Damon Wayans would find their way onto the show. One of the primary cast, now best known as the voice of Earl Sinclair on the TV show *Dinosaurs*, was Stuart Pankin, who was asked to audition by a friend.

"'You want to audition for something called *Not Necessarily the News*?' And I said, 'What's that?' He said, 'It's a cable show.' I said 'what's cable?' This was the days when there was—pardon the expression—29% cable penetration in the United States, and pay cable was even less." Worse yet, writing for a cable show meant no Emmys; cable shows wouldn't be recognized until 1988. Pankin did, though, take home a CableACE Award in 1987 for best actor in a comedy series; it couldn't have been easy acting opposite what was supposed to be Henry Kissinger.

Scanning through the ABC news feeds—the raw footage that they could license—the *Necessarily* writers would look for something usable, either for recontextualizing on its own or, in the case of an interview with Henry Kissinger, an entire comedy sketch. "I interviewed Henry Kissinger," Pankin explains. "[We were] pretending that he wrote a script." Pankin plays a jogging-suit-clad producer trying to get his head around this supposed script, directing everything at a dead ringer for the back of Kissinger's head. Every time we cut back to news footage of Kissinger, he's either subtly reacting to the suggested script changes, or "pitching" new ideas.

At one point, Pankin throws the three-inch thick screenplay in the garbage to start over and tries to prompt Kissinger with "Your movie is about a guy who . . ." The footage of Kissinger responds with "Well, first, he begins with a lugubrious account—" to which Pankin tries to steer him back to something big, maybe with a naked Matt Dillon on a horse. For pieces like this, you couldn't stray too far from the script, but Pankin did present options.

"I like to say that I didn't write, but I rewrote. I've done that all my life. Sometimes people appreciate it. Sometimes they say, you know, 'shut the hell up,' but I will never stop doing that. As long as I'm, you know, capable of reading English." Early on, anyway, minor rewrites might have been the only perk, given the measly budget at the beginning of the show, where they were shooting guerilla style (in LA, this usually means without permits). "Our first dressing room literally was in the men's room of the Shell station in Simi Valley."

Nancy Severinsen was both location manager and music coordinator, to give you an idea of how thin everyone was spread. "She said, 'Please try to buy gas from the Shell station,'" Pankin recalls. Some people were changing clothes behind the open doors of their cars, and they were eating lunch while sitting on rocks nearby. Eventually they were given a Winnebago to change in, a place to relax. Things got better as cable became more accepted, and the legitimacy of shows like *Not Necessarily the News* became clear.

The show featured desk pieces, the ever-popular out-of-context news footage pieces (the popularity of which once caused actor Danny Breen to complain, "Ronald Reagan is the star of the show"), and a segment so popular it became a book: "Sniglets." Comedian Rich Hall's most notable contribution to the show, a *sniglet* is "any word that should be in the dictionary, but isn't." One such sniglet was *premblememblemation,* or the habit of putting a letter in a collection box and immediately double-checking that it went in. This caught the attention of *Not the Nine O'Clock News* creator John Lloyd. "Douglas Adams and I had written a book called *The Meaning of Liff,*" Lloyd explains. "It's a dictionary of words of things there ought to be words for, but aren't, and all the words themselves are recycled place names." Chicago, for instance, means "the foul-smelling wind that precedes an underground train." "We got a copy of *Sniglets,* and were astonished to see that fifty of the definitions were in our book, including one on the back cover, word for word." Lloyd considered legal action, but it never came to that.

The sketches were wide in scope and level of experimentation. There's the one where an armed robber recognizes a potential victim and they play polite catch-up; another sketch takes place in an airline ticket line where all of the passenger's personal information (including turn-ons) is available to the clerk (because computers). Then there's the fantastically surreal yet simple bit with Pankin's anchor character Bob Charles constantly trying to find his camera, which is variously to his left, behind him, or a couple stories above him, and he can't get his story out because of his frantic search for where to look. Everything was pre-taped, which allowed for a certain level of control.

"In the beginning, we showed the finished show to an invited audience in some studio," Pankin remembers. "We played it to get their laughs. Of course, they offered free beer to these people, so you're not sure exactly how honest the laughs were." That method was eventually shelved in favor of something simpler that was still popular in the '80s: the laugh track.

Joe Guppy, a writer and performer known best for his man on the street bits on the Seattle sketch series *Almost Live!*, recalls seeing the "laugh machine" in person. "The guy wheels in this this hand cart with some complicated playback recording equipment with about 200 cassette tapes. A few titters here, and a couple of guffaws there, and he's got all these different kinds of laughs and he 'sweetens' the laugh track." Joe had been brought on as on-air talent, playing a reporter and, along with co-writer Nancy Guppy (also his wife), hired to write for *Not Necessarily the News* for its second-to-last season.

"They hired us as a writing team, which was a huge thing because we went to LA into a union job," recalls Nancy. "We got into the Writers Guild; that got us an agent." With a thirteen-week stint, they secured for themselves the possibility of bouncing to several other TV jobs, getting union benefits and pay. Seeing the Hollywood sign outside their office window was a thrill, too—they were in the middle of it—but it had its share of surprises, like the hours.

"Give 'em three meals a day, and they never have to leave the office," Joe recalls of the not atypical writers' room approach. "It is fun, you do laugh a lot, that's for sure. Even as you're under a lot of pressure, and everybody's trying to claw their way to the top." Some people had cemented their place in Hollywood, like "The Punch-Up

Guy," who *Necessarily* brought in to help meet the "quota" of three jokes per page. No more, no less, or so it seemed. "This is a guy who just, I guess, he travels around from show to show and he throws in jokes . . . if you got two jokes on that page, he'll bring the third one to you." While the couple returned to Seattle four years later, only Nancy returned to *Almost Live!*, putting those hard-earned Hollywood lessons to good use in local comedy.

Future director Troy Miller was one of the crew who started at *Fridays* and moved on to *Not Necessarily the News*, first as an intern, then Production Assistant (PA), then moving up to a variety of jobs, often at the same time. "While I was in film school, I was working at a gas station and I met John Moffitt," Miller recalls. "After berating him for years, I finally got tickets to a rehearsal show. I snuck backstage—literally with my friend distracting security—and then found Christie Stentz, who was the production manager at the time, and the rest is history because they trained me up there."

This, like many first industry jobs, was where the rubber met the road for Troy, as an amateur photographer and a comedy lover. He would often sneak into clubs he wasn't old enough to get into so he could watch his favorite comics, like Larry David, on stage. As PA on *Necessarily*, Miller ran the location segments, less to be near the comedians and more to be near the cameras; as a result, he ended up the de facto camera assistant on this five-person location crew, as well as the boom mic operator, all while still grabbing coffees for the folks on set. Meanwhile, he was playing close attention to the actors, as well as the directors, to get a handle on how to translate his love of comedy to the screen.

Miller recalls keeping an eye out for how not to do it, as well, noticing that some directors, "would do ten takes with no notes to actors, no change in the camera." He could see the problem, but despite holding multiple jobs, including sometimes driving the camera truck, it wasn't his place to speak up. He could speak to Moffitt or the rest of the team, later. "The next one, if I just direct it, it's going to save us so much money." This became his method to climb up the ladder. "I would direct your show if I produced it as well." His approach is "high production values, low dollars," a DIY aesthetic that has paid off; among Miller's credits are *The Ben Stiller Show, Mr. Show with Bob and David* (which Moffitt would also go on to direct), the Mr. Show movie *Run Ronnie Run*, *Tenacious D*, comedy specials, sitcoms, and the opening films for the Academy Awards featuring dozens of perfect re-creations of famous movie scenes (sketches in their own right).

The actors from *Necessarily*, while not all household names, have mostly had long careers, which included a brief stint as improv teachers. In 1985, HBO sent Stuart Pankin and co-star Lucy Webb out on the road to teach improv. They got a little refresher from co-star and Second City improv old hand Danny Breen on the Spolin basics, and headed out to show acting students how it's done. "We got to go all over the country, teaching master classes in comedy and improv," Pankin recalls. *Not Necessarily the News* ran from 1982 to 1990, with a special airing in 1996 for the election called *Not Necessarily the Election*, featuring stars like Janeane Garofalo, Kevin Pollak, Andy Kindler, and Paul F. Tompkins. The legacy of the show, while impressive in terms of the number of writing and directing careers it launched, is that it, if not directly inspired, helped pave the way for, other satirical news shows like *The Daily Show* and *Last Week Tonight*. It is also one of the many shows to have been touched by the hands that made Seattle's favorite sketch show.

---- 5 ----

The Show that Bumped SNL: Almost Live!

There are countless stories of professional entertainers who died on stage. Harry Parke, father to Bob Einstein and Albert Brooks, died after falling into Milton Berle's lap while roasting Lucille Ball and Desi Arnaz. Dick Shawn, famous as LSD in Mel Brooks' *The Producers*, died in the middle of one of his avant-garde comedy performances. US Senator and former US Vice President Alben Barkley, while not a comedian, was a celebrated orator who had perfect timing while giving a speech at Washington and Lee University. "I would rather be a servant in the House of the Lord," he said, "than sit in the seat of the mighty." He immediately fell to the floor, dead, right there on the stage. In 1995, in Seattle, an episode of the local sketch show *Almost Live!* Was about to wrap, after a solid half hour mixing both locally-focused sketches and more universal bits, including a sketch called "E.R.R." "Our strongest sketch, out of act one, was a spoof of *ER*," *Almost Live!* Writer and co-star Tracey Conway explains.

"I didn't collapse right after that sketch. Pro that I am, I waited till the very end of the show." The last sketch of the night was skewering Brad Pitt, featuring Conway and co-stars Bob Nelson and Kim Evey. "Right before we went on, [Bob] said, 'Oh, god, I'm really nervous. I'm gonna screw this up. My heart is just pounding.' And then we went on, and we did it just fine." Like *Saturday Night Live*, the folks at *Almost Live!* Waved goodbye to the audience at the end of every episode. The feed was cut, and the cameras stopped.

Conway turned to Bob and said she didn't feel too good, herself. "And I went down," Conway explains, no memory of anything after that for some time. "The audience was all there, and I'm sure that they thought, 'Oh, I wonder if they're going back to *ER*, you know, that's a very convincing faint she just did.'" Conway had a heart attack on the spot. Perfect timing.

The show's host, John Keister, asked for medical help from the studio audience. "We're not joking here," he was compelled to announce. "Something's wrong with Tracey. Does anybody have medical training?" A volunteer firefighter happened to be in attendance, keeping Conway's heart going until emergency services could defibrillate her. Still, the show must go on. Not *Almost Live!* They'd ended their broadcast for the week. "They had to move the cables of the cameras over my body to go into Studio A so they could do the eleven o'clock news."

Conway was rushed to Harbor View hospital, and the show's cast and crew followed, including brand-new intern Joel McHale and visiting show veteran Bill Nye, of *The Science Guy* fame. In the waiting room, the TV was tuned to KING-TV, so all of Conway's friends were forced to watch what could have been her final moments on earth. Fortunately, she pulled through, though the prognosis wasn't good. She might not ever have the same quality of life. It might be months before there was even a semblance of normalcy.

Two weeks later, she was back on the air, performing sketch comedy; she didn't miss an episode. In fact, they had an episode ready to shoot the week she was out, but an earthquake prevented all regular KING-TV programming from airing that night. She may have only had one line on this next show, but she was back. She stayed with *Almost Live!* Until it went off the air after fifteen years, in 1999. There are no second chances in comedy, only resurrections.

Almost Live! Started in 1984, the creation of two men at Seattle's KING-TV: Pat Cashman, often called "*Almost Live!*'s Phil Hartman," and Bob Jones, who worked at the NBC affiliate. Cashman and Jones had spotted stand-up comedian Ross Shafer on Alan Thicke's talk show, *Thicke of the Night*, and approached him to develop a local late-night show of their own. "I didn't want a TV show," Shafer recalls. "I thought it would take me off the road, where I could make money. TV offered very little at that time." Shafer proposed a half-talk-show, half-sketch idea—a "Letterman-type show," and they put something together with their relatively small local Seattle crew, calling it *Take Five*.

They didn't want to do *Saturday Night Live, but in Seattle.* They wanted their sketches to have a beginning, middle and end, and didn't want them to drag on, as they felt *SNL* sketches did. Cashman, who had been responsible for the 30-second promos at KING-TV, was an expert at squeezing beginnings, middles, ends and a little comedic punch into the tightest possible space, to get people to stick around for the next show. "He was a genius," Shafer says. "He taught us how to do television."

KING-TV liked their pilot, and ordered thirteen episodes of the now-renamed *Almost Live!* Shafer was able to schedule the show around his lucrative nationwide stand-up career, and they brought in music journalist John Keister, who was writing for the Seattle paper *The Rocket*, which reported on local music from 1979 to 2000. Keister was also working on the local music show *REV*, where he often did comedic opinion pieces. Keister was new to TV at *REV*, and recalls some of the first advice he got: "Anyone who doesn't wear a suit on TV looks like a fucking idiot." He put on the one sport jacket he owned and used his music expertise to craft some simple screeds, performed in front of a blue screen with context-appropriate images—simple, effective pieces. Eventually, these caught the eye of the programming director, who suggested *Almost Live!* Try Keister out on their show.

"They didn't really know what I was about to begin with," Keister explains, but once it was clear he could be funny, he felt like part of the team. As long as you could get laughs, you were in. He felt that Ross worked well as a host, and that his amiable, traditional appearance let the other sketch actors shine on a show that, while local, was based in a place that is the "big city" to people all over—Washington, sure, but also Montana, Oregon, Colorado—a big chunk of the country. Keister thinks the show worked because Seattle is a magnet for the right kinds of creatives. "You get a lot of really creative—but kind of a little touched, a little weird [people]—it's where all the serial killers are, all that sort of shit." The show's energy knows that, and with probably the smallest budget of any long-lasting sketch show, it does a lot.

While known for its Seattle-centric humor, *Almost Live!* Never failed to make the show relatable, especially through use of solid pop culture pastiche. On their miniscule budget, with each person eventually getting about $300/week, they were achieving surprisingly cinematic looks. With video cameras, even if you take the time to light your scene as you would a film, it takes extra finesse to make it look and feel even close to a movie. With certain sketches, though, they nailed the visuals, like in the sketch "Alien Gumbys," which, through deft use of smoke and single-point light sources, gives you a sense of what it might feel like if the stop-motion green weirdo Gumby was hunting people on a spaceship. The premise doesn't make an ounce of sense or have a logical reason to exist, but their commitment to the bit sells it.

Local humor gets the pop culture treatment in sketches like "COPS in Ballard," a *COPS* parody set in the Seattle neighborhood of Ballard, using an already tried-and-true format to make local jokes work for everyone. If Python's UK-centric jokes worked for kids in the Midwest, Seattle jokes could work in Montana. Even in the instances where the references were hyper-local, sometimes those pieces gained them the most notoriety. In 1985, for instance, Ross Shafer proposed on the air that "Louie, Louie," as covered by The Kingsmen, be the new state song; it got as far as a resolution being introduced in the state senate, and snagged *Almost Live!* Plenty of national attention.

That same year, Shafer created a scientist. Bill Nye, an engineer at Boeing, had recently quit his lucrative job to get paid about $75 a week writing and performing on *Almost Live!* The name "Bill Nye the Science Guy" was something Shafer says he "blurted out" during a bit, and it stuck. Instead of playing Speed Walker, "the physically fit superhero who fights crime while maintaining strict adherence to the regulations of the International Race Walking Association," or one of the "High Five'n White Guys," suddenly Nye had a persona only he could play.

It was a persona that he used outside of TV, too: He was already a stand-up in Seattle clubs. One night, after The Science Guy was formed in Ross Shafer's lab, Nye opened for Joe Guppy's band, Acoustinauts. He handed out blue index cards to everyone in the audience and asked for science questions. "He just pulled the science questions up and he just started flipping through them and answering them and it was just genius. It was so funny," Guppy says. Like everyone else on the show, adapt and grow seemed to be the Bill Nye motto; that method was making a lot of local celebrities out of *Almost Live!* Personalities.

"I got a tape deck stolen out of my car, and I had to have it replaced," recalls Keister. "My wife said, 'Well, how're you gonna get to the station?' And I said, 'Well, someone will drive me.'" John dropped his car off to be repaired, before work at KING-TV, and headed outside, standing on the corner. "A car pulled over and [the driver] went 'John, what are you doing here?' And I said, 'Could you take me to the station?' And they're like, 'Yeah, sure.' That's the way things were." One other key element to the show's success and staying power was that Eric Bremner, then Vice President of KING-TV, was also head of the NBC affiliates board, which made the major scheduling decisions for all NBC affiliates, nationwide.

"So he used that muscle to push *Saturday Night Live* back half an hour," Pat Cashman recalls. "*SNL* then ran around midnight, and our show preceded it." *Almost Live!* Had been an hour-long show, running at 6 PM on Saturday, but shortening it to half an hour and putting it in the *SNL* slot improved the ratings noticeably. "We were now in a time slot where people actually, you know, were looking for comedy." "This guy was an extremely well thought of person within the NBC community, and he could call in that sort of shit," Keister says.

Even with the power to bump the mightiest of the mighty, *Almost Live!* Was still a low-budget enterprise. This meant the show was also stuck finding people new to comedy, many of them from around the KING-TV offices, who had no on-camera experience. Tracey Conway was no exception, and, even though she was a trained actor, she didn't have writing experience. On *Almost Live!*, like many sketch shows, many of the cast were also writers. Conway was secretary to the head of HR before she was ever on air. She hadn't written much before, but she put together a packet, at the producers' request, and they brought her on.

"I was the only woman on the staff, and it was both wonderful and nerve racking." Now she had to bring sketches in for the group to read. "My friend who was a theater director [said], 'Hey, just go in and do something to break the ice. Take this little windup toy, and put it on the table and see, you know, it might be kind of funny.'" She did as instructed and placed a little wind-up, pop-up penis on the writer's room table. "It was not funny at all, but they're such good guys. They laughed politely. It was an auspicious beginning."

The writers knew Conway would pop on camera. N't long before this, she'd made her debut on a very memorable episode. The show had been interrupted, mid-credits, in April of 1989 by breaking news. A booming baritone interrupted the show almost as soon as the episode began. "We interrupt our regularly-scheduled programming for the following special report." An understandably concerned reporter then explained that, only minutes before, a horrifying tragedy had struck Seattle. One eyewitness was on the street, hurriedly explaining to the news crew, "I heard this sound, it was like thunder, and I . . . I looked up and it was swaying, I—it just, it was—and it just, it went over. It was like somebody kicked the bottom out of it, you wouldn't believe it." Seattle's famous Space Needle had fallen. The episode eventually resumed, but the damage had been done.

"I didn't know anything about it till I came to my job as a secretary [at KING-TV] on Monday and, you know, all hell had broken loose," remembers Conway. She knew plenty about the sketch, of course, but had no idea what impact the Space Needle bit had actually had. After all, she wasn't part of the cast yet, so no one could be expected to recognize her bespectacled face when she appeared to tell the world she'd seen the Needle fall. Hundreds of people had called the police and the station, as well as the offices of the Space Needle itself.

This was just over fifty years after Orson Welles' The Mercury Theatre on the Air did the very same thing to New Jersey with a simple radio broadcast of *The War of the Worlds. Almost Live!* Didn't play the live studio audience's reaction over the "news footage," and in fact used an actor, Michael Schauerman, who wasn't part of the cast, as their news anchor, selling the reality, at least a little. The chyron (the onscreen caption) running over the bit, however, did clearly include the words "APRIL FOOLS DAY."

When the '90s hit, *Almost Live!* Was poised for another run at national attention, at the hands of former producer Jim Sharp. Sharp had left a few years in, when Ross Shafer went to Los Angeles to host the final iteration of the doomed *Late Show*, Fox's flagship (and first-ever broadcast) show, originally hosted by Joan Rivers. Sharp then moved on to work on other Fox shows, where he produced the short-lived mix of licensed sketches and found footage mélange known as *Haywire*, hosted by Gilbert Gottfried. The show could be anything from footage of people trying to do stuff like drink or put on makeup inside a carnival ride, to video of people on the beach dubbed over by "comedians," to animals edited to "dance" to music. They even— shocker—allowed audience submissions. It's not likely any of those ever aired. "It was on for thirteen weeks," remembers Sharp. "We bought a lot of Comedy Central pieces for that show."

Keister recalls speaking to Sharp during this period. "He called me and he said, 'This show I just came on; it is a shambles. They don't know what the fuck they're doing. Put some [*Almost Live!*] stuff on tape, send it down to me right now.' I did. And he's like, 'Fuck, yes, keep this pipeline going.'" As the shows aired, people around the station started being surprised by checks from AFTRA (one of the two screen actors' unions at the time), something none of them had experienced before. It should be noted that the only thing that works on *Haywire* is stuff that had already aired on *Almost Live!*

"That's when Jim was like, 'Fuck, we could just do this, you know?'" Keister remembers. "'We'll sell this show.'" So Keister and Sharp got together for the first time in a while and put together a pitch to Comedy Central, the network from whom Sharp had already been licensing terrible material. Comedy Central bought sixty-five episodes of *Almost Live!*, to air over two seasons. They shot all sixty-five half hours in a single summer. With perhaps the best timing of the bunch, Nancy Guppy had just returned from her stint in Los Angeles after working on *Not Necessarily the News* and a spate of other comedy shows.

"I said, 'Well, I don't want to just be an actor. I'd want to be on the staff,'" Nancy says. Keister agreed, and for the first time, Nancy was an *Almost Live!* Comedy writer. "My favorite part of that job, by far, was writing the pieces, and then producing them, because we got to have our hands in everything." Even with Comedy Central money, for your own sketches, they lived or died by your decisions as a producer. After the two seasons at Comedy Central went by, Nancy remained at *Almost Live!*, writing and on-camera, including some fantastic on-the-street pieces, and in a series of mock-talk-show sketches entitled "Me!" where she plays a self-centered host who ruins interviews. One stand-out, from around 1995, has her interviewing Dave Grohl, played by himself, and eventually trying to wrestle the guitar from him, breaking the neck off of it.

This wasn't just a one-off musician appearance, either. Since the beginning of the show, people in the Seattle music scene were part of *Almost Live!* Grohl even told KING-TV in February of 2022, "*Almost Live!* Was like my summer stock." The musical connections were largely thanks to Keister's experience writing for *The Rocket.* In the '80s, he promoted a band of fourteen-year-olds called "Shadow," who later told him that they stuck with music because *The Rocket* ran their photo. One band member was eventual Pearl Jam lead guitarist Mike McCready. In the early '90s, Keister also put together a sketch called "How the Grunge Stole Christmas," an absolute who's who of Seattle rock, featuring McCready, Bruce Fairweather, Tommy Gunn, Ron Nine, and Kim Thayil—with Keister as the Christmas-hating "Grunge."

Almost Live! Was there for the birth and death of grunge, having fun with it throughout its lifecycle. Meanwhile, they kept a fairly stable cast and crew, and the only mayflies of the group were, as expected, the interns. Some of them worked harder than others, like future star of *Community,* Joel McHale. While training at Theatresports, being on stage four nights a week, he was told by his mother to apply to be an intern at *Almost Live!* "We had a buttload of interns on *Almost Live!* Over the years," says Pat Cashman. "I remember I came in from doing my morning show into the *Almost Live!* Offices, and there was a guy laid out on the couch, and he was sound asleep. And I said, 'Who's that?' They said, 'Well, that's our new intern. This is his first day.'" Conversely, McHale's work ethic was engaged and inquisitive, asking about lighting and cameras and getting himself on shoots.

Before long, McHale found himself co-starring and starring in sketches, playing a little bit of everything. He played Eddie, a dim-witted sycophant to Cashman's Lenny, a street tough who threatens to do nice things for people, like give them a five-dollar bill and tell them to pay it forward. McHale was Jim Carrey as James Bond in "GoldenButt" (with Bill Nye as Q). "I just watched one that Joel was in where he's being followed by a cop," says Presidents of the United States of America front man Chris Ballew. In the sketch in question, Joel and actor Jeff Weatherford are imaging how pissed the cop must be that they're speeding. For two and a half minutes, they continue to yell—unheard—about how there's nothing the cop can do to them. "And the cop pulls off the road, and they get really sad. And they're like, 'I miss the cop.'" It's a perfect build to a sad denouement.

"I would make a point of tuning in to see *Almost Live!*" recalls Ballew. "It was great. I loved Bob Nelson. Any skit he was in was a shining example of dry, ironic wit." Chris may have been one of the few musicians to actually play on the program, although writer/performer Nelson regularly played guitar in the sketches, as the bitter children's show host, Uncle Fran. His deadpan skills gave *Almost Live!* Its own personal Bob Newhart. Like most everyone else involved, though, he didn't come from entertainment.

"I worked at the *Seattle Times* in advertising. They were just a few blocks from KING-TV," Nelson says. In 1988, tired of his job, he dropped off a packet to KING-TV's front desk. They had just hired Ed Wyatt to act and write, though, so they didn't have a vacancy. The next year, as Nancy and Joe Guppy headed for Los Angeles, Bob resubmitted and got in, probably because he submitted an entire packet of sketches. Producer Bill Stainton told him after he was brought on that most people only submitted one sketch for consideration. Twenty-six years after submitting his impressive more-than-one-sketch, Nelson would find himself nominated for an Academy Award for screenwriting, for the Alexander Payne-directed *Nebraska*, which also happened to star two sketch comedy luminaries: Will Forte and Bob Odenkirk.

"I could have never written *Nebraska* if I hadn't gone through the sketch comedy grind for all those years. It does teach you every word is important," Bob says. "You probably can see that a few of the things are actually sketches inside of the movie. I tried to camouflage it." I had noticed, but was embarrassed that it might be a stupid question, because I was so deep into this research that everything looked like a sketch to me. "When they steal the air compressor back, it has the rhythm and build of a comedy sketch, as well. Those rhythms, and being economical with your words, is a big thing."

By the end of their tenure of fifteen years (one year longer than *MADtv*'s, it should be noted) in 1999, *Almost Live!* Managed to keep most of the people they'd taken under their wing as cast members or writers, instead of cycling through new flavors of the month at the beginning of every season. Internet video was barely a thing, yet. YouTube was six years away. *Almost Live!* Is the perfect, intensely-local microcosm for what sketch comedy of the '90s was and what it prepared the world for, namely: singular, often writer-driven sketch comedy, done on a budget by a close-knit group of overgrown theater camp kids, given to the world for free, in the hopes someone would pay attention. *Almost Live!* Was just one—if the least well-known—of over a dozen sketch shows that helped define '90s television, most of which lived and died within the decade in which they started.

They were a ragtag group, most of whom had practically fallen into comedy because of the show simply existing and always being on the lookout for new people. They put together props and sets on the cheap, because of their bordering-on-nil budget. They subsisted on word-of-mouth advertising for the same reason. If they went viral, it was because they struck a nerve. They created not just memorable sketches, but they launched careers—some of which you've heard of, some of which you haven't—just like every other sketch comedy show of the era managed to do.

Almost Live! Didn't rotate their cast, but they also didn't start with a core of performers who had known each other for years. They grew together as performers and writers, and weren't afraid to learn from one another. There's also the inherent charm of a show that feels like public access because of how local it is, only there's still a non-zero budget and actual skilled writers and performers behind it. In practice, it remains illustrative of the fact that you can learn comedy on the job, and be successful at it. Like a bunch of theater kids, they also never wanted this thing to end; the show inspired two short-lived Seattle TV sketch shows: 2013's *The 206* (starring Keister, Cashman, and Cashman's son, Chris) and 2015's *Up Late NW* (starring Cashman and son).

6

And The Simpsons!: The Tracey Ullman Show

I n 1981, the *Southall Gazette* in London ran a piece saying that Tracey Ullman was "fed up" with the label of "comedy actress." Her agent at the time, Lou Coulson, said, "She is not aiming for comedy shows." Two years later, she'd release a cover of the song "They Don't Know," in a bid for a music career. Two years after that, she found herself on the ITV sitcom *Girls on Top* starring Dawn French and Jennifer Saunders, who would go on to co-star in the sketch series *French and Saunders*. Whether she liked it or not, Tracey's comedy star was rising, in the UK at least.

By 1986, Allan McKeown, Tracey's husband—and an established producer with six big hits on UK TV that year alone—signed a co-production deal between his company, Witzend Productions, and Paramount Television in the US. He began putting together a series for his wife, entitled *I Love New York*, but the script and/or the script-writing process didn't work out. At the same time, Coulson was spreading the word via VHS tape in the US, and that tape eventually landed on the desk of James L. Brooks (creator of *Taxi* and *The Mary Tyler Moore Show* and director of *Broadcast News*).

"He had left television," explains writer Paul Germain. "He was basically kind of a giant in both, you know . . . one foot in television and one foot in features." Germain worked under Brooks in many different capacities, including production assistant and script reader, and continued on with Brooks when *Tracey* came along. Brooks and his company, Gracie Films, were based out of the Fox lot in Hollywood. "And Fox basically said, 'whatever you want to do, we'll do.'"

After seeing what Ullman could handle, Brooks took it upon himself to mold the perfect show for her. "He basically decided, 'I'm gonna make a variety show around this comedian,'" Germain continues. "She was a mimic. She could do any voice, she could play any character; she would just become different people." Assertions had been made in the press about the state of variety TV programming by the time *Tracey* came around (mostly that it was dead), but this is the rare case in television programming where precedent and the suits have almost no say in what gets to air. Instead, whatever aired was whatever James L. Brooks wanted to see on television.

In 1986, the Fox Broadcasting Company, or FBC for short, was developing seventeen new series for its launch, including an adaptation of *Down and Out in Beverly Hills* and *Karen's Song,* starring Stockard Channing as a forty-year-old woman who is in a relationship with a twenty-eight-year-old man (the scandal of it!). It was also announced by this point that James L. Brooks was developing a show with and for Tracey Ullman who, in the US at least, was a relative unknown outside of a 1985 Meryl Streep film entitled *Plenty.*

On October 9, 1986, the renamed Fox Network officially launched with *The Late Show Starring Joan Rivers*, a show with a tumultuous history that started not long after it first aired. Before its premiere, Fox COO Jamie Kellner fairly damned the show with a fun mix of hubris and humility, saying, "We're not competing with *The Tonight Show*," then going on to say "We're providing an alternative and making an impact."

The following January, Fox announced their eight shows that were going to "change the face of television," including *The Tracey Ullman Show.* Ullman herself told the press that she got a twenty-six-week commitment and didn't have to shoot a pilot (*Variety* told it differently). Shows like *Jump Street Chapel* and *Married with Children* were also announced, with one of those two shows changing its name to *21 Jump Street.* Gannett ran a piece by journalist Mike Hughes who said that *The Tracey Ullman Show* "could be the one that makes Fox stand out," and on April 5, 1987, the show premiered. A month later, Fox lost its flagship's host when they fired Joan Rivers from *The Late Show*, beginning a rotation of hosts from Arsenio Hall to its final host, the former host of *Almost Live!*, Ross Shafer.

Early on, *The Tracey Ullman Show* wasn't looking like it would "change the face of television." The ratings weren't great and, whether they had planned them or not, some felt the show looked desperate by bringing in guest stars like Steve Martin early into the show's run. It's hard to pinpoint exactly what might not have worked with the show early on. Its pacing and speed can feel terminal, but Ullman herself is a vocal chameleon, even when she's doing accents it's inappropriate for a white person to be doing. The live audience energy is there, and the characters, while often built off of a voice or an accent, often come in fully fleshed-out. What's more, the show had years of experience backing it.

Among the production team were *SNL* writer Marilyn Suzanne Miller, *SCTV*'s Paul Flaherty and Dick Blasucci, Cameron Crowe, Heide Perlman, and nearly everyone who was there for the beginning of *The Simpsons*. They also brought in a crew that knew how to shoot film instead of the traditional video, because this show had to look good. Gregg Heschong was the director of photography for most of the show's run. It was his first multi-camera shoot, and with the production values through the roof, he looked at *The Tracey Ullman Show* as a "loss leader;" in other words, it wouldn't make its money back, but it would get people in the door to look at everything else. "Doing the show was like doing a pilot every week," Heschong says. "There were no standing sets. We wouldn't revisit characters and sets; you'd have to start all over again."

For the art of it, you couldn't beat producing a sketch show with this much variety. "We did these enormous musical numbers. There was one I remember, it was completely in the rain. [We had] airplanes on stage, we did a boat on stage in a storm. I mean, this in front of an audience, it was terrific. Nobody was doing that." No one would really end up doing it again, either.

One reason some might hesitate to call *The Tracey Ullman Show* a sketch show is that the sketches were not typical. There are no blackouts (where you're in and out with the joke and the lights drop to signify the end), no quick and easy premise sketches; though, on the other hand, there were also no one-joke premises stretched to ten minutes for no reason. Instead, the show was mostly character studies, sometimes with a solid sketch premise, like two window washers (Sam McMurray and Dan Castellaneta) who settle down for lunch, only for McMurray's character to suspect Castellaneta's of sleeping with his wife. When Castellaneta describes how his lover acts in the throes of passion, McMurray is relieved, since he's never seen his wife do any of that.

The sketches were denser than American audiences were used to (If not always longer, thanks to *SNL*), and were closer to one-act plays that, as pointed out, sometimes culminated in a big song and dance number. If anyone knew the tastes of American audiences, it was James L. Brooks, and he knew the show needed something between sketches.

"He had this great big office on the Fox lot, and I remember sitting in on this," recalls Germain. "[Brooks] says, 'You know, I'm thinking I'd like to put little interstitial pieces between the sketches to kind of break them up.'" Someone in the room asked Brooks what he had in mind and, perhaps before considering short films about Post-It Notes or his own socks, he pointed to a gift on his wall, from producer Polly Platt. It was an original "Life in Hell" comic strip by indie artist Matt Groening. "Brooks thinks for a second, he goes, 'Let's get that guy!' and he points to this poster." Thank heavens no one had given him an original H.R. Giger piece, or *The Simpsons* time slot would've been much darker.

Germain's twenty-six-year-old go-getter energy really shone through that day, when he volunteered to do the groundwork. "I was just kind of dumb and enthusiastic, I jumped up and said, 'Oh, that's

a great idea. I love those.' And [Brooks] goes, 'Great. You're in charge.'"
They needed three minutes of animation per week, and when Germain explained he knew nothing about animation, Brooks simply told him he'd better learn. Flipping through *LA 411*, a guidebook to all of Hollywood's production services companies, Germain called every animation company in it, big or small, and sent them *Life in Hell* strips so they'd know what they wanted the shorts to look like.

He soon ended up with boxes upon boxes of VHS tapes with bids rubber-banded around them, which sort of just sat there until he was asked which company appealed to him most. He picked a company called Klasky Csupo, who had been specializing in animated company and show logos of late. That wasn't what appealed to Germain. "Gabor [Csupo] was from Hungary, and he had this kind of interesting Eastern European animation that he had been involved in making and producing in Hungary before he came to the United States." It was edgy, not like anything other US-originating animation houses had in their back catalogues. They put in the best bid and got the job; they needed scripts to do that job, first, however.

Germain was a former film student, so he used the screenplay format he was used to, rather than the typical TV script format of two columns, and sat down with Groening and started working on short scripts for these new characters of Groening's. They had been originally drawn on napkins and named after Groening's parents and siblings: Homer and Marge, Lisa and Maggie. At some point, the show also developed shorts with cartoonist M.K. Brown to alternate episodes with The Simpsons, but those didn't stick. Really, none of the cartoons fit in with the style of the show. They were a weird choice. So if any one of these one-minute comic refreshments took hold amid ten-minute odes to a character it took seven minutes to get a handle on, that's what people were going to notice.

Germain got together with Groening and associate producer Jeffrey Townsend and recorded cast members of the show so they could create audio tracks to be animated to. "It was like this little underground operation," Germain says. "Nobody was looking over our shoulder. We could do anything we wanted." The shorts were popular. So popular, in fact, that Brooks stopped hiring a warm-up comic to get the audience excited before and during the long live shoots. "We just had a reel of these cartoons, you know, and we'd just play them." At the time, though, The Simpsons seemed destined to sit between the live sketches. By season two, Brooks was bringing in new blood to come up with new sketches.

Writer/producer Jay Kogen (*The Simpsons, The Wrong Guy*) started out as a PA on many shows, including *It's Garry Shandling's Show*, with producer (and future *Simpsons* co-creator) Sam Simon. Kogen and writing partner Wallace Wolodarsky presented a spec script (a sample to show your skill) to Simon, who loved it, even if they couldn't use it on *Shandling's Show*. "I remember him saying 'This is great, and this is wonderful. I'm going to show this to my other show,'" says Kogen.

Simon passed the script to Brooks, Perlman, and the rest of the producers. "They read it and they said, 'good enough.'" While still Pas at *Shandling's Show*, both Kogen and Wolodarsky were then asked to pitch sketches to the young show. Coming up with ideas for this relatively new series was not the easiest process, either. Kogen and Wolodarsky watched VHS tapes of the first ten episodes, to get a feel for it. "My partner and I were looking at each other going, 'Oh, this is not our favorite show.' But we're young, and we needed a job. So, we'll get excited. We'll work on it." Kogen, like many sketch writers who grew up on *Monty Python*, wanted good concepts and jokes and wasn't attracted to ending a sketch on a song, as the *Ullman* show would sometimes do. "I think that's kind of a cop out. I think the sketches were there to give Tracey the ability to sort of do characters and wear makeup and that kind of stuff . . . I've grown into a writer who cares about character more, but that's not where I started."

Per their mutual agreement, Kogen and Wolodarsky got excited about it and started writing up concepts based on what they'd seen. "We took our lunch break, ran over to 20th Century Fox, pitched them, I think fifteen different sketch ideas, and they bought one. We wrote that one sketch in about three days." They were shortly both hired as staff writers for the second season. By this time, though, the writing was on the wall, at least to some at the show. Germain recalls talking to young executives on set, who were adamant that adults didn't want animation.

"You got an audience of mostly adults, and look at them. They're dying laughing. They're not gonna laugh as hard at the [*Tracey Ullman*] show. But they're laughing at this, you guys should be thinking about this." The same minds tried to intervene when Brooks pitched *The Simpsons* as a TV show. "'Yeah, let's do it anyway, because I want to,'" Germain says, paraphrasing Brooks. Bart Simpson starred in a commercial for Butterfinger candy bars in late 1988, and the final "The Simpsons" piece to play on *The Tracey Ullman Show* was on May 14, 1989, not long before Groening was approving Bart Simpson dolls to be sold at stores. On December 17, 1989, a special aired, titled "Simpsons Roasting on an Open Fire."

In 1990, after the first season of *The Simpsons* had aired, the property made $750 million in merchandising alone. Later, believing her contract gave her a cut, Ullman sued 20th Century Fox for what she believed to be her share of *The Simpsons*. The final episode of *The Tracey Ullman Show*—which never picked up much in terms of ratings—aired in May of 1990. Two years later, Ullman lost her suit against Fox.

The Tracey Ullman Show paints a clear picture of what you can get done in sketch comedy with enough money, specifically: anything you want. What it didn't have—even with some of the best, most skilled writers, producers, actors and directors in the business—was cohesion. It's only "glue," to borrow a term often used for Phil Hartman's job on *SNL*, was Ullman, who was in most of the sketches. Those sketches served her ideas for characters, not the other way around. When the cheap cartoons, produced with autonomy by a skeleton crew and a low-bidding animation house can outshine all the wigs, makeup, fresh sets, and guest stars you can muster, you've perhaps miscalculated.

Author's note: I reached out to a particular cast member of The Tracey Ullman Show *for an interview, but only received a reply from someone in Disney's intellectual property department (Disney now owns Fox). He explained I'd need to pay a license fee to include any I.P. from the show in this book. I said I wouldn't be including any. What follows is an excerpt from a script about the neurotic Kay, one of Tracey's most enduring characters.*

INT. KAY'S ROOM – DAY

KAY is nervously knitting a doll shaped like James Garner. In walks WALLY, a no-nonsense dog groomer (Castellaneta). Kay looks up from her knitting.

> KAY
>
> Is this a real script from the show or is it just in here to see if Disney will try and flag us for copyright infringement?

> WALLY
>
> I think it's the latter, ma'am. It just said"an excerpt from a script," not one from the show. Solid trolling.

> KAY
>
> Thanks, Wally. Would you like this James Garner doll?

> WALLY
>
> My, but you're strange and endearing. Such a lasting and memorable character.

> KAY
>
> That's me! Kay…

The audience erupts in spontaneous laughter and thunderous applause. Cue Simpsons short.

7

Easy to Beat Up, Hard to Kill: The Kids in the Hall

"We started in improv theater where, you know, you weren't allowed to have a prop: it was *verboten*, which is the word I like to use," says Kids in the Hall co-founder Bruce McCulloch. He and Mark McKinney started out together at Theatresports in Calgary, performing at The Loose Moose Theatre. Meanwhile, the "Kids in the Hall" consisted of three members, in Toronto: one Kevin McDonald, another Dave Foley, and a Mr. Luciano Casimiri. Bruce's trajectory into Theatresports was unexpected, but once he and McKinney teamed up, it still seemed like the pieces were falling into place.

"Mark and I had had fairly quick success. Looking back, it felt like as a young person, it always takes forever. We had gone from doing Theatresports—improvised, competitive comedy—to saying, 'Hey, can we write our own sketches, and put them on after Theatresports?'" They were given the go-ahead, and people started sticking around. After about six months, people started lining up around the block just for this group that called themselves "The Audience." Bruce was the artsy punk kid among the group, from the very beginning, and that lent itself handily to doing comedy theater on the cheap. "I do remember going, 'What can we do that's different?,' and making angel's wings out of cardboard and spray painting them, and then coming down on a rope from the rafters."

Even with the young pair's DIY aesthetic, which came from financial necessity, Bruce saw something more for them. He felt the drive to use the group's success for a leap to a bigger market; he suggested he and McKinney move to a bigger market. McKinney said they should hold off for two years. "I said, 'No, no, we're going in three months, and we're going to Toronto,' and so I went to Toronto."

A few years prior, Kevin McDonald and Dave Foley had met at Second City Toronto, and also performed in that city's franchise of Theatresports. Once The Kids in the Hall and The Audience finally met up, in bits and pieces at first, they eventually combined forces. One group, The Kids, was a comedy juggernaut some called "vaude-villian" and the other, The Audience, was not going to be doing the modern version of "Who's on First." "Mark and I were doing beat poetry with flashlights under our faces and we'd have weird lights and you know, throw some water on the stage . . . I was more influenced by dance and all that stuff, where somebody with the right light moving forward with a wind machine can do all in the world that a hard set can't." It was the kind of experiment that, at that time, no other established improv or sketch comedy group was going to touch.

As the group came together after meeting in Toronto, their styles began to cohere, with each member able to keep their own style while finding a unified group voice. They also began to find a midway between The Audience's overt theatricality and The Kids in the Hall's no-nonsense comedy approach. They used the stage more like a TV director uses a camera, sometimes by making other parts of the theater "part of the stage," through simple lights that focused the audience's attention there. This was perfect when, for instance, they needed to stage what became the TV series' opening sketch—where Tiffany and Tabitha call each other at the same time and "love it when that happens." On stage, Scott is off to the side, but a light lets the audience know he's still in the sketch.

Fortunately for us all, the group eventually voted for the name "The Kids in the Hall" over "The Audience." Ironically enough, the next and final member of the group would practically throw himself at them from the audience of one of their shows. He was going to be a serious actor until he saw The Kids in the Hall performing in Toronto. "It was love at first sight really," Thompson says. He saw writers and actors onstage, and wanted that; as an actor only, he felt like an interpreter, where instead he now felt like he could do what The Kids were doing. "I was with my friend, Darlene. I remember saying to her, 'I'm going to be in that group.' And she was like, 'We don't even know them.' And I just went, 'I know, but I just have a feeling.'" His opening move? To interrupt a sketch by throwing donuts onstage (which were intended for a sketch), for which they gave him serious shit when they met him after the show.

Scott did, eventually, will his way into the group as a wildcard who wasn't cutting it as an actor, to his own satisfaction. "Maybe that's why I wasn't getting much acting work because the truth was, I had a hard time sticking to scripts. I had a hard time, you know, doing a play where I would go 'well, I have a better line.'"

As McCulloch tells it, "Mark likes to say that [Scott] was formed from a pile of wigs, on a street in Toronto, that was hit by lightning, and then he joined our troupe. That's the real story." The Kids in the Hall, in their final form, started performing at The Rivoli in Toronto, the group again drawing audiences nearly too big to fit in the performance area. In a period when *Saturday Night Live* was in a serious slump, it wasn't long before the newly-rehired Lorne Michaels got word of The Kids.

"Lorne found out about them from [*SNL* scout] Pam Thomas," remembers director John Fortenberry. "Lorne liked them, they were really rough around the edges at the time." They soon found themselves performing for Michaels, auditioning not as a group, but as five separate writer/actors. For the first time, they had to compete with one another for attention on stage, rather than concentrate on the success of the scene. Only two of them (Mark and Bruce) would end up chosen to work as writers on *SNL*, in a year where no one knew what to make of the show.

The entire cast of *SNL* just prior—which featured Billy Crystal, Jim Belushi, Christopher Guest, Julia Louis-Dreyfus, Rich Hall, Martin Short, and Harry Shearer—had left after season ten in a mass exodus. By this point, Michaels had been gone from his show for five seasons. For season eleven, he was in a position of having to re-staff his show, practically from the ground up. The new cast included Robert Downey, Jr, Anthony Michael Hall and Randy Quaid, and among the writers, long-time staple of the show Robert Smigel was also hired for this season. For Bruce, these miserable few months shaped how he felt about sketch as a form.

"It helped me redefine that [what] I loved about sketch was The Kids in the Hall," McCulloch says. "It's almost like romantic or chemical attraction . . . Someone can be technically beautiful, but you're not attracted to them, and you can be quite attracted to sort of a slutty Kid in the Hall." There were also the practical considerations, like realizing he had a very different comedy brain than the people around him, established and green. "I had never realized in a way that my ideas were as weird as they were to other people, because I'd been in the bubble of The Kids in the Hall." A perfect example is the promo he wrote up for *SNL*, entitled "Thirty Helens Agree."

"Thirty Helens agree this is a pretty good show," the narrator would've said.

"They went nuts on me. 'There's no stars in this promo! "*Agree* it's a pretty good show?" Do you know what a promo is?' So the way I was looking at the world, I realized, was different." On the other hand, he did get his first experience learning about camera placement. He also learned from Lorne Michaels that whatever feels important during the week may not matter at all once the sketch is going out, live to the entire country; the "not ready for prime time" attitude may have helped Bruce defer to the material a little more. "I learned to trust how it chemically came onscreen, and how the audience related to it, and how quickly things could change."

Meanwhile, in Toronto, there were three pretty bitter Kids in the Hall, still performing, but with understudies for the two guys they couldn't be sure would ever return to the group. One actor who stepped in was Deborah Theaker. "I played Mr. Cabbage Head, all of their parts, and filled in for them at The Rivoli, which didn't go well. There were characters that didn't translate." Though Theaker would eventually appear on the TV series, she recalls not being invited back to the stage show, for reasons she wasn't totally sure about. "I think they were their own unit. They jelled so well together. They didn't need to bring somebody from the outside in." To the surprise of the Toronto Three, the New York Two did indeed come back after a disappointing single year at *SNL*, in May of 1986. By October of 1987, they'd be performing their first gig to a paying audience in New York City, courtesy Lorne Michaels.

The Kids would be honing their act in preparation to shoot a TV pilot, at places like Caroline's at the Seaport and the West Bank Café. "There was one night at The Seaport," remembers Fortenberry, "I swear to god, there were two people in the audience. I had to go back to say to them 'What do you want to do, guys? Do you want to do the show for two people or you want to just call it?'" They didn't go on that night, but did thank the audience for showing up. In May 1988 they got a press boost when *Rolling Stone* published the piece "Is America Ready for the Kids in the Hall?" which chronicles their time in New York, from their first, boo-laden show, up to their final performance, the last piece of the puzzle to be laid into place before they could shoot their pilot.

"We got everything down," Fortenberry recalls about prepping the pilot. "A director named Robert Boyd had worked with The Kids and they knew him, and it was going to be shot in Toronto. He's a Canadian director, so he was sort of on the inside track." In Toronto, a few months later, The Kids had their soundstage at CBC's location on Mutual Street, former home to Canadian music program *The Tommy Hunter Show,* and they had their crew, some "borrowed" from *Saturday Night Live.*

As for Boyd, "It turns out, he was a little green. So Lorne called me, and I sort of directed the pilot," Fortenberry says. He was not credited for directing the pilot, though he was offered the opportunity to direct the studio portions of the series, with Boyd shooting filmed pieces. He chose to stay in New York.

"I was actually at the first taping and I had been at most of the Rivoli shows," recalls musician and journalist Paul Myers. "It was just exciting to see them building sets and that they brought The Shadowy Men from a Shadowy Planet band over to play live, raised above the audience on a platform." The audience that night was treated to two performances of this pilot (which was occasionally billed as a special, but always intended as a pilot for a series), with an unheard intermission that included a livid Lorne Michaels.

"The first one, they were blowing it. What I didn't know—because I didn't go backstage between shows—is that Lorne had read them the riot act between one and two. They basically trashed the dressing room and said, 'We've got to win this thing. We've got to show Lorne that we're good.'" Two of them insist they did no trashing, but instead peed in the sink as an act of mini-rebellion. Whatever the method was, it worked, and the audience ate up that second show, and in November of 1988, the pilot aired, with HBO soon committing to buy twenty shows.

The Kids in the Hall officially debuted on HBO on July 21, 1989. It's easy to say that an entire generation of future comedians grew up on this show as the next *Python* and went on to create their own comedy, but they were also affecting their own generation of comedians, including future Upright Citizens Brigade co-founder Matt Besser. "Adam [McKay], me, and Ian [Roberts], we had a goal of being like *Kids in the Hall,* specifically. We saw the route they'd gone, and it seemed like, if they could do it, 'Why can't we do something like that?'"

This first season was groundbreaking for North American sketch comedy, firstly because it had been some time since a pure sketch show had been on TV (with no variety elements like musical guests). In the United States this was probably the first sketch show where we'd be able to hear swear words in a sketch, or see openly gay characters and an openly gay actor without that being some kind of punchline. "When I first started out, I was openly gay, and nobody was back then, especially in my business," Thompson recalls. "You couldn't be an openly gay comedian; that would be a death sentence . . . But then when I saw The Kids in the Hall, I went, 'Oh, I can hide in these characters until the world is ready, if that makes sense.'" He compares it to waiting for nuclear fallout to clear before you can come above ground. "I never even really thought before that I could even do that. But they made me think that I could."

When *Rolling Stone* asked if America was ready for *The Kids in the Hall*, the answer wasn't clear. In Canada, though, journalist Richard Ouzounian both hated that the show's actors used their personalities and world views for potential laughs (sort of the key to writing comedy) and admitted that his own reaction to them mirrored the reaction older people had to him loving *Python* when he was a kid. He weirdly excludes any commentary on the few things that actually deserved such ire, like the use of blackface. He didn't think the show was Canadian enough, either, and praised other sketch shows' "send-ups," something *The Kids* most definitely were avoiding, along with commercial parodies, and felt that "anyone anywhere in North America" could make the show. HBO, on the other hand, felt that no one nowhere should be doing it, and canceled it after the first season.

After a spate of CableAce nominations, and a win by Mark McKinney for best actor, though, the show was picked up for two more seasons at HBO. It spent its final two in the late slot on CBS. Throughout their run, they continued to experiment, and to demand perfection. "I was a production designer's nightmare," says

McCulloch, "I'd just come rip posters off [the wall], like, 'He wouldn't have a fucking Nike poster,' you know? Our [onscreen] environment once we got to TV was super important to us." Their brand of theatricality translated perfectly to being cinematic. Even sketches shot on video would often pay close attention to angles and lighting to add layers to elevate their sketches beyond "here are some guys on a stage."

By season four, they'd reached the creative juncture that sketch groups often dream of—the pretentious and unwieldy phase— best-exemplified by the McCulloch-directed "Love and Sausages." Even if you love a good short, elegant sketch, for some writers the easiest way to break the current mold is to try something you never would have done before—and maybe with good reason—to reassess where you're going. "Love and Sausages" is a surreal short film about a sausage factory worker (McCulloch) who falls in love with the lady at the factory who kisses each box of sausages as they go out. Meanwhile, he's tormented by Thompson as his father (or grandfather, it's not quite clear) with cries for more sausages. It took two days to shoot, and didn't have the confidence of the whole group. It might be a weirdly brilliant metaphor about giving your love to the right people, and something about capitalism. It's also gross and kind of beautiful, like love.

The Kids are a rarity for the '80s and '90s, in that they were a group before they were a sketch show. Assembling a group for the sake of a sketch series is not at all uncommon, but their particular brand of camaraderie is what allowed them to gang up on an idea and see it through. Somehow, despite on-set difficulties or egos, fifth season writer Diane Flacks describes the *Kids in the Hall* writers' room as the "sanest one" she's worked in. "What often happens in writers' rooms is, first of all, intense competition, enormous game playing, and a kind of fakeness that is so antithetical to good writing.

"I felt competitive to get the best material out there, but I didn't feel like anybody was trying to take anybody down in any way." Whether this lack of politics in the writers' room was the result of five years on stage and four years on the air is up for debate, but it was clear during this season that it was the end for the show. The Kids would eventually continue to tour, but they ended their TV show with a tearful goodbye that ended in them all shedding their wigs for what could have been their last time on TV as a group.

Once the tour was in place, Foley had been cast to shoot the pilot for the sitcom *NewsRadio* with fellow Canadian and sketch comedian Phil Hartman. Though he offered to compensate the group for any lost ticket sales because of the scheduling problems, the group started to fall apart, and arguably disintegrated, just as they were about to film what they assumed would be their first movie, *Brain Candy*. "We're horrible with business, even to this day," McCulloch says. "We were sort of told by ourselves, by society, by the arts community that we should do a film. That's the thing you do after a show. And I don't know if we really wanted to."

McCulloch explains the feeling as sour, and rewrites upon rewrites didn't help. The pieces felt stronger than the whole, and that wasn't how The Kids in the Hall operated. "We didn't know what to do, so we tied ourselves to the success of that movie to tell us what to do, which was wrong."

They were probably as zombified by the post-show exhaustion and the stressful rewrites as the patients in their film end up after taking the "miracle drug" Gleemonex, only instead of living inside their happiest moments, they seemed stuck in the most bitter cycle possible, made worse by the production of a movie that felt even cheaper than their series had been. "We were in the arms of a cruel producer who wanted to know, 'Could we have titties in the movie?' You know, and like, 'What?'" On top of this, there were personal problems interfering with the project, too, and the lack of fun was a clear barrier to getting it done right. "We'd always had tension, but it was the first time that it had been no fun, not one day of it." Even if the movie still enjoys a following today, the box office receipts weren't great.

A syndication run for the series on Comedy Central and a new tour eventually helped them patch things up, and in 2010 they released *The Kids in the Hall: Death Comes to Town*, a mini-series rather than a new season of their sketch show. It would be a dozen years before they'd revive the original series—twenty-seven years from the end of the original run—on Amazon. It deals with many of the same ideas the original show did, but doesn't deny the passage of time, nor the realities of being on a relatively censor-free streaming service.

"They did age-appropriate versions of *The Kids in the Hall*," Paul Myers says. "It's so punk to walk around as a naked middle-aged man in the first episode." He's referring to a sketch in which Foley and McDonald are approached by the cops (McCulloch and McKinney) only to convince them the men they're looking for are fully clothed, while they are completely naked. Which they very much are, complete with bouncing up and down. "They managed to find a new way to be shocking, at their own expense."

The show is well-rated and fans of the original show love it. They should; it's not a reboot, just a new season. While it's hard to age into comedy after three decades and not come across like a bunch of whiny grandpas who are afraid of change, they just keep moving. They go the completely cinematic route (no live performances) and embrace the several weird notes they left us on. Still, the terrible business sense is at work. "What do we do with the success of our new show?" McCulloch imagines the group asking itself. Then, in a dumb kid voice, "Well, we don't know."

8

Canadian Content: Sketch Shows from the Great White North

Comedy in the United States would be worse off without Canada. In the '70s and '80s, the influx due to *SNL* and *SCTV* were integral to us getting films and TV shows that are still celebrated today. Even as the Canadian government has tried to bring more Canadian content to their own airwaves, they export so many skilled writers and performers that their culture has surreptitiously integrated into ours irreparably, and that is a good thing.

Codco

In 1973, Newfoundland's Traveling Theatre Company started picking up actors who would eventually perform in the comedy stage show *Cod on a Stick*, written by Tommy Sexton and Diane Olsen. "I think we got $40 a week and we slept on gym floors," recalls Codco's Mary Walsh. The show poked fun at stereotypes about Newfoundlanders being bumpkins, or worse—stereotypes well-known enough that the comedy would play across Canada. Eventually becoming Codco (short for "Cod Company," due to Newfoundland's large cod fishing industry), members of the group bounced in and out of active membership for the next thirteen years. The group, though, never stopped being about comedy with an agenda.

"Our whole raison d'être, when we started out, was to stop the *Newfie* joke bullshit," says Walsh. "When we started in '73, in Toronto, if people asked you where you were from on an elevator, people from Ontario would fall down laughing, just because you said you're from Newfoundland." A particular brand of bigot was convinced that Newfoundlanders (some consider the shortened version of this a slur) were backward and a drain on Canada as a society. With such a seemingly narrow focus for their comedy, one could fairly assume that they were only a hit with Canadian audiences.

"We got some great reviews in Philadelphia, from a guy named Walter *Herring*, which was funny, because he was reviewing *Codco*." Herring's review in the *Philadelphia Daily News* paints a pretty clear picture of how much satire you could find in their 1975 show, including a sketch about the IRA, one on the typical Newfoundland family, and something called "Morton the Child Molester." On top of taking a lot of chances, they integrated home movies into their shows—a bit more complicated in 1975 since it was all on film, meaning a huge portion of their show was at the whims of a working film projector. "We were a big hit in a very minor way."

The core of the TV group—Andy Jones, Cathy Jones, Greg Malone, Tommy Sexton, and Mary Walsh—had worked with the live show throughout the years, along with Diane Olsen, Bob Joy and Paul Sametz. In 1986, the group started touring again, and were approached by producer Michael Donovan. They then started developing their series, though it wouldn't first air until 1988, put into a difficult Thursday night slot on CBC designed to siphon off viewers from NBC. Not long after *Codco*'s premiere, *The Kids in the Hall* would premiere, and it would become a block of daring, original Canadian sketch comedy.

"*The Kids in the Hall* had a broader appeal than we did because they were suburban," Walsh says. "They were from a larger area. And we were more, can I say parochial or provincial, but I think we were equally funny." The appeal of *Codco*—even if a lot of the references, accents, and more will fly above the average American's head—is that the show has a strong, relatively new-seeming point of view.

The show was actually written by and starring both men and women, and both Sexton and Malone were openly gay. For any of its failings (such as all sketch shows have) the group use specificity to their advantage, and demand that the audience play catch up. There's no character representing the audience unfamiliar with Newfoundland or the issues of the day in any of their sketches. "We were specific, very specific. Except, of course, Tommy and Greg always loved doing television parodies."

They were never worried about the specificity being a problem, though. "We were very inspired by *Monty Python* and *Beyond the Fringe* . . . What do I know about Liverpool, really? What do I know about the British character, except, of course, they did own 93% of the whole fucking world at one point, so they kind of made an imprint." For a show in 1988 to feature jokes about mansplaining before it was a term, or a commercial for "Tamponettes," which were "small enough for a man, but made for a woman," it would have to be Canadian. These were not issues being broached by American sketch shows. There was drag (often played just as real as it would've been on *The Kids in the Hall*) and if a social or political view demanded it, they'd have fun with it. Whatever it was, it was the point of view of a native Newfoundlander.

An article in the *Ottawa Citizen* in 1986 ends on a quote from Andy Jones that sums up their almost militant devotion to local humor. "The more local and specific you are, the more universal the humor, because it is real. People who set out to do 'generic' comedy, that isn't based on a particular place or particular individuals, usually fail because no one comes from 'everywhere.'"

This Hour Has 22 Minutes

Toward the end of *Codco*, in 1993, Mary Walsh and Cathy Jones joined forces with frequent collaborator Greg Thomey and comedian

Rick Mercer to create the satirical news show *This Hour Has 22 Minutes*. At the time of writing, the show is in its thirtieth season, meaning an entire generation of Canadians have grown up with it, and many of them have gone on to work on it, like comedian Graham Clark. "My parents knew *Codco*, and that was their lead-in to watching *22 Minutes*," Clark recalls. "It was our version of the *SNL* news."

"I had this idea for a news of the week thing, loosely based on [English '60s topical satire show] *That Was the Week That Was*, or that kind of show," Mary Walsh says. To her great fortune, Ivan Fecan, director of television program at CBC Television, was looking for something just like that. She approached most of the *Codco* team, including Cathy Jones, who lived just down the street. "She said, 'Well, I don't even care about the news. The news makes me feel violently, physically ill.' And I said, 'Well, that'd be perfect, because that is a whole other view than anybody else will bring in.'" Many of her busy friends turned her down.

"Everybody else knew how much of a time commitment it was. I didn't." Starting from scratch probably should've been more daunting: In five days they were expected to put together an entire, topical comedy show with sketches and "news reports," which would air only days later. The show was bought for a six-episode run, though CBC continued to add episodes to their order, even if Mary wasn't available the entire time to fully appreciate it. "I wasn't even there right from the start, because my back gave out and I was in the hospital having back surgery." After recovery, she found she was no longer head writer of her own show, but she kept going.

"I must say I was full of rancor and resentment. Crying, crying, crying. But also, I really believed in the show, and I believed, quite wrongly, that we could make some change in the injustice and fairness [in Canada]." Walsh would often approach politicians in character with a microphone and camera, trying to catch them out and expose them for what they really were. "By the end of my time there, politicians were calling us up and asking us to ambush them because it made them look like, you know, *hail fellow, well met.* Good sports and stuff like that."

"I served as their West Coast correspondent," says Clark. "The producer at the time wanted to have somebody out here because they very rarely would focus their energy west of Ontario." Since Canada's biggest story the year prior had been the Keystone pipeline and protests against it, the show realized they'd missed out. "A lot of the stories I did were just silly, Vancouver-based stories." These included, among other things, the "worst bus stop in Canada," which was behind cement barriers on a freeway, and a Vancouver otter that was eating tens of thousands of dollars in local koi.

While *22 Minutes* is decidedly, and importantly, a Canadian show, it hasn't managed to keep everyone in Canada. Perhaps the best-known recent export is deadpan weirdo Nathan Fielder, who started out in a segment entitled "Nathan on Your Side." This segment was a clear tonal precursor to his series *Nathan for You*, featuring interviews with real people clearly not prepared for his onscreen persona. While Canadian shows are certainly reservoirs of comedic skill, Graham Clark sees being on a show he grew up with through a pretty practical lens. "It's funny, Canada's comedy business is so small that eventually you will run into somebody that you idolized as a child. It's not big enough a scene for that not to happen."

This could explain why leapfrogging from Canadian comedy show to Canadian comedy show makes segues simple. Mary Walsh explained to me that *Codco* and *The Kids in the Hall* were ordered by the CBC at the same time, by the same executive. In 1992, that same CBC executive ordered *22 Minutes* and *Royal Canadian Air Farce* in the same go. As Graham Clark reminds me, "If you're around long enough, you'll just meet everybody."

Royal Canadian Air Farce

Like *Codco*, *Royal Canadian Air Farce*'s history also begins in 1973, or at least that's when the name begins. It originated as an improv troupe in 1970 in Montreal, as Jest Society Company, with a cast comprised of Roger Abbott, Martin Bronstein, Gay Claitman, Patrick Conlon, and John Morgan. By 1973, the new cast of Roger Abbott, Dave Broadfoot, Don Ferguson, Luba Goy, and John Morgan were known as Royal Canadian Air Farce, landing themselves a radio show the same year (which would run for twenty-four years). Then, in 1993, the *Royal Canadian Air Farce* TV show premiered, which ran regularly for fifteen years, with specials each year up until 2019.

Air Farce was topical, a mix of sketches featuring actors playing world leaders and people making the news, various fake news desks (often from different countries) and the sketch show staples of commercial parodies and straight sketches, infused with daily news items. Jessica Holmes, who joined the show in 2003 after having her own sketch show in 2002, was less familiar with *Air Farce* than some of her contemporaries. "I wasn't allowed much TV growing up, but I knew my grandparents had listened to them on the radio," Holmes remembers. "It just sort of got ingrained in me, this Canadian thing of *we're supposed to poke fun at the government, we're supposed to poke holes in politics*." The way she sees it is that they were attempting to keep people honest through comedy. At the same time, they chose their targets carefully. "They really never believed in punching down. They only believed in punching up and speaking truth to power; they're just such good people. They never took the wind out of anybody's sails who wasn't kind of living the high life."

The show also had plenty of high-profile Canadian guests, like Tommy Chong. When Chong showed up, Holmes played an anti-marijuana advocate and he played himself. At one point in the sketch, Chong lights up some prop marijuana. Holmes remembers the sketch distinctly. "He got the prop people to switch out the fake pot with real," she says. "No one told me, so during the live show, we were all getting a little buzz on in the studio." When they weren't being switched out, props and costumes were a huge part of the show, since *Air Farce* actually had a reasonable budget for those things.

"On Mondays, you'd get your script, and you'd work on the script," Holmes recalls. "Then Tuesday we would go in for hair and wardrobe. It was just so exciting to see [that] Luba's doing the Queen again, to see them pull out the wig and the giant outfit. Seeing characters come to life, especially when the show first started, the budget was astronomical—no limitations on what we can try and who we could play."

Perhaps because of the standards of the producers, you wouldn't call *Air Farce* biting satire, but that approachability probably made it so that at least some satire was getting into the homes of people who wouldn't be watching *22 Minutes*. The characterizations could be big and goofy, but the goal was as noble as any other satire. It was also a show that appreciated the fickle nature of entertainment and liked to keep their people happy. "There's a loyalty on *Air Farce*, unlike anything I've seen before on other series. There was a member of the crew going through a really hard time; it was literally like, 'Hey, whatever you need, we're here for you. You take as much time as you need. And there will always be a home for you if you want to come back.' And so that was really beautiful."

Holmes was given the same treatment when they found out she was pregnant. On most shows, she'd have been written off. Instead, they built sets to hide her bump, and even gave her some advice. Two producers told her, "If you want to have another baby, go ahead and have it now." The show was good to its people, and to some, played a part for underserved comedy audiences.

"I think the show did a service for people by filtering news through the comedy machine," Holmes says. "*Air Farce* was not seen as a cool show, it was not seen as cutting edge as other forms of comedy . . . *Air Farce* was comedy for rural populations or for central

Canada, for the East Coast. So I was grateful that we were connecting with people who don't often get to feel heard on TV." It's helped her with her stand-up comedy career, too. "If I had never had *Air Farce*, I would only ever be doing one type of job to please one type of people. There's a whole other world out there."

In 2009, after over 300 episodes and consistently good ratings, the core crew of *Royal Canadian Air Farce* made the choice to end the show. Their final season had aired live, and for the next ten years they would get back together for a yearly reunion show. Their place had been cemented in history, and Don Ferguson said the group had done "pretty much everything we wanted to do."

The Vacant Lot

If I didn't know better, I'd say Lorne Michaels has been planning the slowest takeover of the United States in history. In the early '90s, he tried to repeat his success with *The Kids in the Hall* with a Toronto group called The Vacant Lot. Consisting of Rob Gfroerer, Paul Greenberg, Nick McKinney (brother to Mark), and Vito Viscomi, the group was blessed by the hand of Michaels and got to shoot a season of six episodes of sketch comedy called, appropriately, *The Vacant Lot*.

"I moved to Toronto in 1986, and I had been doing sketch comedy and improv in Ottawa," Nick McKinney says. "My brother had mentioned this troupe, which was, at the time, Vito Viscomi, Paul Greenberg, Rob Gfroerer, and Alex Karzis." The group had been performing at Ryerson University, a public technical college (now known as Toronto Metropolitan University). "Shortly after I moved there, I met them at a party at Scott Thompson's house. We all just really hit it off instantaneously; [there was this] sort of stylized mixture of absurd and dark that we were all into."

Soon enough, the Vacant Lot were performing at the Rivoli, the old stomping grounds of The Kids in the Hall. They opened for The

Kids and other groups, including music acts, at venues all over Toronto. Where some acts might tweak and cull from the same set of sketches over time, McKinney estimates they were putting together two shows each month of nearly all brand-new material. They slowly started combining their best material into a single show and put it on at The Theatre Centre in Toronto. "We first got scouted by a guy called Jim Biederman, who worked for Lorne Michaels." Not long after, they got the call from Michaels.

"This is typical Lorne, it's the same thing he did with The Kids in the Hall. He scooped us all up, we went to New York for I think two months." They were put up in an apartment hotel and expected to put on as many live shows as possible, in a town still relatively unaccustomed to live comedy theater, ironically enough for *the* theater town in the US. They performed at legendary places like The Village Gate, which in the '70s had hosted *National Lampoon's Lemmings*, featuring to-be legends like John Belushi, Chevy Chase, and Christopher Guest. Like The Kids before them, Michaels expected The Vacant Lot to get used to tougher crowds, meanwhile, "We're starting to write the first season of what we thought the show would be."

Once the show was greenlit, with the CBC, The Comedy Network and MTV all bought into it, The Vacant Lot headed back to Toronto to write their little Canadian hearts out. They workshopped their bits live before committing anything to film, a hard transition for any comedian in a time when universal pocket cameras didn't exist. "Midnight at the Rivoli is very different than hitting your mark and editing stuff," McKinney says. Even with a few missteps, like any show (including some regrettable brownface and accents), *The Vacant Lot* manages to be unique from the jump, perhaps one of the few short-lived series of this early-'90s era to have more potential than its short run hints at. It has one of the great openings of any sketch show—all four members in a living room, in slow-motion as a giant fan blows them and their belongings across the room. Eventually, the back wall falls—*a la* Buster Keaton—and leaves them covered in wall bits and window frames. "That was unplanned. I mean, they were breakaway windows, but we didn't know that one of them was going to end up hanging off Paul."

The show was not shot live, though about half of it was shot in studios. All of it would likely have been played for an audience to record their laughs after the show had been edited. One of their more well-known sketches is about the song "Blinded by the Light," where three of the guys argue over the lyrics to the famously mumbled song. "Held up like a loofah by the foreman of the night" is the first suggestion, and they get dumber from there, until one of them angrily corrects the group with the real lyrics and storms off when they laugh at him. One of them then says, "Somebody's a little hot under the colander."

In one series of sketches, Jesus Christ finds himself in a modern-day middle school, failing in wood shop and being called out for cheating at swimming by running on the water. A simple concept, but it works. Every episode features one well-produced musical number—something listenable and maybe even danceable, *a la Not the Nine O'Clock News*. They're mostly quite quick half hours, full of energy, and definitely big "sketch comedy acting," but harnessed in a way that makes a lot of the sketches play well. "In hindsight, I wish I'd understood the process better," McKinney says. "There would have been little things I would have tweaked along the way. Because we did very broad comedy that was then sometimes also filmed in a very broad way. And I think that would have been something I would have liked to have changed in a second season."

That second season didn't happen, even if the one they got was the culmination of years of sweat and toil. "In Canada it takes six or seven years to make an overnight success," McKinney says. The group eventually split up, with Gfroerer and Greenberg moving to

LA to act, and McKinney and Viscomi moving to New York to write. In 1996, the two writers worked up something for Lorne Michael's Broadway Video, who had a brand-new digital department. They had partnered with Microsoft to experiment with a live-streamed comedy show, broadcasting from the Catch a Rising Star comedy club in New York. Streaming video was not really a thing, just yet, which is why McKinney and Viscomi like to call this the "six-million-dollar mistake."

They hired most of The Upright Citizens Brigade (fresh to New York at this point), with Todd Barry as one of the writers, and Marc Maron hosted. At one point, Gilbert Gottfried brought out Phil Hartman during a show—there were a lot of names, because there was a lot of money being thrown around. "The only problem was that the only people who could see it with any great regularity were these, I don't know, fifty people at Microsoft in Redmond who had the bandwidth and the technology to support this stuff. We could watch our numbers live, say two thousand, three thousand people would tune in, but because of technical glitches, you would just be losing audience all the way along." Needless to say, this experiment was about fifteen years ahead of its time.

McKinney would go on to harness his writing skills, and love for documentary, by working at the fledgling *The Daily Show*, and he recently produced the documentary *Kids in the Hall: Comedy Punks* for Amazon, based on Paul Myers' book *One Dumb Guy*. The rest of The Vacant Lot are still working actors and writers, infiltrating comedy one show and movie at a time.

9

Poets and Geniuses:
iO / ImprovOlympic

Davidshepherd was addicted to starting improv groups. After The Compass and its satellite theaters were no longer a going concern, he continued to try out new ideas. In 1965, he worked with Janet Coleman's The Loft Theatre in New York to create improvisational workshops. Then, in the early '70s he started something called Improvisation Olympics, a way to put Spolin-original and Spolin-inspired games on stage, in front of an audience, but with a twist. The Olympic part was as literal as you could get; improv teams competed, and were rated by judges, on three criteria: Content, Commitment, and Cooperation. Not too long after, Keith Johnstone's Theatresports would start in Canada, with a very similar aesthetic and approach.

By the time Shepherd brought the Improvisation Olympics to Canada, where it flourished, Charna Halpern was a student at The Players Workshop in Chicago. Sometime after, it was shortened to "Improv Olympic," or "Improv Olympics," plural. The games caught Halpern's eye. "I thought, well, you know, if you're not one of the six people on The Second City stage, you're not performing. Because there was nothing else," Halpern says.

One night in 1981, as she was driving back to the suburbs after an improv class, Halpern had a brainwave. "'We have so many of us who have nowhere to perform.' I just turned around and I went right back downtown to go meet with him." She knew David was in town putting on a show called *The Jonah Complex*, and approached him, proposing that she bring Improv Olympics to Chicago. First, he made her audition. She got the role of god. "Which I was very excited about. Sounds like a big part, but it turns out god is just the person doing the lights, the disembodied voice. So I never even got on stage."

Later that year, Halpern was running ads in the papers announcing training and competitions for ImprovOlympic (it seems she may have been the one to smash those names together first). She and Shepherd worked together to formalize how the training and games would run, usually out of whatever space Halpern could find, with playoffs being held at Second City. "After just about a year, I had to separate because David was a little bit crazy. So we agreed that he would go to New York, and I would do Chicago, and maybe we'd have this big contest together in the future."

It soon dawned on her that she was getting tired of the games being the main aspect of their shows and, again, decided to find the one person she knew who could help her realize her improv dreams. "It was Halloween. I knew I couldn't stand the way ImprovOlympic was at the time; it was still this game thing. So I thought, 'I'm gonna seek out Del Close.'" Close, while already something of a legend, both for being involved in and teaching improvisers for a couple decades, and for his involvement with chemical substances, wasn't what you'd call a recluse. You could find him.

Halpern knew that Del was doing a show at an art gallery. She showed up to find Close wearing a robe and brandishing a magic wand, surrounded by lit candles and a room full of people. Close was a practicing witch—something Halpern didn't know—and at the moment, he was invoking demons. "At that time, I was doing [transcendental meditation]. I was learning how to meditate, and they tell you to 'white light' yourself and protect yourself and not let demons in. I was watching this and I was horrified. I was like, 'The nerve of this man to invoke demons!'" She forgot why she'd even showed up in the first place, and tore into him for his invocations.

"Hey, you have a lot of nerve invoking demons in front of all these people!" she said.

"I protected the building," Close responded.

She left and headed back to her performance space at the Cross-Currents Theatre. "I was hitting myself in the head like, 'What did I do? I blew it. Now the guy hates me.' Then someone says to me, 'You know what Charna, he's always high . . . You'll see him again, in a month or so, and he won't even remember you.'" She took advantage of Close's drug-addled state and approached him about a month later.

"Hey, how'd you like to make two hundred bucks and some pot?" she asked.

"What do I gotta do?" he asked.

"Just teach one class," she said.

"I figured, let's see what I can steal from him, you know?" Halpern recalls. Close asked if he could do whatever he wanted in his class. She was firmly in favor of his making the class his own.

"Can I invoke demons?" he asked.

In a way, so it seems, he did. He taught a single class to a group of experienced improvisers, one of whom Halpern remembers as one of the best improvisers she's ever seen. They were cocksure and ready to blow Close's mind. Instead, he had to raze and then re-lay the foundation of everything they thought they knew about improv.

"We left in shock," Halpern recalls. "He tore us apart, you know, but that's where we learned everything." This is where—instead of learning how to compete for points in a scene—they learned to say "yes, and" in a scene, so that you don't deny the reality of it and stop it dead in its tracks. This class is where they learned the lesson of playing to the top of your intelligence: in other words, play your scenes as smart as you are, and the audience will follow along without a problem.

"Treat the audience like poets and geniuses and that's what they'll be become," he would often say. It was also about making everyone else on stage look good, to interlace everyone's ideas into something cohesive as the scene goes on.

"He just really opened the secret to the universe to us about what this really was," Halpern says. He wasn't kind about it either, asking them why they were playing like "little children." After this class, she gave Close a ride home and they stopped off for some coffee. "There's got to be something more for improvisation," she said, dreaming of expanding what she was doing. "And he said, 'Well, maybe you're not at a twit after all.'"

"Let's close down your little game theater and I will work with you," he offered. Halpern got exactly what she wanted, and exactly what Chicago needed. You'll read in other places that Close was the co-founder of iO which, in a sense is true: He helped it become what it is best known for. Eventually they'd go from ImprovOlympic, to ImprovOlympia, then get threatened with a lawsuit by the International Olympic Committee and decide to go with, simply, "iO," and Del was there when that happened, too. So, yes, Del Close elevated iO, but Halpern, through sheer determination and insulting the right people, got the whole machine going.

As for the name change, "I hated that cheesy name anyway, and Del and I were doing something so much cooler with long-form. So I wanted to get away from the name that had a competition aspect." Long-form improvisation—namely: the Harold, which Del had started developing with Myerson and Mathieu at The Committee—was going to be their bread and butter. The first several years were a struggle, especially until iO finally had its own theater on Clark Street in Chicago, in 1995. During those critical years, future comedy stars would come to iO, sometimes working at Second City, too. The members of The Upright Citizens Brigade, which in the early years counted among its members Matt Besser, Amy Poehler, Ian Roberts, Matt Walsh, Rich Fulcher, and Adam McKay, cut their teeth at iO. Also there at the same time was future *SNL* star David Koechner.

"I was reading in the Chicago Tribune—they had a Sunday arts section—I read about this cat named Del Close, and Charna Halpern, this place called ImprovOlympic, and he sounded fucking amazing." Koechner decided he was going to study with Close, even if he'd actually moved to Chicago to go to Second City. "I don't know why. Like, why would I abandon the thing I came there for? But everything in that article told me *go there.*" Shortly after starting his study under Close and Halpern, they started introducing more levels—opportunities for more dues revenue, sure, but also more ways to hone your craft. "Del doesn't do basics. You know, you're supposed to have your technique by the time you get to his class."

Koechner eventually also studied at Second City at the same time as iO, and checked out Mick Napier's Metraform, a precursor to The Annoyance Theatre. During his years in Chicago, Koechner crossed paths with innumerable people who were also shaping the future of comedy. "This was a special, once-in-a-millennium group," Koechner says. "Also, they weren't there to get famous. That was the very big difference. Everyone that was there at the time I was there, they were there to be good—to get good . . . Everyone wanted to be the best that they could be."

The list of names who would come out of both iO and LA's iO West (Ih opened in 1997) and move on to *Saturday Night Live* and other comedy powerhouses is too big to put here, but includes Bob Odenkirk; *30 Rock*'s Scott Adsit, John Lutz and Jack McBrayer; Stephen Colbert, Kevin Dorff, Jon Favreau, Danny Pudi, and Andy Richter; *The Office*'s Kate Flannery and Angela Kinsey; *MADtv*'s Phil LaMarr; *SNL*'s Vanessa Bayer, Aidy Bryant, Bill Hader, Tim Meadows, Jerry Minor and Cecily Strong; and improv legend David Pasquesi "Still one of the most brilliant minds ever," Koechner says. "He's the person we all still revere as a god. David Pasquesi was our everything."

Phil LaMarr is a founding member of Yale's The Purple Crayon, a long-form improv team that started before most of the group had ever even performed a Harold. One of his buddies, Eric Berg, had gotten the full experience. "He had spent the summer taking workshops at Second City and ImprovOlympic," LaMarr recalls. "He really loved it, so he got a group of us, his actor friends together." None of them really knew what improv was, so Berg walked them through it. "I remember sitting down with Eric in the dining hall, and he took out a napkin, and he sort of just made a diagram of what a Harold was. And that was our introduction to long-form improv."

Not unlike Halpern's own mind-expanding moment, LaMarr recalls that the tenets of improv just "clicked" for the whole group. "I've just spent since I was thirteen learning that conflict is drama, but now you're saying agreement is comedy? So we can build a scene by just collaborating positively? That's such a much better life philosophy!" It's easy to see how Del would've gravitated toward people learning the Harold off of a napkin, too: It was being woven into the fabric of comedy through the oral tradition. "Basically, he was putting out a principle. Einstein didn't have to teach everybody relativity." It didn't just click, either; the group absorbed the whole worldview. Soon, The Purple Crayon were invited by Halpern to participate in a Harold competition, which the young group won.

That same week, Del Close visited the home of LaMarr's friend Adam Gross, and put on an impromptu workshop with The Purple Crayon in Gross' basement. Gross' father was an attorney, which caused a genuine freakout when Close decided to smoke pot in their basement. Panic aside, that little workshop caused the whole group to head back out for a pilgrimage to Chicago that summer. "We would do Wednesday night workshops with Del, and then we would do a Saturday morning workshop at Second City," LaMarr remembers. They would perform at iO's space at CrossCurrents and spend their summer absorbing improv and comedy.

A few years later, Yale was hosting a Harold competition. The Purple Crayon were approached by Halpern. "Del wanted me to give this to you," LaMarr recalls her saying. She then reached into her purse and pulled out a tiny, three-inch magic wand with a gem on top.

LaMarr recalls thinking, "Oh, god. Is it okay to touch it? Or will I go into another dimension?" That was Close's power—even with a genuine, sincere gesture you had to wonder if there was something more behind it. At the end of the day, Close just wanted his people to succeed. This is the same reason why, eventually, Second City wasn't the only game in town where you could expect to find *SNL* scouts. Halpern recalls a night that future *SNL* writer and *30 Rock* co-star John Lutz saved his own ass.

"Back then, we were doing a different kind of audition for Lorne Michaels. He was letting us do improv," Halpern says. Improv is no longer sufficient for Michaels, she says; characters and writing need to come through, rather than just thinking on your feet as a performer. During the improv days, Michaels was in the audience as the show was being prepped backstage. "I put the group together and I have so many amazing people, I just somehow forgot about John Lutz. John is amazing, it was just a total mistake on my part." As the cast is getting ready to come out, Lutz runs up to Halpern. "'Please can I play? I feel so ready.' And I was like, 'Oh my god, baby, I forgot about you. Yes, yes! Go! Hurry, get backstage!'" Lutz made it onstage just as the lights came up. He was hired based on that performance. "It was just so lucky that he had the guts to come up and beg me to play."

Halpern's job developed and changed over the years, too. After Del Close passed away in 1999 from emphysema, she was the new figurehead, on top of still running much of the show. Spotting comedic skill became just as much a part of her job as making sure iO ran smoothly. When it came to *SNL* auditions in more recent years, she would prepare for months in advance. She knew Michaels wanted to see her fifteen best performers, so every Monday night she would see fifteen people herself, then whittle them down so that by

June, she had a list in her head of who will go up for Michaels. One July, before season thirty-eight, she was locked in; auditions were over.

Cecily Strong was working in the box office at the time, and Halpern walked by, asking why she hadn't auditioned. "She was one of my top women, she was in The Deltones, a musical improv troupe—she was really funny," Halpern says. Strong didn't believe she had enough material yet; she'd wait till next year. "Come upstairs, let me see what you have," Halpern said. Strong put on a standalone audition for her with short, succinct character pieces with clear jokes to them. "So I said, 'You're going up,' and she was so scared. 'No, because I don't think I'm ready,' and I said, 'You are ready, you're going up.' And I put her up, and she got hired."

Finding a place to teach you improv, as well as to give you the skills to do immersive, long-form improv while also trying to help you find work is not as common as you might think. iO doesn't have a touring company. They never had a TV show, in the '90s or otherwise. In the early days, especially, Halpern would even be called upon if a movie, TV show, or music video shooting in town needed extras who could follow direction. You can see Halpern and other iO folks as extras, featured and otherwise, in the music video for "300 Pounds of Heavenly Joy" by Big Twist & The Mellow Fellows, a music video by Johnny Winter, and one iO member ended up in *Wayne's World*, even if you can only see the back of his head. Oscar winner Adam McKay once got hooked up with a job through iO that saved Matt Besser's car.

"I dropped out of college senior year, because I heard about this magical place Chicago, where you could go on stage and whatever you kind of dream up can happen, so long as you don't say no to someone else saying something," remembers McKay. He was at iO, but wasn't making money—he was broke. "Matt Besser was leaving town for a week, and I didn't have a car, I was riding a bike . . . It was great, I had a car for a week. I parked it near this apartment I was at and I came out and it was gone. And I was like, 'Oh shit, someone stole Matt's car.'" He called the police—no help. He then looked back where he'd parked it. "It was a snow zone. Even though it was like seventy-five degrees out." He called Besser to tell him what had happened.

"Dude, I have like $3,000 of parking tickets on that car!" McKay scrambled for options, figuring that whatever his solution, he'd have to head back to college, because he couldn't afford to live in Chicago after bailing out Besser's car. "I was really thinking about hanging it up." He spent his last $120 getting the car out of impound, and no one—for whatever reason—mentioned the tickets. Still, McKay was now without money for food, rent, anything. "Right at that moment Charna Halpern called me and said, 'A friend is doing a big PR thing for that Nine Lives cat food, and they're going to run [Morris the Cat] for president. They need a campaign coordinator.'" McKay went to the audition—something he almost never did—and got it. It paid $700 per appearance, for about fifteen appearances.

"They did a big thing at the Winter Garden Theatre with the cast of *Cats*, they flew me into New York, put me up at a fancy hotel, they had me go around the country. With that money, I was able to get an apartment with a roommate. And off of the leverage of that—we were already doing Upright Citizens Brigade, but I was able to keep doing that—I auditioned for Second City, and I got it. From there, it all went pretty well. But without Nine Lives, and Morris the Cat and his handler, I probably wouldn't be here right now."

As I interview Charna Halpern for the second time (we spoke a few years back on the *Comedy on Vinyl* podcast), iO is in a transitional phase. It doesn't seem that way—the most recent theater space had closed down due to the ongoing pandemic, then was purchased and reopened not long after we spoke—but it is. I asked Halpern about iO's legacy because it seemed like that might be pertinent at the time. "We changed the face of improvisational comedy," she says. "It used to just be games that help build Second City shows or sketch material, and we really showed everyone that we can actually think intelligently on stage and create things that are worthy of a play, and create art, and create something that's worth fighting for." She reminds me that Second City co-founder Bernie Sahlins used to say that it wasn't worth it to pay to watch improv, that it was only a tool to be used in the creation of something else, effectively . . . "We proved that that's not true."

When Close passed away, he had not long before been surrounded by friends from the improv community, including Halpern. "He thanked me on his deathbed for putting his dream on stage," she says. "It was something he was experimenting with in the '60s. It was basically unteachable and unplayable at the time . . . When we started working together, we took some of my games from the ImprovOlympic, and plugged them into this form." When Harold Ramis was interviewed during Close's final birthday/going away party, he said the best lesson he ever got from Close was that an improviser's job is to make everyone else look good. If everyone on stage does that, then everyone looks good. The community aspect of Paul Sills' dream for The Compass also lived on in Close.

At his party, Close, with a long gray beard underneath an oxygen mask, talked about legacy, but not his own. He's on the phone, talking to members of The Upright Citizens Brigade. At first you might think he's talking about all the hard work they've done in improv when he says "We haven't done such a bad job," but it's soon clear he's talking about humanity. "It's a conspiracy of geniality and hope, and we need to investigate it some more." It's final, but not. He implores everyone listening to keep digging into the meaning of things, even if those things are good and pleasing—maybe especially because of that. The clarity of his last hours comes through, with a solid mix of acceptance and hope when he says, "Let's hear it for the fuckin' human race."

— 10 —
Unskied Snow:
In Living Color

Tommy Davidson's big break was auditioning for and getting *In Living Color*. If you ask him, though, the show itself still hasn't gotten its break. For comedy lovers, *In Living Color* was the place to get a taste of a kind of comedy that was brand-new to television. It was television from a Black perspective. Davidson illustrates why the show's success deserves more accolades: "White guy and a Black guy at a race. They're going to run the 40-yard dash. Black guy's got a ball and chain on his ankle. He's holding a baby, a dog is chasing him. Pow! The White guy beats him by a fraction of a second, but the headlines read 'White Man Better than Black Man.'"

He's not talking about people remembering the show, either. People clearly remember it. It made some huge careers, and pretty much everyone in the original cast is still working regularly in entertainment, with one of them at one point becoming the highest paid actor in film history. There's at least one book out there about the show, too. What's missing are the seemingly little things: lists of all-time great shows, stuff that keeps its memory alive a little longer, introduces the show to new generations. He thinks—rightly—the show should continue to be recognized that way.

The first sketch in episode one of *In Living Color* is a parody of the old game show *Love Connection*, with Keenen Ivory Wayans as Mike Tyson and Kim Coles as Robin Givens. Jim Carrey is Chuck Woolery and is toned down, for Jim Carrey. Tyson and Givens were part of a very public relationship and divorce, with Tyson accused of abuse, and Givens called "The Most Hated Woman in America," after CNN ran a poll asking who was at fault in a relationship no one in the public had a window into. The sketch paints Givens as a gold digger, and Tyson as a violent idiot who overuses the word "ecstatic" and spells it "E-X-K-I-T." Carrey's Woolery ends it with a sign off of, "May all your dates be a matter of public record."

Like sketch shows throughout history, *In Living Color* does get around taking sides by using the old "equal opportunity offender" cop out. For all the sketch's weaknesses, the undeniable reality of its importance is that, until 1990, this sketch couldn't have aired on any other sketch show. Mostly because there were rarely ever two—and definitely never more than two—people of color on any sketch show for any substantial amount of time. Who else was going to play them? That's a trick question with only one (bad) answer. This time, Keenen Ivory Wayans was in charge, and he'd been doing this kind of comedy, both professionally and otherwise, his whole life.

The Wayanses grew up poor, eventually fitting twelve people into a small apartment in New York City. Their dinner table was their first writers' room and comedy revue, where impressions and tearing into one another for laughs was the name of the game. Keenen made moves toward comedy early, and by 1980 was palling around with Robert Townsend, who showed him the ropes of the comedy business. They wrote together for some time, including an extended sketch called "Black Acting School," a commercial for a fictional school that teaches black actors how to play all the great stereotypes they'll be offered if they get into entertainment, like slaves and butlers.

They'd end up self-funding the filmed version of this sketch, and eventually wrote an entire film around it, entitled *Hollywood Shuffle*. That film was also self-funded, on credit cards, seven years before Kevin Smith got so much attention for doing the same thing with *Clerks*. And *Hollywood Shuffle* is mostly shot in color. It's the story of Bobby Taylor (Townsend) who aspires to great things in the acting world but, as you can guess from "Black Acting School," he's stuck auditioning for thug stereotypes or "Eddie Murphy types," which means no room for making a role your own. The movie is a narrative, interwoven with sketch; all of the sketches are a mix of fantasies in Bobby's mind or things he's seeing on TV, which he also imagines himself starring in.

Throughout the film, Bobby is told by his family that "there's always a job at the post office," which is not-so-subtle code for "acting won't pay shit," but he persists, culminating in his most screen time yet. The role is another gang member and, when he sees the look on his visiting family member's faces during the shoot, he quits. Another desperate actor steps right up and takes it, because, well, throw a rock in LA. The end of the film sees Bobby finally at the post office; he's filming a commercial where he gets to play—imagine it—a normal guy, working at the post office. Like so many pieces of anti-racism satire, it's all about fighting to be allowed a sliver of humanity. The year after, Keenen would write, direct and star in the Blaxploitation parody *I'm Gonna Git You Sucka*, a strict narrative that uses even more stereotypical Black roles to tell the story of taking back the streets from the perspective of a pretty dumb kid who doesn't know how to fight back.

Tamara Rawitt, producer of *Sucka* and *In Living Color*, was involved in every element of the show's creation, from choosing every writer for the show's first three seasons, to designing the look of the series. "We went in to meet with Fox, and I know Keenen really desperately wanted to be an action movie star. But what he didn't realize is that he had a better chance of becoming a business magnate, by letting us put this show together for him." It took some convincing on Rawitt's part, but Wayans eventually agreed to move in this new direction. Rawitt saw the potential to bring a black sensibility to TV sketch comedy that she believed had essentially left after Eddie Murphy exited *SNL*, years before. Off of the success of

Sucka, and the pep talk by Rawitt, a new, majority-black sketch show with dance numbers performed by the "Fly Girls" throughout was soon greenlit by the still young Fox Network.

Writer Rob Edwards was the first writer hired on *In Living Color,* writing for a lot of that first season. "I think that Keenen's original dream was to invert the model of *Saturday Night Live,* where there was always a cast of characters, eight famous comedians, and then one black guy. If you got a black woman, then that was even more miraculous, but it was usually a guy in a wig and a dress." Edwards had never written on a variety show; he was more of a sitcom guy, with a little stand-up experience, but he was excited about this show idea. Head writer Buddy Sheffield was later brought on because of his extensive work in variety. His brother David Sheffield and writing partner Barry Blaustein also came on board—both had written for Eddie Murphy in recent years—as well as stand-up comic Jeff Joseph. Also, of course, the Wayanses.

"You would just be sitting there kind of trying to come up with ideas, and then all of a sudden, Damon and Shawn [Wayans] would run in the room and say, 'Hey, we were talking about this at dinner. What if there are two critics . . .'" Jim Carrey came in the room, riffing on this idea he had about a fire marshal.

Edwards and the rest of the writers' room would then take frantic notes and try and sculpt these wild ideas into something cohesive. "It was a lot like animation in that way. Ideas come from all over the place, and you just kind of try to harness lightning in a bottle . . . My thing was just trying to give shape to a lot of these crazy ideas that were coming in, and [helping] Keenen shape what was going to be the voice of the show." Seemingly, that voice started scaring the shit out of the Fox Network.

Originally, the higher-ups at Fox had agreed to make *In Living Color* a one-hour show, but eventually scaled it back to a half an hour. "Fox kind of lost its nerve; they never really understood what the show was, who it was going to be for, all that kind of stuff. So they changed it from a one-hour show to a half-hour show, then from a half-hour series to a half-hour special," Edwards says. So, by the time they were ready to shoot—cast, sets, props, wardrobe, that now-iconic steamy rooftop set—it was going to be a one-off, hardly what Keenen had shot for in the beginning. Still, they planned to shoot ninety minutes' worth of material and edit that down to an undeniable thirty minutes of TV, with their loaded cast: Jim Carrey, Keenen, Kelly Coffield Park, Kim Coles, Davidson, David Alan Grier, Damon and Kim Wayans, and T'Keyah Crystal Keymáh.

"That hour and a half wound up being just cannibalized into the entire first season and a little bit of the rest of it," Edwards says. "Just about everything that we looked back on all the seasons as being great, a ton of it was on that first night." The first sketch Edwards pitched to Keenen, during his interview for the job, was something called "Great Moments in Black History." The first approach was hitting at the idea that when television does feature Black people, it has a tendency toward pandering, more than reality. Edwards' first suggestion was to set one of the "Black History" sketches at the 1935 Academy Awards. "Stepin Fetchit versus Mantan Moreland versus Hattie McDaniel . . . everybody was like 'Oh my god, we can't, we can't go there!' But we went to these other, better things."

The second sketch of the first episode wears the show's goals right there on its sleeve: It's an announcement that the show is about something, that it's not just pop culture parody. It's the first evidence of the show taking sides—specifically, the right side of history. With a clearly provable offense, like 400-plus years of oppression, there's no wiggle room, if you're doing it right. The first "Great Moments in Black History" gets right to the heart of it. It's a PBS-style mini-documentary hosted by Tommy Davidson that tells us the *true* story of the Apollo 11 moon landing. We all know about Buzz Aldrin, Neil Armstrong, and Michael Collins, but until today we'd never heard of Slick Johnson. After landing on the moon, with only enough fuel to return three astronauts, they "sent Johnson out to find a nice place to play volleyball." They leave him behind, and Slick Johnson (played by Jeff Joseph) is wiped from the history books.

Edwards recalls the feeling of freedom in terms of subjects they could write about on *In Living Color*. "Because it was unskied snow, the entire thing, you could just point at any aspect of Black life and do something really, really amazing with it." The audience, of course, felt the same way; they were waiting for this show. "They had been aching. We're like, 'Oh, Eddie Murphy—Yay!' and then, nothing. So they were just ready to bust." And the cast and crew were waiting to see if they'd offered up something this audience wanted. Any live performance is going to cause anxiety, so the group who had worked so hard on this show would be waiting until the first joke hit to know if they still needed to worry or not.

"It took about ten seconds after the first thing we did, but they were like—I don't know if you've ever been to a black church when things get going; it was like that. It was that cathartic. People weren't laughing, they were stomping their feet, and they were running up and down the aisles and high fiving everybody, it was like a sport." As this was happening, the Fox execs turned to Edwards and asked him if the show had paid the audience members to react like that. "How much money would it take to pay people to run up and down the aisles and high five each other, sweat, cry, laugh, cheer at the same time, where it's deafening in the room?"

Still, Fox wasn't convinced, even if they knew *In Living Color was good*. "They liked it a lot," remembers Rawitt. "But they were terrified of it, because it was all black, and [the Fox executives] were not all black." Their fear was alienating a community they knew very little about. This led to a screening for the NAACP in hopes to get some cultural approval in advance. "Most of the members at that time were well into their late fifties, if not older, and once you empower people to say 'no' and 'I don't like,' they use that power very gleefully." It was too much for the group that they screened the pilot for. "They were chastising us for being so daring and raw, and they just they couldn't get with it, and that scared Fox."

As a result, the pilot was shelved for six months, something which usually spells death for a new show. Fortunately for *In Living Color*, Rawitt's number of powerful connections in the media from coming up in marketing was unsurpassed. The tape was making the rounds, too, on purpose. "I heard from everybody, like, 'Why isn't this on the air? Why didn't this happen?' It gave me the impetus go rogue." Rawitt pulled up every journalist in her rolodex, and one of them—Martha Frankel, then at *Details* magazine—agreed to watch the tape. Frankel loved it, and wrote an unassigned piece on the hit show that never got a chance. "I tore it out of the magazine, faxed it to [founder of Fox] Barry Diller's office and I said, 'Now, what are you scared of?' The next day we got picked up."

"Within a week, *In Living Color* was a hit," remembers director Paul Miller. "It was a very exciting time, because the response to the show was overwhelmingly positive." The audience was there, the press liked them; they even ended up on the cover of *New York* magazine, which got them even more notice. "I remember pulling into the garage at Metromedia, where we did the show in Hollywood, and there were brand new cars for every member of the Wayans family, as gifts from their brother, who was a very generous guy." Miller recalls Keenen telling his dad he could retire. Things were changing for their family, just as the family itself was actively changing what TV looked and sounded like.

Writer Becky Hartman Edwards started at *In Living Color* at the beginning of season two. Like many of the show's writers, she found the schedule daunting. "I really quickly realized, like all the ideas I've ever had my entire life for sketches, you pretty much ran through [them all in] the first month," she says. The Monday pitch meeting could be difficult even if you did have material. She recalls Keenen being difficult to read. "If you pitched an idea that was terrible, it could be very brutal." If your sketch was picked for the next episode, there were 4 PM run-throughs with the actors to consider, which would come with notes from Keenen, which could come late if he was slammed with meetings.

"I feel like I was there almost every night till at least midnight, usually till sometimes even like 3 AM, or you would sleep over." The actors would need the updated scripts by 10 AM the next day, so it often went in cycles like this. Of course, if the actors decided to improvise, it started to look like you weren't doing your job. "These actors are amazing improvisers . . . Then you would get notes from Keenen about, 'Why wasn't my note done about the Jesse Jackson sketch?' It actually was in there. Now, I'm not saying that what one of the actors improvised wasn't better, but you can sometimes feel like you got caught a little bit between that." For Hartman Edwards, *In Living Color* was "writing boot camp."

Early in the show's run, Keenen took no prisoners, even slamming people on air who he knew well in real life. He lampooned Arsenio Hall, a fellow member of Eddie Murphy's crew, giving him a horse laugh and making him an inveterate name-dropper and ass-kisser. He was unrelenting in finding mannerisms and body parts (long fingers, big butt) of Hall's to exaggerate. Keenen also occasionally chose to play Marsha Warfield in sketches. Keenen knew Warfield well from the clubs and, like anyone else, if they were public figures, they were fair game. Keenen chose to make his version of Warfield hyper-masculine, yet oddly empowered within that framework.

"It's weird to see what people think of you," Warfield says. "I appreciate it much more now. But I wasn't mad at him for that. But seeing somebody do impressions of you, it's really interesting the mannerisms they pick up and what they hear. Your first instinct is to go 'That's not me.' And your second instinct is 'Quit lying, you know good and well he got you.'" Hall never appeared on *In Living Color*, for obvious reasons, but in season five, Warfield played herself in a sketch where Ace (Jamie Foxx) and Main Man (Davidson) deny her entry to a theater, per their raison d'être of getting in everyone's way, as well as their own. It was a show to be seen on, throughout its five seasons. Warfield, as herself, gloriously puts both characters in their place.

In Living Color was experimental in just about every facet of its creation, from the casting, to the makeup of its writers, meeting an apparent niche cultural need that turned out to be a national one. By season three, not content to simply change the world of comedy, *In Living Color* accidentally changed the world of sports, too. By the '90s, the Super Bowl halftime show was a travesty of entertainment, a mix of okay pop acts, university marching bands and the occasional aging comedian. By putting a live episode of *In Living Color* up on Fox at the same time as the halftime show, they not only siphoned away viewers for half an hour, but they purportedly changed the way the Super Bowl programmed their halftime from then on. The next year the Super Bowl's only performer was Michael Jackson. *In Living Color* as a whole sometimes gets credit for this change, even if the idea came from specific people behind the scenes. "I joined several people in coming up with the idea to do the show as a live halftime special to counter [the Super Bowl]," Rawitt recalls. "There was not a thing that I wasn't involved in. But of course, as a female your value is discredited, and many times you're put in 'the Patty Hearst closet.'"

In Living Color was such a hit that Keenen had designs on expanding the show, as well. There were rumors that some Fly Guys might come in to add to the sex appeal of the show, while the Fly Girls were on a different trajectory, maybe even toward their own TV show. Keenen wanted to make them a pop group, even before Jennifer

Lopez joined in season three. The story Keenen's manager, Eric Gold, relayed to author David Peisner in his book *Homey Don't Play That!,* is that the Fly Girls almost got signed, but that Paula Abdul overheard them insulting her in a bathroom during their pitch meeting, and she gave Virgin Records an ultimatum, so the Fly Girls never got signed.

Marty Lester, a sound designer and audio engineer, wasn't anywhere near the Fly Girls around this disputed incident, but he does have a different perspective on it. "I was working in a studio in Los Angeles. I was just [an] assistant engineer. This up and coming producer, Dave Pensado, came in with a project . . . it was the Fly Girls. They came in with the songs, I think, pretty fully fleshed." Marty says the Fly Girls at the time—Deidre Lang, Carrie Ann Inaba, Cari French, and Lisa Marie Todd—showed up to add their vocals. "One or two of them could actually sing," he says, indicating he worked mostly with those one or two; he also met their to-be famous choreographer.

"Rosie Perez came in one day, and she hung out and she was kind of cheering them on and hyping them up . . . Everyone was professional, everyone was real nice." The following day, Lester headed into the studio, and the session had been canceled. "What I heard was is they had aired a sketch that Paula saw, freaked out about it, and called up [Virgin Records] . . . Paula was, you know, their bread and butter, and they only had a few acts." That sketch, a parody of Abdul's song "Promise of a New Day," was a body shaming anthem sloppily entitled, "Promise of a Thin Me." Lester doesn't buy that Paula didn't know about the Fly Girls and then found out about them in a bathroom.

"That's bullshit. [The Fly Girls record] was a known thing, and if it was hidden from Paula, I'd be surprised. LA is a small town." The Fly Girls never went beyond *In Living Color,* and the Fly Guys never materialized. Keenen and the show kept trying to push beyond the limits of the TV set, eventually getting close to producing a movie around Damon Wayans' angry children's performer "Homey D. Clown," but that also fizzled. As the show's final two seasons came around, *In Living Color* would see considerable cast changes, such as the loss and return of Damon Wayans (he came back for $75,000 *per sketch*, as opposed to the rest of the cast's $25,000 per episode) and the eventual exit of Keenen from the show. As usual, the writing staff continued to lose and bring in new blood.

T. Faye Griffin wrote on seasons four and five, a newbie along with Al Sonja L. Rice; they were the only two Black female writers on the staff. "I think we were primarily hired to bring the Black voice into the room. What they didn't anticipate, I think, is that we wrote harder than they expected. We weren't relegated to just writing the girly stuff. We kind of went toe to toe with the fellas." In a season where so many of the characters were fully established, and with the *In Living Color*'s voice in danger of wavering, this energy clearly helped a show that could have stagnated or become The Damon Wayans Show. This was especially important as Jamie Foxx was officially one of the stars now, after two seasons of being simply "featured."

Season five was almost entirely new faces, too, with only Carrey, Davidson, Grier, and Keymáh lasting all five seasons. Over hiatus, Tommy Davidson was working on the film *Strictly Business* with Anne-Marie Johnson (who had co-starred in *Hollywood Shuffle* and *I'm Gonna Git You Sucka*). Johnson was about to leave her current show, the adaptation of the film *In the Heat of the Night*, and Davidson suggested she join up, talking production into bringing her on. Johnson recalls, "I got that phone call and [they] said 'Welcome to *In Living Color*.' So Tommy Davidson got me that gig."

She'd been working on high profile TV shows for some time, so Johnson wouldn't have had the opportunity to even audition for the show before this. Like the rest of America, though, she was more than aware of it. "I was a huge fan of *In Living Color*, and I could not believe it that I was on it . . . *In Living Color*, especially for African

Americans, we were like, 'Okay, this is unreal,' and its continual social comment was very reminiscent of what we did on *Hollywood shuffle*."

There have been stories floating around that Carrey's film endeavors were frequently laughed at on set. Perhaps it was his try-hard energy, busting out three films in 1994 alone. "Fox asked me to come back as a producer and director," Paul Miller says. "Jim Carrey was under contract to do another season. I said, 'You guys, this is an opportunity to rebuild the show.' We had Chris Rock on the show, still a great cast." Carrey told author David Peisner that he had no intentions of continuing, but that he wished the show had continued on, anyway. The three films Carrey released that year were *Ace Ventura: Pet Detective, The Mask,* and *Dumb and Dumber.* Carrey was literally inescapable, and by year's end, his films would end up pulling in more than $700 million in box office receipts. With dropping ratings and nary a Wayans to be found, the writing was on the wall. "There was a lot of potential there to rebuild it, but at the end of the day, Fox decided to cancel it after that season," Miller says.

For a large group of people who hadn't seen themselves on-screen tenfold before like White people had, *In Living Color* was an opportunity to see an opportunity. There had been no weekly sketch show starring majority Black actors that ever lasted more than a few episodes. It helped normalize the idea of majority Black casts, too, by simply being as funny as possible, and being undeniable. *In Living Color* told stories that anyone could understand without denying any Black perspective, and without letting the audience assume any sort of monolithic culture of Black ideals or sense of humor. Like *Python* before them, if there was a joke you didn't get, it didn't matter. The specificity was part of why it worked: *no one comes from everywhere.*

The impact *In Living Color* had on TV was already being seen, with increasing numbers of black-led shows on TV, like *Living Single* and *Martin.* The show's broad but committed acting style was its own beast as well, with a whole generation of kids growing up imitating Jim Carrey—some of them on TV in the '90s themselves. For some, like Skye Townsend (*A Black Lady Sketch Show*), the show's boldness was key. "When you really line up all of the characters in a row, the range is absolutely wild," Townsend says. "That started to form who I wanted to be as a comedian, because I felt like on that show specifically, they would walk right up to the line and almost cross it and be like, 'Our toe is dangling over the line. Let's see how far we can take this.'"

For Townsend, *In Living Color* also was a demonstration of how to share the stage, even if some of the stars were breaking out as the show went on. "Playing to your strengths is the key in sketch. You have to know when to pass the ball . . . When you see a comedian who's a ball hog in a sketch, it bothers you. On *In Living Color* they knew how to alley-oop it to somebody if they had a stronger joke coming up. They just could feel it."

While *In Living Color* never saw a spinoff film (RIP Homey), it did see an attempt at a TV revival in 2011, but that show was canceled before it ever aired (Townsend herself was nearly cast on that, too). It should be noted, though, that with the insane box office of the *Scary Movie* franchise (almost $900 million) and the fact that it "inspired" numerous similar films ending with the word "Movie," there is at least a Wayans legacy of parody, going all the way back to Keenen co-writing *Hollywood Shuffle*. The satire legacy starts there, too, continues with the best of *In Living Color*, and carries through to the beautiful Spike Lee Mini DV feature film *Bamboozled*, starring Damon Wayans, Tommy Davidson, Jada Pinkett Smith, and Savion Glover.

"[*In Living Color*] was the first time a lot of White people began to understand what our humor was and is," Anne-Marie Johnson says. "[They] began to understand historical references and issues of the day from the African American point of view. Comedy has always been used as commentary, but to see all these brown people doing sketch comedy, it was like, 'I didn't know Black people could be funny like that.' So it was really groundbreaking."

"It was a long shot and a long way to get there," Warfield says. "But it didn't just happen. There was a lot of groundwork laid." The slow desegregation of unions and of writers' rooms, and other results of equal opportunity and the civil rights movement were notoriously slow to show their results. "You have to give Keenen credit for seeing the landscape and exploiting it the way he did . . . It was a remarkable feat when you know all of the things that that went into making that opportunity happen and maximizing the opportunity."

Rob Edwards recalled how critical *In Living Color* was, especially after being so titanically underestimated. "It was a moment in time where you absolutely needed a show like that, [in terms of] social change and what was going on in the media. We were right on the precipice of *The Fresh Prince* and all that stuff. TV was changing radically . . . here is the cornerstone of it."

— 11 —
A Taste that's Oddly Familiar: The Ben Stiller Show

You don't have to dig deep to hear *The Ben Stiller Show* that aired on MTV often spoken about in the same breath as the Fox TV show of the same name. In fact, they're frequently treated like the same show, for no reason other than the title. In 1989, MTV announced their first major programming shift toward original content. For five years, it had been the place for music videos alone, and some of these original shows were designed to "keep people interested between the videos," as MTV's senior VP in charge of programming, Doug Herzog told the *LA Times*. Thus was born the vidcom (a combination of music videos and comedy pieces). One of the first shows announced along with this change in programming was the sketch series *The Ben Stiller Show*.

There are definite links between the two versions of this show. They're both shows about being shows, effectively: Ben Stiller is playing a version of himself in both of them. On the MTV version, he's too big for his britches, and co-creator/co-star Jeff Kahn is ostensibly the straight man for these parts. When they get to Fox, it's Stiller on camera between pieces, talking to his co-stars, like Bob Odenkirk and Janeane Garofalo, or that week's guest (anyone from *Star Trek*'s James Doohan to Sarah Jessica Parker), in bits that highlight how "Hollywood" Ben has gotten. Then there's the pop culture parody and pastiche, with which Stiller had already made a name for himself.

In 1987, Stiller co-wrote and co-directed a short film entitled *The Hustler of Money*, a parody of the Martin Scorsese film *The Color of*

Money. In it, Stiller premieres his Tom Cruise impression, and is joined by John Mahoney (later of *Frasier* fame), playing Paul Newman's "Fast Eddie Felson." In reality, though, they're both also playing Cruise and Newman gunning for awards. It's six minutes of meta Hollywood jokes and references to things like Newman's Own salad dressing. It was shot on film, looks great, and was funny enough to get a spot on *Saturday Night Live* that same year, even though no one involved in the film was a cast member or writer yet.

"We met at John Cusack's rented house during the filming of *Say Anything*," recalls Jeff Kahn. "It was a crazy little house on Outpost in LA." The house was a to-be comedy who's who, with Joan Cusack, Jeremy Piven, future indie film darling Lili Taylor and future co-writers of *High Fidelity* and *Grosse Pointe Blank* Steve Pink, and D.V. DeVincentis rounding out the roommate situation. Kahn didn't know what to make of Stiller at first. "I was like, 'Who is this kid in a Hugo Boss suit?' We were all in shorts and cut off shirts." Kahn and Stiller ended up begrudgingly sharing a bedroom, and seemingly didn't care for one another. "But somehow I made him laugh, and because I didn't realize who his parents were, I didn't really give him much of the time of day. I think he probably liked that, so we got to be friendly."

The two would eventually part ways—Stiller for his hometown of New York City and Kahn for his hometown of Chicago— and meet up again when Stiller was in Chicago shooting the film *Next of Kin*. "He got this guy who wanted to make a short feature with him in Chicago, and he gave him some money to do it. He had written ten minutes of it." Kahn and Stiller would end up co-writing the short film, and Stiller would direct. This awkwardly-edited, twenty-some minute film, *Elvis Stories*, would end up featuring, among others, John Cusack, Jeremy Piven, Mike Myers, Joel Murray, Stiller, Kahn, and Chicago's David Pasquesi. A series of chunked-together near-sketches with a through line about purported supernatural Elvis sightings, *Elvis Stories* isn't exactly a clear line to *The Ben Stiller Show*, but it does show Stiller's propensity toward directing shorter pieces with a clear visual style. If nothing else (and nothing else), *Elvis Stories* doesn't feel like anything else from 1989.

Stiller and Kahn sold the film to Rhino Video, though the money from the sale wasn't enough to really get anyone paid, especially as they shot it on 35 millimeter film stock, which has always been expensive. After this experience, which was a mini-film school for Kahn, Stiller invited him to New York so they could room together and work on stand-up at the same time. The stand-up work ended up getting Kahn a manager, and a gig writing for an MTV pilot called *Patio Party*, for which he made all of $500. "I didn't have a computer and I didn't type at that at this point, so I wrote it and Ben's parents' assistants typed it for me."

While *Patio Party* didn't end up happening, the folks at MTV were interested in Kahn's stand-up career. "They realized that I was working with Ben, and they were like, 'Oh my god, we'd love to work with Ben.'" At the time, Stiller was working on *Saturday Night Live* for what would end up being a brief, four-week stint, before leaving when it was clear he wasn't going to be making more short films *a la The Hustler of Money*. "Mike Myers was breaking really big and it didn't leave any room for another talent like Ben, who was sort of generationally the same as Mike. They covered a lot of the same territory in a way. They had different takes on comedy, but there was some overlap, and I understand why Ben would have felt frustrated at that time." When Stiller left *Saturday Night Live*, the pair were offered an MTV show called *It's Your Hour*.

MTV

"Ben actually had auditioned to be a VJ and auditioned to be the host of *Remote Control*," Doug Herzog recalls. "We gave him his first paying director's job. He directed a half-hour special for Colin Quinn called *Back to Brooklyn*, which is basically a series of sketches—pop culture parodies." The young network and its young executives were pleased with *Back to Brooklyn*; that's when they offered Stiller his own show. In January of 1990, the show was advertised as *Ben Stiller: It's Your Hour*, though it would shortly be known as *The Ben Stiller Show*.

"By this point, I was working on *Remote Control*, which was their big breakout hit game show," Jeff Kahn says. "They said, 'We want to do a Ben and Jeff show.' And I was like, 'Oh my god, my dreams are coming true finally.' I told my manager and she was very happy. Then I got a call from her, and she said, 'Actually, it's not going to be The Ben and Jeff Show. It's just going to be The Ben Show. But they still want you.'" The show's sketches would be a mix of fake behind-the-scenes footage, which frequently become the sketches themselves, and some slightly more traditional, character-centered sketches. Stiller and Kahn would co-write and co-star, and Stiller would, of course, direct. There would be no live audience, either: Everything would be pre-taped and run without a laugh track.

"The premise was, Ben was the star of his own cable show—a little bit of an egotistical jerk, but within that, that's how that all these sketches would happen," Herzog says. Each show had a loose theme that the sketches could play with, and then led into specific music videos. After all, this was part of the vidcom experiment, and MTV wasn't about to let anyone forget that they were still the music video channel. In a music themed episode, for instance, Stiller is trying to start his own music career while Kahn tries to talk him out of it. Stiller lightly pastiches each band before their music video comes up and, by the end, he's roped Kahn into the whole music career thing. They end up on a rooftop, *a la* U2 and The Beatles, where Stiller premieres his Bono "impression" with "Where the Streets Know My Name," all about Bono's ego. He'd bring Bono with him to Fox, too.

The show goes the meta route from the jump, as a sketch show about a sketch show. The credits sequence is Stiller in a suit, in a studio, contemplating possible openings to the show; he raps in one opening, there's a cheesy talk show theme and graphics in another, the third is just big and bold graphics of the show's title, and the final is a no-frills slate with the show's name and length on it. By the sixth episode, they're "out of ideas," so they instead run a "6th Episode Anniversary Show," a fake clip show of sketches that had never actually aired before this, many of which suddenly have a laugh track.

"Back when our first episode went on the air, a man named George Bush was president. The decade was young, and so were we. We were all trying to find ourselves," Stiller tells the audience. One fake clip is a "blooper," wherein Stiller spits a mouthful of something into Kahn's face because of Kahn's sort of Scottish-ish accent. Another is a half-entendre-prone, proto-Stuart Smalley called "Edwin Love" who says "suck my energy" a lot, because this sketch was supposedly produced when the "censorship codes were different," six weeks ago. In another clip, Kahn accidentally kills a goat, to the disgust of the "audience."

"It was artistically very freeing, because they were like, 'Okay, you can do whatever you want.' It was really fun for us, this show within a show," Kahn says. The format was so loose that they could experiment, often bringing in ideas from their stand-up to the sketches. Conceptually, they played with the format for all thirteen episodes, including one that called out their lack of budget. "We did a show called 'The Fox Episode,' where the premise was that we hated MTV because they didn't pay us any money, so we were trying to get on Fox."

FOX

As a young network, Fox was made up heavily of former MTV staff. Youth, hipness and an ability to effectively run a network was in high demand at the newest network. "I got the Fox episode to Joe Davola at Fox," Kahn says. "He was like, 'We want to do a show with you.'" The network was based in Los Angeles, and Stiller and Kahn, who were now writing a movie for Norman Lear, were splitting their time between the coasts. Fox liked their sketches, but wanted a premise. "'Where's the show going to be? In a clubhouse?' They worried about these weird things."

The development process for the new show went on so long, that by the time the Stiller/Kahn team were both in LA full time, Judd Apatow had been brought on as a producer, who in turn got HBO involved as the production company. Still, they couldn't quite figure out what the show was, besides the obvious showcase for their sketch ideas. "We shot, I think, three different pilots. One set at a clubhouse." The pilot that aired and that you'll find on the DVD set of the series contains pieces like the *Cape Fear* parody "Cape Munster," with Stiller as a grown-up Eddie Munster, and these sketches remained the same among the three different pilots. The premise, though, continued to change.

"On that first one, they were forcing us to wrap it around with a sitcom," recalls director John Fortenberry. "Ben and Judd hated it, but they were trying to play ball." The central characters of Stiller, Odenkirk, Garofalo and Andy Dick were to live in the same apartment together, and these scenes would somehow interweave with or simply support the actual sketches. "We literally shot, I think two episodes, maybe four, before there was just a revolt from everybody and I think Fox saw this is just not working."

Kahn recalls, "We finally said, 'Let's just use the talent that we have for wraparounds, and we'll just have them talk to Ben.'" This new premise—not far off from the original "behind the scenes of a sketch show" at all—worked well enough for Fox to give it the go ahead. To direct, Ben Stiller took the reins for nine episodes, and the rest were split amongst Troy Miller, Paul Miller of *SNL* and *In Living Color*, and Fortenberry. Among the writing staff for the Fox season were Apatow, Kahn, Stiller, Robert Cohen, Garofalo, Odenkirk, Dino Stamatopoulos, Andy Dick and David Cross (who joined as a mid-season replacement writer).

Odenkirk had been performing an updated version of his (sort of) one-man show (also featuring Dick), *Half My Face is a Clown*, now entitled *Show Acting Guy*, at the Upfront Theater in Santa Monica after moving to LA. "I was writing at [the Chris Elliott sitcom] *Get a Life* and then on Saturday night, I'd do this show." Garofalo brought Apatow with her to see *Show Acting Guy*, at which point Apatow purportedly decided to cast the show there instead of auditioning people he wasn't familiar with. It would take some disparate, weird sensibilities to make a series seemingly centered around a single personality stand out.

Even if the pop culture pastiche or parody was nothing new to the world of sketch, this particular group of creative brains was about to raise the stakes for TV sketch, production-wise. Especially in the cases of film parodies, which were shot on film, the show made it a point to match the production values of the original films wherever possible. The easiest way to do this was to make sure they had plenty of other sketches that could be shot on video and would be okay to look like they were shot in a studio. Doing this would allow them to earmark production money for bigger pieces, like "Die Hard 12: Die Hungry," in which Stiller plays Bruce Willis as John McClane, trying to stop a supermarket burglary, headed by a nameless villain of indeterminate European origins played by Taylor Negron.

In this extended trailer, McClane crawls through piles of produce instead of an air duct, pops out of a pile of vegetables to yell "Hey, fellas, you gotta eat your greens!" before unloading a gun on them, and the stand-in for Reginald VelJohnson's Al Powell yells at the cops that McClane is running out of one liners. Toward the end, *Die Hard*'s "Yippee-ki-yay" becomes "Yabba dabba doo, dabba dooba dabba deebee dabba." Because HD and 4K video are now as commonplace as they have become, it may be a little harder to appreciate how expensive and difficult shooting on film can be: This cost a lot more, and took more time than any digital short on *SNL* would now, even if it all takes a ton of skill to do right, regardless of format. Dedicating this kind of time and money to a half-hour sketch show, this regularly, was new to TV. No sketch show was trying to be this cinematic. Even in parodies of teen dramas like *Melrose Place*, they made it look as good as possible.

Like seemingly every other sketch show of the era, *The Ben Stiller Show* also took on the reality show *COPS*, where cops were followed as they arrested people (hell, even I parodied *COPS* when I discovered my VHS camera had a light on it—it was just a thing you did at the time). *Stiller* puts a spin on it, with the show being set variously in places like ancient Egypt, or during the Salem witch trials. Fortunately, there were also moments of pure absurd sketch comedy joy that don't require any other point of reference, that, in hindsight, came from the most obvious place.

"It wasn't my forte or style, the kind of parody stuff," remembers David Cross. Cross had been in a sketch group at Emerson College in Boston, but even then, parody wasn't part of his group's language. "Not that I had disdain for it. It just wasn't my thing." Working on *The Ben Stiller Show* was a learning curve for him. "Ben wanted to do something where he was Bono, or he wanted to do something where he was Tom Cruise or something. So you're sort of shoehorning these ideas into that." Where Cross shone, along with his future writing partner Bob Odenkirk, was in writing original stuff.

"The one sketch that is purely me that made it on to the show was a thing called 'The Legend of T.J. O'Pootertoot.' That tells a story, and that's something that I've always been drawn to, whether it's sketch or stand-up or anything else I've done, long-form or short-form, it's telling a story." This sketch about a theme restaurant with a cannibalistic cult behind it is a densely-packed short film, with supernatural mustaches, drinks like Sex in a Hamper (with or without milk) and the Miserable Whore, and food options like Curly Ribs, Atomic Liver Crisps and Pooter Balls.

"What kind of meat is in that?" asks a customer.

Faith, Your Food Gal (Garofalo) replies, "It's Pooter Meat, with a taste that's oddly familiar." Company spirit and earning Pooter Points are key to success, and complaining could get you sent to Pootertoot Spirit Camp. There is a hint of what is to come for *Mr. Show*, including one of only two onscreen appearances for David Cross on *Stiller*.

This was Cross' first Hollywood job, and it says something about the show's standards that a sketch this far out of the show's vibe actually made it to air. While its bread and butter was parody and pop culture mashups, it didn't shy away from a good concept or character piece. Despite having control over the show's aesthetic, Stiller was open to input on how the sketches needed to look and feel. "Ben was really great; I didn't know anything and I'm still like whispering in his ear," Cross says. This was also the first regular staff job or co-starring acting job for the likes of Garofalo, Odenkirk, and Dino Stamatopoulos (*Moral Orel, Late Night with Conan O'Brien*). Some of the show's writers, like Odenkirk and Rob Cohen, had already made a bit of a mark.

"I'd written an episode of *The Simpsons*. It was in season three, called 'Flaming Moe's,'" recalls Cohen, who was doing punch-up on a film with Jeff Kahn before the *Stiller Show* got greenlit. His episode of *The Simpsons* likely played a part in why he was hired, making this his first regular writing gig. "It was such a formative amazing experience, especially for me; that was my first staff job as a writer. The quality—given our incredibly small budget and how incredibly disinterested Fox was in the show—we just got to do the greatest stuff."

In a typical writers' room, there are the staff writers and the head writer (or writers); the staff writers pitch ideas to the room and, depending on the head writer, good ideas are praised and move on to the next step, and bad ideas are either cause for in-the-room tweaking or belittlement and shaming. *The Ben Stiller Show* was much more of a *do it your own way, on your own, and come back with something* type of room. "Every Friday we would turn in sketches into the packet as it as we call it . . . Sometimes people would team up, and if it was an idea we were really excited about, we may go pitch it to Ben or to Judd," Cohen says. If they were told no right away, the sketch stopped there, easy enough.

"We got to be involved in every facet: writing and producing and editing and sometimes acting. It was like an indie film show in all areas, but we got to do stuff that just looked great." In a group of Gen-Xers, it was also helpful that their pop culture references were the same. "Almost all of us knew exactly the minutiae of it, and how to make it a seven-layer bean dip of weird stuff that called back *The Six Million Dollar Man,* or *Batman,* or *The Monkees.*" On the *Stiller Show,* they premiered "The Grungies," with four Seattle grunge rockers— Jonsie, Dolly, Tork, and Stone—a laugh-track-laced goofy romp about over-serious musicians. It's a sketch that, at seven and a half minutes, should feel long, but looks and feels the part so much, you don't care. Doing this level of work with such a low budget is a testament to the crew.

The budget was so low, in fact, that food and snacks around the office, which are a TV and movie set staple to sate writers and other crew working long hours, were not a thing. "They were not enthusiastic about our presence on their network," Cohen says. "There was a big complaint once and somebody at Fox sent us one giant tub of Twizzlers, but it was stale. And it was intentionally sent as stale. I remember admiring that, because somebody had to go out and buy a tub of Twizzlers and let it get stale." Someone on the cast or crew eventually threw the tub against the wall out of frustration. "The Twizzlers shattered like glass because they were so old. That was the perfect example of where we were, cash-wise and partnership-wise."

There are some comedians of the opinion that making your sketch comedy cinematic has the potential to elevate it, in the same way that playing a comedy bit extra-straight sells the reality of a piece and makes the joke that much stronger. Others feel that sketch comedy deserves to be lo-fi whenever possible, letting the staging and *mise-en-scène* be funny, too, giving the entire production a DIY vibe. Some shows fall into the latter by accident, where some, like *Mr. Show with Bob and David*, would eventually lean into it despite their reasonable budgets. *The Ben Stiller Show* is not exactly auteur comedy—that's just about impossible, anyway—but it does have the benefit of having the name in the title being the person whose attention to detail drove a heavy number of the show's sketches. "I've said this to him a million times, but I'm so happy that he's directing serious stuff now. He's got a great eye," Cohen says.

The show was known for being cinematic as a rule, whenever they could, despite the asininely low budget. Coming from the "do it for the exposure" network of MTV, right into the arms of a network that didn't know what to with them (and didn't want to give them snacks), in order to survive, it became the first DIY sketch show to actually start, and end, in the '90s.

The Ben Stiller Show never found its footing in the ratings, even as it ran on Sunday nights as the 7:30 PM lead-in to *In Living Color*. Only a few weeks into the run, it was pushed to 10:30 at night. It was canceled after thirteen episodes, one of which didn't air until 1995, on Comedy Central. Eight months after being canceled, *The Ben Stiller Show* won the Emmy for Outstanding Individual Achievement in Writing in a Variety or Music Program. "I wrote three of the five sketches on that episode. Ben gave me the envelope the day we won,"

Odenkirk says, giving credit to his brother Bill for coming up with the premise of one of the sketches in that episode. "'Three Men and an Old Man,' that was Bill's and then I wrote it up as a sketch."

"I think they made a decision to put their chips on other shows," Cohen says, making it clear this is speculation. "We were literally the lowest rated show on television, because we didn't get any promotion. But, they also just ignored us. I think the president of the network at that time thought we were this crappy little sketch show. I don't think he appreciated humor in any form." The Julie Brown sketch show *The Edge* briefly took the late spot after the *Stiller Show* was canceled, but *The Edge* only lasted eighteen episodes, itself, leaving *In Living Color* as the standalone Fox sketch show, yet again.

12

No Time to Breathe: The Weirder Side of '90s Sketch

Thanks perhaps to MTV and the youth-centric "edgification" of everything in the '80s, by the early '90s, comedy was also perceived to need extra teeth. Often, in search of what makes something weird and different successful or interesting, executive types will latch on to one thing inside that success and expand from there, with mixed results. "Oh, they swear a lot," or "The humor is just *so* dark," or "They tell it like it is," and that's how edginess is born. The edgy thing doesn't fit into a box, hence the edginess, but then a new box is built to fit around it, and people start to use that box to define their comedy tastes. And, since we are all monkeys making copies of copies anyway, this is when art gets out of hand and people like me start saying dumb shit like "Why can't they make them like the Marx Brothers did?" There's a workable middle-ground, but these shows weren't playing there. (Also, they did effectively make a Marx Brothers movie in 1992, called *Brain Donors*, and I don't know if I can vouch for it or not, it's been a while.)

In the early '90s, the alt comedy scene was starting to take off in New York, in places like Luna Lounge, and Los Angeles at Big and Tall Books and The Diamond Club. Comics at these clubs—stand-up, sketch, performance art, and otherwise—were trying stuff that was, reductively, not in a suit in front of a brick wall, talking about airplane food. At the same time, some TV sketch shows were very much throwing angry spaghetti at a wall and calling it "pushing the envelope." This was a populist approach to "alternative," which very much depended on the tropes of the status quo for effectiveness. In and amongst the weird for the sake of weird, though, you might find some gems, if you can find them to watch them.

Pirate TV

The day after *The Ben Stiller Show* premiered on MTV in 1990, TV pirates in a barge just outside of New York took over the cable channel, playing the videos they wanted and doing the sketch comedy bits they'd like to see. Perhaps a stronger premise than the *Stiller Show*, and in keeping with MTV's pseudo-rebel image, this vidcom was given just as much room to play as everybody else.

"I was very fortunate to work at MTV when it was very cool," remembers producer and director Deborah Liebling. "I grew up with the network; I was one of the original staff. We were all producers, and we were all young, and we just did stuff. There wasn't much structure. They were just like, 'Go do a thing and go do that and get on a plane and go be with Prince and go come back with the show.' So we were sort of making it up." MTV hired a group from morning radio to create a sketch show on a shoestring budget and—smartly, like *SCTV* before it—the show was designed to look like it had even less of one.

Created by song parody writers Steve Kerper and Dave Kolin, *Pirate TV* was designed to take their skillset and direct it toward TV. Cheaply-produced parodies, without complicated sets or expensive costumes, was probably music to MTV's ears. They brought in writers from *Letterman*, like Boyd Hale, and actors who they literally found on the street, like Tim Blake Nelson (*O Brother, Where Art Thou?*). "I put my card in his hat," Liebling recalls. "He was performing and I said, 'You're funny. I work at MTV, call me.' Then the very first thing he ever did was on *Pirate TV*."

Based solely on Liebling's memory and the memory of the internet, Nelson's stand-out character seems to have been a character named Scab O'Hooley, who raced pet rats on the deck of the ship. There was a commercial for "Reejok," an inflatable pump-style jockstrap that parodied pump sneakers of the time. There was a sitcom where the characters were played by drawn-on popsicle sticks, and an interlude where a man says "Four out of five dentists recommend *Pirate TV* for patients who chew TV." This sampling is 97 percent of what is available on the internet or in the memories of people I've spoken to about this show.

This was also a period of time where shooting guerilla style in New York City was actually possible. "You could go into New York and just say, 'Hey, pizza shop. We're gonna bring our cast and our crew in here for a couple of hours,' and they're like 'Hi! Sure! Come on in!'" Today, every place is hip to the idea that cameras *must* equal a budget (they do not). They shot a parody of Jacques Cousteau's films that took place outside of the water, where their Cousteau walked around in a snorkel and flippers at a laundromat in Hoboken (now you know 98 percent of what is available). When asked about the budget, Liebling isn't certain, but "I'm sure it was disgustingly low."

To make up for the lack of money, there was very little oversight. "There weren't seven layers of clearances and approvals," Liebling says. You'd go off and shoot what you shot, and it would air. Occasionally a higher-up wouldn't like it, but that didn't affect the show. "'Too bad, there'll be another one next week.'" Through her work at MTV, Liebling admits she fell into comedy, but found a niche for herself as someone who could speak to comics, when other executives didn't know how to. This was not an opportunity that would normally go to a woman, either. "There weren't as many women who were playing in that arena at the time, and I'm just so happy that has changed radically, but you had to sort of be one of the boys when you were in the comedy space because it was pretty male." She'd eventually work with the *Pirate TV* crew on an HBO show called *Hardcore TV*, and would go on to be the person who discovered *South Park* and brought it to Comedy Central.

The Idiot Box

Just before *The State* started establishing a handheld look that would bleed quickly into the future style of MTV, there was a show that oozed the energy MTV was chasing for years after. *The Idiot* Box features the quickest cuts, canted-est angles and plenty of distortion in a combination so anxiety-inducing that I find it difficult to sit through an episode without needing a break. It's not necessarily the kind of thing you'd necessarily expect to come out of a *de facto* art collective—which is what Alex Winter (Bill of *Bill & Ted's Excellent Adventure*) and Tom Stern would eventually create in their Venice, California apartment.

Stern and Winter went to NYU together, just a few years before the comedy group The State, and partnered together on short films. They eventually headed out to Hollywood, and sent one of their college films to their filmmaking hero, Sam Raimi. "He wanted to work with us," remembers Stern. "A dream come true. So he commissioned us to write an anthology comedy in the vein of *Kentucky Fried Movie*." They wrote the whole thing up and Raimi optioned the feature from them, paid them to explore a way to get it produced. "We made like five hundred bucks to write a feature." While Raimi was a fan, the film didn't work out, so the two of them had a movie's worth of sketches that could be shot; the problem was that they had no other connections to get it made.

In February 1989, though, things changed, practically overnight. "*Bill and Ted's Excellent Adventure* came out and was a surprise hit, so that all of a sudden Alex had cachet and was hot in Hollywood." Through the general moving and shaking that follows a box office surprise like *Bill and Ted*, the two made a connection at MTV, who asked if they'd want to make anything for the cable network that was just about to get into comedy. "We pitched them the idea of doing a sketch comedy show, *The Idiot Box*, and they said, 'Yes, here's no money, go make it.'" Stern and Winter each made about $250 a week to film six episodes (and a single, actual "Best Of" episode), which they'd co-write with Tim Burns (*An American Werewolf in Paris*).

"Tom and I lived together," Winter recalls. "We'd be working during the day, either making our own stuff or I'd be acting, and we'd kind of write all night. Tim usually wrote on his own, and then we'd have conference calls or he'd come down to our place in Venice, and we would huddle together and go eat cheap Thai food somewhere and bash out stuff." The rooming writers were always making short films and music videos or writing on other projects, often pulling from The Actors' Gang theater when it came time to cast. "We were making music videos for Ice Cube, or the Chili Peppers or whoever, and our crazy shorts." They were doing this at Propaganda Films, as well, then the premiere production house for music videos, where directors like David Fincher and Michael Bay were honing their craft. "They looked at us as these kind of weird, fringe, punk rock guys."

Winter was raised on the comedy of Spike Milligan and Peter Sellers, and admired the troupes that they often worked closely with, and he soon started bringing in his *Bill and Ted* friends to his own group, too. "It would often involve hanging out, a bunch of people at our apartment at all hours of the night. There were costumes everywhere, Tom would be in costume, I'd be in costume. It was all very theatrical, and it was really our life. It wasn't like we turned it on and turned it off. It was just kind of how we lived for a chunk of time."

The Idiot Box was shot all at once, in the style that a movie would be shot, rather than like a series, which is shot one episode at a time. With so little budget, they frequently used the offices at Propaganda for their sets, like when Winter plays a "Rock Accountant," who does accounting for musicians during the day, but when five o'clock hits, he destroys his cubicle. "I think my Rock Accountant thing is Michael Bay's cubicle, which we totally fucking destroyed. Everything we shot, we shot at like two in the morning when nobody was there, obviously." The collective would come in at the wee hours, dress the set, and often make props on location.

Stern was particularly adept at this; one character on *The Idiot Box* is "The Burrowing Bishop," whose pope-hat-like head covering is a giant drill bit that lets him travel through the ground. Stern glued a bunch of Styrofoam pieces together and sculpted them with a wire brush on a drill to make a giant augur that would fit on Winter's head. This was, as Winter points out, their lifestyle. Their apartment doubled as a workshop and tripled as a costume house. Their impromptu studio started expanding, too, when their NYU friends made their way out to LA. "We rented like four of the apartments so that little funky-ass building became The Stern/Winter Studio; it makes Corman look like Paramount . . . We were building shit and making costumes, making sets, making art department props, all out of this house, at all hours of the day and night."

Every episode of *The Idiot Box* (which premiered in 1991) is loaded with sketches, with a pace that is hard to fathom. There are no lingering shots, and the acting is amped-up, with an energy designed to mimic the cartoons Winter and Stern grew up on. "To try to make something that felt like a Tex Avery cartoon, but in live action, just required a certain aggressive energy," Winter says. "Our biggest influences at that time were *Python*, Tex Avery, Sam Raimi [and] what he had done with *Evil Dead II*, which had this incredible energy and dynamism to it." The other influence was Max Fleischer, and the *Popeye* cartoons. "I loved how there was this constant manic narration track that just constantly rumbled along through it. All of that stuff sort of fed into what we were doing."

Winter describes the group's work methods as "ragtag, but with purpose," and *The Idiot Box* reflects that. That energy continued later with their feature film, *Freaked*, which has developed a cult following, as has *The Idiot Box*. The show only lasted one season, but you can see a parallel, if not a direct influence, in what internet video first was and, in some ways, what it has become again. Due to bandwidth and technology, early internet video had to be quick pieces, in and out in a few seconds, maybe ninety at most. Vine, and now TikTok, have shortened what is postable and acceptable, and it doesn't always have to be a story, just a recognizable joke or premise, and doing it with a budget is almost pointless, especially if you haven't caught fire yet.

The Idiot Box did well enough that it could have kept going, even if the budget would likely have remained the same. "It was a hit," Winter says. "They were very eager for us to do another season. By then, my career was taking off as an actor, so I was getting more recognition. We were able to parlay that and the success of *The Idiot Box* into *Freaked*."

Hardcore TV

After *Pirate TV*, Deborah Liebling had left MTV and was out on her own, developing new shows like the NBC kids' show *The Guys Next Door*, which was basically if New Kids on the Block lived together like The Monkees did. Her next job would be the polar opposite, since it was going to be on HBO. "HBO was doing a lot more, you know, overtly sexual programming," Liebling says. "The same writers for *Pirate TV* pitched *Hardcore TV*."

The bump in budget didn't necessarily help this show out from the miasma of weird '90s sketch comedy, though it did help sell some concepts that would have looked a lot cheaper over at MTV, like putting Bullwinkle the cartoon moose (here a person in mascot-style Bullwinkle costume) into movie parodies like "Raging Bullwinkle." With actors like Mario Cantone, Lauren Graham, Michael Imperioli, and Kristen Johnston, *Hardcore TV* was pulling actors some of the same places, but using them perhaps a little better than MTV allowed them to.

The standout, though, is Tim Blake Nelson, specifically as Bob Ross in a series of sketches entitled "The Joy of . . ." various things they maybe couldn't do on MTV. Like "The Joy of Tattooing" (a woman's bottom), "The Joy of Bikini Waxing," or "The Joy of Circumcision." Tim Blake Nelson does the best Bob Ross impression you're likely to see, and the baby who is "circumcised" is played by Liebling's relatively newborn baby son.

The writers and creators adapted some of their original *Pirate TV* ideas for HBO, but primarily leaned into doing whatever they could get away with on pay cable. Swearing and boobs? Well, that's what they did and showed, whenever they could, in sketches like "This Old Whorehouse," the concept of which you don't have to think hard to figure out, or "Fairy Tales from the Dark Side," where a lady reads filthy, upsetting fairy tales, with seemingly fully-illustrated books for each sketch (there's the budget at work).

One great piece in the series follows an ad for the Miracle Stick, which is "ten workouts in one," "an ear swab," and "a dictionary," and "*not* a plunger handle." *Letterman* writer and actor Joe Furey worked on the series, too, playing a guy in the commercial who says "it's a belt!" The commercial is followed by an extended interview with Joe Furey as "The Guy who says 'It's a belt!'" who is really hoping to get into directing.

Hardcore TV lasted through 1994, though information about how many episodes were produced and who was involved is sparse. Liebling does remember having an idea of where the show was on the HBO hierarchy. "I remember *Mr. Show*, because they were at HBO, too, and they thought *Hardcore TV* was, you know, beneath them. Which it was. I mean, I get it, we were Walmart, and they were Neiman Marcus. We were fine with that, but it was definitely a slightly different class of respect and status and stature in the in the comedy community. But they didn't kick me out, which I appreciate. I still got to be in the clique."

The Edge

For some unexplained reason, every episode of *The Edge* begins with the cast of the show—Julie Brown, Jennifer Aniston, Tom Kenny, Wayne Knight, Carol Rosenthal, James Stephens III, and Jill

Talley—getting murdered in some way or another. In one they're all decapitated, in another they're set on fire: Pick a gruesome way to die, and there's your cold open. It's not realistic, nor is it actually a comment on being edgy. It's just sort of there. The rest of the show is a mix of great premises, actors giving their best despite the direction and some of the writing, and a few bits that have so much potential it's a shame to see them mixed in with everything else.

The Edge was a Julie Brown vehicle, and while she'd already had a sitcom pilot that wasn't picked up by NBC, they gave her another deal to develop a show, which she decided would be a sketch show. NBC didn't take it, but Fox was interested, probably to add to what they hoped would be a growing lineup of shows like *In Living Color*, which was pushing the envelope in terms of taste, but succeeding for still managing to push some of the boundaries that mattered.

The cast, including occasional guest stars like Alan Ruck, Paul Feig, and Rick Overton, was a strange mishmash of great actors in a very weird ensemble. The show was cast by Brown herself and show creator (and Brown's then-boyfriend) David Mirkin. "The everyone dying thing was David's idea," Brown says. "I never liked it. It was okay. But that was his for sure idea." Brown and her writing partner, Charlie Coffey, she estimates, wrote half of the sketches that got into every episode. Also on the writing staff was Charlie Kaufman, whose sketches never made it to the top of the pile. "I didn't like that. I didn't get to make the choices even though I probably should have. David was kind of maniacal. I really thought Charlie Kaufman was really funny in a very offbeat way. Even at the time, I thought he was hilarious."

As for production of the show, some of the cast felt they had whatever they needed to make each sketch work, more so than your typical sketch show. They had a prosthetics team, great costumes and props, and more sets than you'd find on another sketch series. The cost of these sets alone must have been astronomical, and the days were long, too. "You're there like a movie; every split second of every day, all week, every week," Rick Overton says. He was brought in primarily to do impressions, which were aided by the quick-moving prosthetics department. For his audition, he had a few impressions in his quiver already, including Client Eastwood, Larry Fine of The Three Stooges, and Chewbacca.

"They said make something up and so I just made up some silly commercial about barbecue sauce," remembers Alan Ruck, about his audition. "I think I called it 'Bull Paste.' It was just some silly-ass shit. But, you know, I got a couple of laughs out of David Mirkin, so I figured it was okay." Coming from a solid theatrical background, Broadway shows under his belt and with *Ferris Bueller's Day Off* on his resume, Ruck still had to contend with the realities of auditioning—in this case, while wearing a colander on his head. "One way I describe it is that I was a character actor without a lot of character. I was just kind of like this, you know, inoffensive white guy, you know, and so even though we're talking about *The Edge*, there was nothing particularly edgy or dangerous or anything about me like that."

Ruck would end up hired to alternate weeks with future *Bridesmaids* director Paul Feig. "They were looking for some sexy breakout guy, but you got to figure if there's some sexy guy who's that funny, he's probably got his own show already." The alternates would get large roles in some sketches, though, such as when Ruck plays Luke Perry in the show's *Beverly Hills: 90210* parody, with his hair spiked about nine inches tall. Tom Kenny plays Jason Priestley, with a wave just as high. Neither of them wear shirts throughout the extended sketch.

When *The Edge* ventures into pop culture mashups, they get a little more mileage, like when they have The Three Stooges perform an exorcism. It isn't perfect, but the impressions are good and the grossness of the sketch is justified by the source material. When the show has real promise—like a series of sketches featuring "The Armed Family," a trigger-happy family who always carry loaded firearms and shoot at anything they aren't sure of—they often aren't directed strongly enough, even if Wayne Knight's ability to look convincingly stressed out at the drop of a hat is fantastic.

The Edge lasted only eighteen episodes, if you don't count the "best of" compilation that aired after the series left the air. Creator David Mirkin said in a 2012 interview that Sony, the show's production company, intended that *The Edge* would only continue with a slashed budget. Mirkin then left the show, because he didn't feel it could continue on two-thirds or possibly one half the budget. After it ended, two of the main cast, Jill Talley and future husband Tom Kenny, would go on to make up part of the cast of *Mr. Show with Bob and David*.

Limboland

Comedy Central's early experiments in sketch TV were often as high concept as those at MTV. For *Limboland* it was "sketches that take place in a white void." The show was originally titled *White Cyc*, because that void of a room with only curves to connect the walls, to avoid shadows, is called a "white cyclorama." In twenty-two minutes of TV, you'd get about as many sketches on *Limboland*. A promo, narrated by Penn Jillette, pitched it thus: "Anybody can do comedy with a bunch of props and a set. Watch what *Limboland* does with just four white walls."

It should be noted that Comedy Central and MTV were both properties of Viacom, which should give you an idea of why this concept was appealing to them. *Limboland* was conceived by Lol Creme, of the band 10cc. Creme had been a commercial director for some time, and Winchell and then-husband Mick Kuisel hired him to direct for Nissan.

As the three started working with new actors for their commercials, Creme began putting together a potential cast in his head for this sketch show he'd been wanting to produce. Creme's record label at the time bankrolled *Limboland*, which would feature, among others,

Winchell, Gino Conforti, Eleanor Reissa and Harvey Levine. It was to be hosted by "The Late Jackie Lenny," a CG skeleton voiced by comedian and writer Dana Gould (likely a reference to Lenny Jackie, a terrible stand-up character created by comic John Byner in the '60s).

Winchell recalls shooting the entire series of three episodes in as many days at Raleigh Studios in Hollywood. It was quick and dirty, and with what she describes as a British sensibility—specifically, more music hall and broad than of the dryer variety of British humor. The episodes would open with Levine playing a painter who painted in a color that was keyed out (chroma green or blue), revealing the first scene. At the time of writing, nothing is available online or on physical media to watch. The single promo floating around shows a rock band, a baseball game, a waiter serving a man in a desert, two people in a horse costume at a bus stop, and a lady dancing in a tux.

For her part, Winchell remembers the most details about one sketch, in particular. In it, she plays an immigrant trying to enter the United States. It is set at a desk, symbolizing the border, and she's given some basic questions about America, but then they get progressively more difficult to answer. They escalate to becoming increasingly difficult math problems—basically, anything that could trip her up, a seeming comment on how difficult it can be to become part of a country that is often ironically afraid of immigrants.

Many of the actors were improvisers, as well, so they might set up a scene—say on a bus, or something similar—and let everyone improvise until they discovered a few funny bits that could be cut into the final show. Stewart Copeland is credited in some places as having acted on *Limboland*, though Winchell believes he composed the show's soundtrack. As to why the show didn't go further than three episodes, she doesn't think the show was American enough. "It was right in that pocket where I don't think it was at home anywhere." The humor could also be a little hokey and goofy. "I liked it, but I could see how it would seem dated, and maybe not everybody's thing."

13

I Am a We, and There's Eleven of Us: The State

David Wain only needs guidelines. As a kid in Cleveland, he'd look in *The Plain Dealer*'s kids' section, called "Cappy Dick," and occasionally he'd send in for one of their contests. "One of them was—I remember this very well—it was a clown with some sort of coloring page," Wain says. "And my thing was, I pasted it onto a larger page and then extended the picture, so that it was even bigger, and that made it novel." He won that week, getting mailed a color change magic trick as his prize; another time, he won a model rocket with a camera inside. *The State* wouldn't have made it onto TV if it weren't for this tendency to make people accept something they never really asked for.

The State is the first major sketch show to start in the '90s that came from an existent core group, rather than being assembled *for the TV show*. They're also the largest group of the bunch, at eleven strong. It seems highly unlikely that a group of eleven nearly complete strangers would form a successful sketch troupe and that all of them would make it on to television, with a little help and some lessons learned directly from *Almost Live!* It is even less likely that that arrangement would last a few seasons and that they'd still be performing together, in various combinations, thirty years later.

The State started out as disparate groups at NYU in the late '80s and eventually, Todd Holoubek, Kerri Kenney-Silver (then Kerri Kenney), Thomas Lennon, Joe Lo Truglio, Kevin Allison, Ken Marino, David Wain, Michael Showalter, Robert Ben Garant, Michael Ian Black (then Michael Schwartz), and Michael Patrick Jann became part of The New Group, in order to stand out from NYU's sketch-comedy-group-in-residence, The Sterile Yak.

"We were just like, 'Whoa, The Sterile Yak, we could never be that good,'" Kenney-Silver explains. For her part, like many comedians in their early stages, sketch comedy didn't even look like an option. "I didn't know you could just *do* sketch comedy. I thought that was *SNL.* I thought that was *Monty Python.* 'I'm not on those shows, so I guess I don't do sketch comedy.' And then I saw [The Sterile Yak]." The New Group developed out of a need to keep a tight group together that didn't have to hold to any official college rules that applied to The Sterile Yak, which was directly associated with NYU. This meant hundreds of people would audition for The Sterile Yak, and only a couple might get in. The New Group meant practical experience, and a better chance of getting in, at least at the beginning.

"At the time, there was no such thing as a sketch comedy course. You know, there was no UCB [Upright Citizens Brigade Theatre]," Kenney-Silver continues. "By nature, it had to be DIY. Even if you were in the theater school, which most of us were, we weren't doing sketch comedy. So it was like putting on your own little play." The group—most of them, anyway—were lovers of *Monty Python*, and sketch comedy started to bond them. Quite closely. "We were using the toilet with the door open in the same room so that we didn't miss a beat with each other."

Todd Holoubek was part of The Sterile Yak almost from the beginning, but branched off not long after to form The New Group. Putting on student shows with no budget, and with skilled performers, meant that they were prepared fully for low-to-no-budget TV. "I think we put a lot into trying to make the theater performance as professional as possible," remembers Holoubek. "I think that tradition is one of the elements that really helped us when we got to TV . . . we were all ready to do it. It wasn't like we had to hustle and be like, 'Oh, how do we compensate for this lack of budget?'"

You Wrote It, You Watch It

On February 13, 1993, MTV premiered a full-length comedy show that was not, this time, a vidcom. It was all original content, but with that classic MTV flavor of getting free material from people whom they didn't pay. The show, hosted by Jon Stewart, featured a cast of actors, including Donald Faison and Toby Huss, reenacting viewer letters about their craziest stories. Frank Santi of Brookfield, CT says that he had "EAT ME" written on his forehead when he fell asleep at a party, and the show acts that out; it embellishes a bit as though he didn't realize the writing was there for several days, including during a job interview.

Brandon Dziengielewski of Depew, New York said that there was a rumor aliens had taken over his school, and the sketch plays out with Faison getting vaporized by a teacher's laser eyes. "I wrote a letter and got back MTV stationery, to basically write a treatment," Dziengielewski says. "I sent it in and didn't think anything of it. And then that summer, I was playing with friends, and one of my friends said, 'Hey, I just watched the show.' He described exactly what I wrote." Dziengielewski explained to his friend that the alien story was something he had written, and no one believed him—after all, the title card with his name was hand-scribbled and only onscreen for four seconds at most. To make things even harder to verify, while they interviewed someone on camera about the story, it was just an actor playing Brandon. "I have a master's degree in screenwriting, and that's the most I've ever had on TV, is what you sent to me. So that it's kind of bittersweet."

The show was looking for new directors not long into its run, and fortunately for him, David Wain had a friend who had effectively loitered his way into a job. "All roads in the early days led to this guy named Jon Bendis," says Wain. "He used to just hang around at MTV, just as like an interloper. Then he started working there and doing stuff." Through Bendis, Wain's short film, *Aisle Six*, had been seen by some folks at MTV, and Wain started interning and getting little production jobs here and there. MTV asked him to bring in something he'd directed to see if he might fit at *You Wrote It, You Watch It*.

"Instead of bringing something I directed, I went back to The State, and I was like, 'Let's make our own version of this.' We made three pieces for them that night, and brought them in the next morning. That's why we like sort of blew everyone else's samples out of the water." MTV had become Wain's new Cappy Dick, and as a result, he became well known for being able to do a lot for a little. "That's sort of been the good and bad albatross of my career. I have come to be known as someone who can get something done very quickly and cheaply, for better and worse." Quick and cheap was MTV's mantra; because of this, Wain knew he had some room to make the show something that The State could be proud of.

"I came in basically saying, 'First of all, I'm not an *I*, I am a *we*, and there's eleven of us, and we're doing it the way we do it . . . Also, nobody tells us how to do it.' We're like twenty-one years old. That sort of cocksureness really served us for the all those early years." MTV moved forward with Wain and, after a while, there was a clear casting change, from a disparate group of actors to a tight-knight group of cocky 20-somethings, getting paid $300 a week. They used their own Hi8 camera, may have borrowed a boom mic, and they all hung out in their single office at MTV while editing and writing. They reported to other people in their twenties who were also still figuring shit out, and had virtually no limits on what could be used in a show. Need hugely popular music? Of course MTV could air that. This would later come back to bite *The State* and numerous other MTV shows in the ass, with new rights fees preventing them from releasing as-aired versions of their shows on DVD; replacement songs didn't have the same impact or intent.

The troupe were pretty spoiled by this creative freedom and flexibility, but that also helped them continue to have a tighter creative vision. Todd Holoubek likens their success to the rarity of a restaurant making it in New York City. "The ones that stay, they either own the building, own the space, have a farm outside of the city where they can get produce . . . they're saving money on one of the larger expenses of running a restaurant." It was DIY because they'd already amassed all the things they needed to create the show, except for the $50/week they had to spend on props. "We could say, 'Let's shoot this five more times, lets shoot it ten more times, there really wasn't a deadline."

By the end of *You Wrote It, You Watch It*, The State already had big-time representation at William Morris, as a group. Meanwhile, producer Jim Sharp was busy on a marathon sixty-five-episode shoot of *Almost Live!* for cable.

The State

Jim Sharp had been busy working in development at Comedy Central, turning rough ideas into workable comedy programs. He knew better than most that, regardless of budget, if a comedy group doesn't have TV experience, they aren't exactly likely to have TV chops, and cable TV isn't the place to slowly find your footing. Sharp was burnt out from making *Almost Live!* for Comedy Central, and in the middle of recovery, he got a call from MTV.

"'Listen, we have these guys from NYU that have done a few things for us. We think there's something there,'" Sharp recollects hearing from the folks at MTV. He agreed to look at whatever they had put together, and MTV sent over VHS tapes of *You Wrote It, You Watch It* to see if it made sense for him to head to New York to develop yet another sketch show. "My wife and I looked at them and went, 'Whoa, there's something about these guys. They're kind of special.'" He noticed that The State were making smart comedy that wasn't too broad, yet still had an obviously silly side to them; their performances are what really stood out to him.

Coming from short-form local sketch comedy, Sharp learned the value of an informal joke quota early. "I'm really like a six jokes per minute guy, you know, really all about the joke. I think I taught them about jokes, and I think they taught me about performance. I can't tell you the number of times where I'd get a script, and I'd go, 'Man, I don't know, this feels like a B' and they'd go, 'It probably is a B, but we'll make it into an A, just let us rehearse it for you.' And they were usually right." After watching their work on *You Wrote It, You Watch It,* Sharp booked the flight to New York City, finding himself face to face with ten guys and one woman, straight out of NYU and still pretty fresh to TV.

"They were full of themselves, and cocky. MTV was kind of letting them run the show," Sharp recalls of their very first meeting, where MTV executives were also in attendance. "These guys really didn't know much about television production, but they had a love of comedy, and thought that they knew everything about comedy." He was, appropriately enough, their thirteenth interview, and it didn't go well. Still, he later got an unexpected call from the group, who asked for another meeting that night.

"'We'd love to talk to you one more time,'" he recalls them saying. "I went back, they had a bunch of pizza and beer in the room—MTV wasn't in the room—and I ended up doing the pilot." Sharp would go on to produce the series for the whole run.

Kenney-Silver remembers how the original meetings with MTV went, before anyone else was brought in. "They said, 'Okay, here's what we're looking for in your show. It's a sketch show, so by nature, what do we look at as a template? Let's look at *SNL.* So we're gonna want topical humor, we want you to do a lot of impressions, a lot of musicians because you're on the music television channel, and we want political jokes.' We said, without hesitation, 'We don't do that.'" There was no further discussion on the matter. The State wanted to make something timeless about the human condition.

"We definitely had a real sort of manifesto in our heads of what this is and what we do," says Wain. "It was decidedly unpolitical . . . we wanted to keep it moving, and we wanted to keep it raw and cool and visual." There was an element of *not being SNL* to how they defined themselves, as well. They didn't want sketches going on too long, and they wanted the sketches to stand on their own, rather than be about recurring characters or the history of the show.

"We were lucky that they agreed to give us a little bit of a break on that, although they wanted catchphrase characters," Kenney-Silver says. This was how the character of Louie came about. You might recall, he was the guy who yelled "I wanna dip my balls in it," illustrated by the ping pong balls he would carry with him. "We said, 'Yeah, fuck you. You want a recurring character? You want a catchphrase, here's your catchphrase.'" *The State* was a solid unit, and they wanted to make it clear that they were not cycling people in and out, and they hadn't come together because MTV needed a show; they were on MTV because MTV needed The State.

The pilot, which never aired, featured a runner throughout with all eleven in elevator, with singer Meat Loaf making an appearance. There was a storyline to the runner, as well, an experiment that has rarely ever worked on a sketch show, before or since, though executives frequently try and find something for the audience to hold on to, besides the engaging, funny sketches. "So often, a sketch show that has a gimmick, the gimmick takes away from it being good, and that's where you've got to be careful," Wain says. In addition to ditching the runner, they also ended up re-shooting some of the sketches from the pilot for their actual first episode.

It was quickly evident who was falling into what roles off-camera, especially with Jann and Wain, the directors. "We did two very completely separate things," Wain says. "He directed the actual sketches that we shot with a real crew on film, usually, or Beta, which was the fancy medium. I continued shooting Hi8, with the camera on my own shoulder and just running around and doing what we called 'second unit,' which was a word that meant 'zero budget.'"

Kevin Allison thinks that some part of *The State*'s DIY ethic comes from being born at the right time. "We were the generation of kids that was coming up when some of these recording devices, like the Super 8 [film] camera, for example, were a little bit more available to middle class kids." By 1983, the first consumer video camera had been released, with Hi8, a broadcast-resolution camera, coming in 1989. The digital revolution was only a few years away, but The State was part of a new breed of sketch comedian who could do a little bit of everything at home, if they needed to. Never mind the cheapness; coming ready to shoot and ready learn made them ideal for MTV.

The State premiered on Jan 21, 1994, to pretty terrible reviews. The most notorious of these contains the words, "It's so terrible it deserves to be studied. Every scene and performance should be examined in detail so that MTV is sure never, ever to produce anything like it again . . . a historic mess." They would eventually cut a promo featuring the worst of their press, with the group reacting like they'd been deeply hurt by all of it. Over the course of the next two years they'd make four seasons, and a total of twenty-four episodes for MTV.

The first episode of *The State* doesn't look like or feel like any sketch show before it, at least on the whole. Every sketch hits, whether it's in studio or shot on location. When they're in studio, the show knows it and we get audience reactions and laughter. When they leave the studio, the show chooses to bolt away with it, with "The Lenny Lipton Show," in which the host, guests, and "audience" are literally running throughout. The news report is similarly on the move. There's no audience reaction for pre-filmed sketches, striking a balance that makes perfect sense, but is rarely explored in other shows. Robert Ben Garant has credited *The State* with defining the look of MTV, with cameras always on the move and never quite completely steady—this is certainly true of Wain's "zero budget" shoots.

The State isn't concerned with being overly cinematic—just cinematic enough to get the point across. They would rather hit the look of a cereal commercial spot-on so that every character in it can spout dumb gibberish, in the simplest, most effective satire of TV ads you're likely to see. "Please Kill Tim," in which an otherwise sweet family keeps praying for the death of one family member, only to have it turn out that God is Tim's biker friend, has a simple sketch premise that, in other hands, might turn into a *Python* homage and never become its own thing.

The one challenge in describing what *The State* is as a living, breathing show is that while it wears its influences on its sleeve, at no point does it creep into the derivative category. Also, despite making it their goal to "not be *SNL*," which was a common call to action for sketch groups at the time, it doesn't rebel without absolute purpose. Even when they had the potential to creep into pretension by season four, they roll over it by going big but delivering. This is best exemplified in the catchy musical number "Porcupine Racetrack," which serves practically as a satire of sketch shows getting cinematic and getting too big for their britches.

"The very first email that I ever sent was to David Wain," recalls Jake Fogelnest. In the mid-'90s, starting at age fourteen, Fogelnest hosted a cable access show called *Squirt TV* that ended up featuring some of the biggest names in music and comedy, before moving the show to MTV. "They invited me up to their office at MTV, and there's a *Squirt TV* public access episode where I go to The State's office and they're writing their show, and they're just being goofy and going through sketches that they can't do on MTV and it's really, really fun. And they were leaving MTV."

Parting ways with MTV was, apparently, the result of a massive miscommunication, complicated further by an offer from network TV: CBS wanted to bring *The State* to the airwaves. "We were not told that MTV wanted more episodes," Kenney-Silver says. "We were told

CBS wants us, and so we said, 'Great!' My mom, all my life, had been saying, 'When are you going to be on regular TV so I can watch you?'"

It didn't hurt, either, that they were getting paid much less than anywhere else was going to offer. "It was not lucrative, to say the least. But I feel like what I got out of it was . . . I would do it again for free. Don't tell them . . . If my lawyer is reading this, I don't fully mean it." CBS had the money, and cable was decades away from the glut of prestige TV shows we've been told exists; network TV had more viewers than anywhere else in the '90s. Viewers, though, don't know a thing is going to be on if the network in question isn't paying for promotion.

CBS

"The State's First Annual Halloween Special" aired in 1952, if we're to take *The State's 43rd Annual Halloween Special* from 1995 at its word. Introduced by comic Alan King, and opening on a musical number with them digging their own graves and opening on their dead bodies at the gallows, the special really seems to know what it is, even if the group themselves didn't. It announces itself to be the last State Halloween Special, and we're told we'll see them in hell, punctuated by a cackling Peter Dinklage, playing Satan.

The special was a great way to launch a new series, which they couldn't even be sure if they had, yet. The only gimmick in it is the use of a few celebrity interviews talking about growing up with *The State* on TV, *a la* the mockumentary *All You Need is Cash* about the fake band The Rutles, and these pieces are honestly fantastic. Not only did Sting grow up watching *The State*, but Ric Ocasek recalls seeing them light a kid on fire and then throw him over a bridge on an episode; that kid would grow up to be Denis Leary.

There's a *Wild Kingdom*-style sketch about Manzelles—men with antlers and nude body stockings smelling their own breath and trying to mate, who tangle with the pack hunters known as Boyotes—similar-looking men but with tighty-whities on. There's a game show called "What Am I Saying," where Tom Lennon's host character's vague Eastern European accent plays a part in what the contestants have to guess. At one point The State introduce an historical moment . . . for the first time in the history of television, a sketch group will put up the fourth wall; they roll it in and the entirety of the sketch takes place out of sight. Topping themselves at every turn, they give us the beautifully brief sketch in which Kenney-Silver directs her own romance scene, telling the booth what shots she wants and which camera to take, stressing to do it with "more urgency." Outside of a performance by Sonic Youth, it's *The State* and, almost beat-for-beat, it's a showcase of them at their best.

"We were all in a room together watching it live on television," remembers Kenney-Silver. "The first commercial that came on was for Geritol. It was on a Friday night at [10 PM], and we said, 'Oh, we're dead.' Michael Black goes, 'Why do I feel like we're probably the only people in the world watching this right now?'" The time slot and the ads for the aging to the side, the group sucked it up and headed back to the office to write the second special they had been contracted for. Of course, as with all writers, procrastination is priority one in the face of a blank sheet of paper or screen.

"Tom Lennon and I were bored and had gone into the kitchen we had in our office, and we had taken all these paper plates and made like a mask out of them, and then we had wrapped ourselves in rolls and rolls of toilet paper," Kenney-Silver says. They were going to spread the potential writers block around and haunt the rest of the group as mummies. "Jim Sharp comes to get us. He's like, 'I need you in my office right now—the head of CBS comedy is calling.' So we go in, we're like, 'Hi,' and [CBS] fired us." They were sent to clean out their desks after a single episode.

Wet Hot American Summer

While it was never officially a movie "by The State," so many people from the group are involved in 2001's *Wet Hot American Summer*, it's as close to a movie by the group as we ever got. The members would go on to make so much new comedy, like *Viva Variety*, *Reno 911!*, *Stella* and too many other shows and movies to count that they are, in pieces at least, a ubiquitous presence in the comedy world. *Wet Hot American Summer* didn't come close to making back its budget in theaters, but it has since spawned a prequel series and a sequel series on Netflix, based purely on it being a cult hit and the aforementioned ubiquity of its players, including non-State members and future stars like Amy Poehler and Bradley Cooper.

The State has broken up, and yet it hasn't. By its nature, it is a sort of evolving group and, when they can, they still put on a banger of a show, fidelity be damned. On June 10, 2020, toward the beginning of the COVID-19 pandemic, The State put on a streaming show over Zoom, featuring classic pieces and great interludes, including an appearance by Kids in the Hall's Dave Foley, who pretended to fall under the common misperception that he, himself, was a member of The State. They'll put on a show by whatever means necessary, provided it's done their way. They won't exactly kick the doors in to do it, but they will have carved their own key so that before you know it, they're inside the house.

14

At Its Best When You Were in Middle School: Saturday Night Live

A Canadian man named Lorne Michaels who once worked on *Laugh-In,* and who had his own variety show in Canada, broke it off with his comedy partner, Hart Pomerantz, and started a live comedy television show based in New York City. He produced that show for five years, then left "for a year," and so did the rest of the cast, but for good. The cast was weird for several years, even if the show did discover Eddie Murphy during that period. Four years after his one year was over, the Canadian man came back to fix the show. That year's cast was strange, too, but the following year he hired fellow Canadian Phil Hartman. In 1990, a different Canadian man named Mike Myers was made a repertory player, mid-season, ringing in the '90s, slowly changing the show's goal from launching careers to finding characters that could star in movies. None of the movies would ever do as well as the first one this Mike Myers person made.

That is a highly-oversimplified version of how *Saturday Night Live* made its way into the '90s, the details of which are in many other books and online pieces think. *SNL,* despite now being a late-night TV and sketch comedy and variety mainstay, has had its share of shakeups. More than its share of cast and crew—writers, actors, directors, producers, the cue card guy—would go on to bigger things (Wally Feresten also does cue cards for Seth Meyers and sells custom cue cards on the side). Despite the headlines in the press reading "Saturday Night Dead," by the '90s, things seemed to be stabilizing, and at places like The Second City, iO and The Ground-lings, their reputation as the pipeline to *SNL* had been solidified.

Jim Wise, who would go on to a guest writing stint at *SNL,* per-formed and taught at The Groundlings in the '90s. "When I would run auditions at The Groundlings, it was clear that people were trying to use The Groundlings to get *SNL,*" Wise recalls. *SNL* had plans to send someone to see Chris Kattan in a show in 1995, at which point Wise got a call from fellow Groundling Will Ferrell. "He says, 'Hey, do you know what's going on at The Groundlings right now?' I said, 'No.' He said, 'Well, Chris Kattan and his managers got *SNL* to come to see the show. They're coming on Friday at ten o'clock, and our director is letting everybody bring their best stuff in.' She refused to put on a Chris Kattan showcase. It was kind of mean, but it was great for everybody else."

Wise himself was then on a self-imposed hiatus from the main company, doing other work, and acknowledges he could've put his best work together to be seen by *SNL,* too, but didn't. "From that show, they took Cheri [Oteri] and Will and Chris and Jennifer Coolidge to audition." Ferrell and Oteri made it, but it would be an-other half season before they hired Kattan. That same year, they brought on Adam McKay, who auditioned first as an actor.

"I don't really do impressions," McKay recalls. You need a polit-ical impression for a *Saturday Night Live* audition. "I had like a C-plus Bill Clinton. I [also] did this schlubby guy who just kept saying, 'You can't fight city hall.'" He then needed a celebrity impression, and pretended to cop out. "I did this preamble of how the greatest ce-lebrity in my life is my dad . . . but then the dad character starts un-dermining my audition, and talking about 'I'm the funny one in the family,' and starts like taking over my audition." It went well enough, but it was, in McKay's words, a "writer's audition." Michaels com-mended it, but McKay immediately handed him an envelope, saying

"I'm a writer, too." A week later, he was hired to write for *SNL*. The following season, he'd be offered the head writer position.

"My first response was, 'I'm having such a good time, why would you screw with this?' And by the way, I wasn't entirely wrong." His then manager told him to think on it: Saying no meant he'd never be offered the head writer job again. "So I said yes, and it did change things, because suddenly, I could feel a little bit of the weight of the show on my back." His response to the pressure was to do something that harkened back to his days at Second City: He started proposing massive changes to the show. Since being head writer is not just about writing, he produced some animated shorts for the show and told Michaels that he thought *SNL* could return to having stand-ups open it, like in the beginning, with George Carlin. At the first show back, dress rehearsal went poorly. "They threw out all the things we had worked on over the summer. My wife, to this day, will tell you that that's about as depressed as she's ever seen me."

That year ended up finding solid footing toward the end, even with the rough beginning. "I love it that I took the jump, I learned so much. I mean, I got the crap kicked out of me." Even then, this was a new *SNL*. A lot of the infamous pressure-cooker nature of the show (a combination of environment, the all-night-all-week hours, and certain personality types) was gone. "Marci Klein, the talent coordinator, would jokingly make fun of us," McKay says. "She would say, 'What's with this fucking group? You guys are like *kum-baya*!'" McKay describes the group he was with as nice, collaborative people, like Molly Shannon, Ferrell, Nancy Carell (then Nancy Walls), Tim Meadows, Ana Gasteyer, and David Koechner. "It was much more laid back. You're all just very happy to be there . . . Some of the old-timers just straight up said it, 'This is the nicest group of people we've ever had here.'"

Koechner had come from a small town of fewer than 3,000, majoring in political science before studying comedy. "I think I'd always really just wanted to be seeking a stage. Because I knew when I was thirteen years old there in Tipton, Missouri, watching *Saturday Night Live*, I said to myself, 'I'm going to be on that show.' Now you don't tell people in small towns your dreams, because they don't hear your dream. They hear 'I'm leaving you. You're not good enough for me.' So they feel a sense of abandonment, that's how they emotionally digest it." Everyone in his cohort in his Chicago comedy days, he points out, grew up on *SNL* as he did, starting with the original cast. There was a special appreciation for the show's history with this new group of comedians.

Behind the scenes, of course, there were just as many artists and comedy lovers as you'd find in the writers' room or onstage. One of *SNL*'s unsung heroes was graphic designer Marlene Weisman, who grew up worshipping Python, sneaking backstage at their live shows in the US, meeting the Pythons themselves. Among countless other things on *SNL*, Weisman designed the "Wayne's World" logo, the label for "Schmitts Gay" beer, and "Steve Martin's Penis Beauty Creme." High-powered computers weren't used for these, either—they had a typesetting machine. "There were two guys," Weisman recalls, "who would sit there all day, waiting for us to give them typesetting assignments." The font types were limited in those days, though, so sometimes Weisman had to draw logos by hand. "I drew 'The Bensonhurst Dating Game' . . . 'It's Pat' was in my handwriting. I drew 'Toonces,' I drew 'Happy Fun Ball.' Those are all literally my hand."

Even though locking in art is critical to a sketch, the art department would occasionally get last-minute changes, too, like when someone decided that one punchline in a sketch would be Christopher Walken holding up a picture of Edvard Munch's *The Scream*; they made this decision less than an hour before air at 11:30. With no internet, they had to find a reference image in their physical catalog. "They finally get a reference . . . They bring it down, it's like 11:15; you know what, it even could have been during air. I had to draw an image that had to read as *The Scream* . . . I was shaking because it was so scary." The actors may not be ready for prime time, but you're fucked if the art is late.

Even though people regularly choose the stress of a weekly sketch show for the obvious career benefits, despite its reputation, not every comedian shoots for *SNL*. "I never really went after *SNL* because I was a stand-up," says Kevin Nealon. Even as his close friend Dana Carvey made his way onto the show, he still didn't look at it as an option. "I couldn't believe I knew someone who was gonna be on *SNL*. I was really proud of him." A couple weeks in, Carvey called from Lorne Michaels' house. "'Guess who's in the kitchen? Bill Murray! . . . Anyway, Lorne Michaels is looking for one more cast member. I told him about you, and I think he's gonna want to see your audition tape.' And I'm like, 'Bill Murray's in the kitchen?'" Nealon eventually sent over a tape, and then was told he was going to be flown in for an in-person audition. "I said, 'Steve Martin's in the kitchen?'"

Like many people I spoke with, Nealon doesn't remember what he did for his audition, but it worked. He didn't exactly fall into the show, but there was a certain element of fortuitousness to it for some people. Robert Smigel, who started the year before Nealon as a writer, nudged the door open by recognizing cast member Tim Kazurinsky on the street from *SNL*. Tim was taken aback (not expecting to be recognized), and would go on to recommend Smigel head to The Players Workshop in Chicago. "He said, 'Oh, you could take this course in a summer, and that sounded good, because I'm afraid of committing to anything ever,'" Smigel says. He returned to Chicago the summer after his time at The Players Workshop to be part of the sketch comedy group All You Can Eat; their latest revue was popular enough that the *SNL* writing team Franken and Davis came and saw them.

"They liked our show, and then a few weeks later, they got hired to produce *Saturday Night Live* because Lorne Michaels came back." The year 1985 truly had the potential to fill *SNL* with young voices revolutionizing sketch comedy, even if Smigel, McKinney, and Mc-Culloch were technically "apprentice writers," paid less than Writers Guild union scale. "I know the Writers Guild thinks we were exploit-ed but *one of us* wouldn't have been hired, you know? We got in the door and [it] led to great things for all three of us." Smigel had been in the perfect spot in the perfect time for his own comedy evolution at The Players Workshop, discovering that sketch was his thing, far more than improv.

"I would see these shows and these improv games, and it was impressive in a very limited way to me," Smigel says. He looked to the act Nichols and May, who developed scripted sketches through improv. "They had used improv as a tool, which is a great thing . . . when I worked at *SNL*, sketches were just written on Tuesday night, by a couple of writers with very little sleep, and they would be good, but they were not uniformly as textured as, say, a great *Kids in the Hall* sketch." Some sketches, though, were developed based on charac-ters that had been entertaining audiences at places like The Second City for some time. Chris Farley's character, Matt Foley, the motiva-tional speaker, was something Bob Odenkirk had created and con-tinued to write for.

"I never auditioned to act," Odenkirk recalls. "I'm surprised and thankful that Lorne let me say probably five lines in the course of [the] four years that I was there." When he eventually left *SNL*, Odenkirk explained to Michaels that he wanted to up his game in the performing arena, even if writing was still his main gig at the time. "Like a lot of writers I thought writing—and I still secretly, between you and me and this book—think that writing is kind of a higher order effort. In that there's aspects of acting that allow you to stum-ble and fall and carry on and come out looking good. I think writ-ing, when it starts to break down, it's just not worth it."

Bob's brother, Bill Odenkirk, who would go on to write for *Mr. Show* and *The Simpsons*, was in grad school studying chemistry as Bob was writing for *SNL,* and remembers the two of them chatting at length during his time there. "I'd help out with things he was working on," Bill says. "Occasionally we would write stuff cold, but it was mostly his material and I was just sort of pitching in and talking to him about it." Bill heard second hand about the stressful nights of writing and the resulting anxiety, all while plugging away at school. "My first trip to New York was to go to *Saturday Night Live* and work with him for a weekend like on some material. So it was a blast. I loved it immediately, it was exciting. We actually got scenes on the air, too." Getting to see his own material on television while effectively still on the other side of the glass was an eye opener for him, too. "I was becoming less and less enamored of chemistry."

"Bill helped a lot when I was at *Saturday Night Live*," Bob says. "He flew in twice for the week and he would help with sketches." There, Bob introduced Bill to the likes of O'Brien and Smigel, Bill managing to keep up with the room. He finished out his doctorate in chemistry at the University of Chicago and came to LA the next day. "From the briefest of interactions on a few visits to *Saturday Night Live* he'd already established some credibility, and that's a tribute to Bill and how funny he can be, and how great he is."

Chris Parnell was seen by Michaels' scouts a few times before the gates at *SNL* were opened to him; he'd seen his fellow Groundlings like Gasteyer, Ferrell, and Oteri get plucked and chosen for stardom. Parnell's managers eventually sent a tape to *SNL* unbeknownst to him, and he was soon flown out to New York. "They wanted three impressions and three characters," Parnell says. Oteri and Gasteyer, though, told him he could do four characters and two impressions, instead. He had a monologue as a preacher, a lounge singer character, and a British drama student performing a dramatization of the children's book *Babar, the Elephant.* His two impressions were Tom Brokaw and the scratchy-voiced MTV VJ Jesse Camp. He also performed a dance to some popular music. "The Academy Awards used to have dance numbers for the songs that were nominated, so I did it as though the theme to *Mortal Kombat* had been nominated."

Not long before Parnell was cast, his fellow Groundling Jim Wise was offered a guest writer spot for two weeks, where he shared an office with the new hires: Michael McCullers, Tina Fey, and Michael Schur. He got some material on these two shows, and some of his material was held over, used on later episodes—not a bad track record. One sketch involved Norm McDonald busting out his impressive Quentin Tarantino impression, so Jim headed to Norm's office to see if he had any notes on the sketch. Norm invited him to sit down with his writers, Ross Abrash and Frank Sebastiano, to get to know Jim. "We do the name game of who we know in common, and then he says, 'So what do you think of "Update?"' And I said, 'Well, I love it, it's the centerpiece of the show. I mean, it's why most people watch *Saturday Night Live* really.'"

One of the writers then says, "Maybe Jim should talk to Don Ohlmeyer," who was president of NBC at the time. Jim didn't get the joke.

Norm says, "Well, they don't like it. They don't like *me*. I think they're gonna fire me."

"No, I—is this a real thing?" Jim asks. Norm's writers affirm.

"Yeah, it's a real thing. This is happening." Norm's assistant then entered the room with a landline phone in her hand.

"It's Don Ohlmeyer for you," she says.

"Norm goes 'Oh, here we go.' He takes phone and I and I'm like, 'I should go. I don't know you guys at all.'" They insisted he stick around, smiles on their faces, knowing Norm was up to the challenge.

He was going to work his magic. As has been rumored in the past, Don Ohlmeyer's friendship with O.J. Simpson meant he didn't like Norm's continued jokes at Simpson's expense, so it seemed in the room. The smiles in the room slowly faded. "These guys were realizing that their gig was going to go away." Norm got off the phone and took a minute with the room: his two longtime writers . . . and Jim Wise.

"Yeah, I got fired," Norm says.

"I should go," Jim replies. Norm doesn't miss a beat.

"Yeah, go tell everybody the good news."

"Who's gonna be the anchor?" Jim asks.

Norm replies, "I think *you* are."

Norm's predecessor to the "Weekend Update" desk had been Kevin Nealon, who would end up developing a considerable stable of characters, in addition to fake newsman duties. Perhaps his most weirdly enduring character was Franz, of the duo Hans and Franz, with Dana Carvey. It was clear by the second time they performed these bastardized impressions of Arnold Schwarzenegger that the characters were catching fire. "The first time it was kind of a tepid response," Nealon says. "The audience is trying to figure out what we're doing and who we are. We let it sit there for a couple of weeks, and then finally I said, 'Dana, we should put up Hans and Franz again, see what happens.' So we did, and it was like a long lost friend. When they saw us, they loved it."

"Pumping Up with Hans & Franz" would continue for another couple of years before it was clear that these characters could be *SNL*'s first feature film since *The Blues Brothers* in 1980. Carvey, Nealon, Smigel, and relative new hire Conan O'Brien all worked on the script for *Hans and Franz: The Girly-Man Dilemma* together. In the script, Hans and Franz leave the fictional Little Austria in New York City (which would have been all in black and white) on a bicycle built for two, heading to California to find their cousin Arnold. "I dedicated most of my time to the script; we wrote it at Sony in an office there," Nealon says. He recalls mostly writing with Smigel. "Some people are just, they're the typers in the room. They're also writers, but then there's the other guy or girl who likes to just sit back and kind of throw ideas around."

"I was told, yeah, Arnold's interested in doing a movie with us where Hans and Franz go to Hollywood to get into show business with [help] from their cousin Arnold," Smigel recalls. Schwarzenegger would end up attached to the film as a producer, so there was a lot of leeway as to what the film could be. "So I hear this, and I say, 'That sounds like a horrible idea, your characters are so one dimensional . . .' And then I was like, 'Well, what if it's a musical? If it's a musical, it'll make the movie not take itself as seriously. Which helps, and it will kill about twenty-five to thirty minutes of a ninety-minute movie, require less plot, and maybe it'll help us fool people into thinking that this thing is actually a movie.'"

The film would've potentially had 'n antagonist named 'Rolf, ideally p'ayed by Dolph Lundgren. Smigel wanted a bad guy who spouted exposition and made it clear he was out to get rid of "girly-men" for good, and one other thing. "It would always be like this extra tagged on thing about how he's going to also hurt the environment." Famously less-than-stereotypically-masculine men like Sonny Bono or (Michaels' long-time friend) Paul Simon would start going missing, and Arnold would play his own grandmother. The film is also a road trip on Hans and Franz's tandem bicycle, of course. "They pick up more and more people and the tandem bicycle just gets longer and longer. I don't know why." At intervals throughout the film and along the trip, there would be visits with movie critics Siskel and Ebert, as well, with Hans and Franz checking in on how the outspoken men were feeling about it.

"At the end of the movie . . . they also save the environment, and Earth opens up its mouth and thanks them in a very gentle voice," Smigel says. Schwarzenegger eventually backed out of the film, so *Hans and Franz: The Girly-Man Dilemma* never saw the light of day; he was making *The Last Action Hero* at the time, so it's possible that another film playing that much with his image didn't seem appealing or lucrative. "If we had written it after *Wayne's World,* it would have gotten made, because other movies got made . . . especially with Arnold in it. I don't think Lorne had that kind of movie juice yet that he could just get anything made." *Wayne's World* would prove to be the odd one out, becoming the only film to be made among these early contenders, like one about Bill Swerski's Superfans (of "da bears" fame) and a purported *SNL* sketch anthology film that actually launched an attempt at a franchise.

David Letterman and Chris Elliott on *Late Night with David Letterman*.

Cast photo of *Not Necessarily the News*—clockwise from top left: Danny Breen, Anne Bloom, Mitchell Laurance, Stuart Pankin, and Lucy Webb.

Title card for *The Tracey Ullman Show*.

Ross Shafer poses with Ed Mc-Mahon and Dick Clark, promoting his campaign to make "Louie, Louie" by The Kingsmen into the Washington state song.

Almost Live! cast photo—clockwise from top: Pat Cashman, Bob Nelson, Ed Wyatt, Tracey Conway, John Keister, Steve Wilson, Nancy Guppy, and Joe Guppy.

Cast photo for *The Tracey Ullman Show*—from left to right: Julie Kavner, Dan Castellaneta, Tracey Ullman, Sam McMurray, and Joseph Malone.

Ullman as Tammy Lee Didawick on *The Tracy Ullman Show*.

THE KIDS
IN THE
HALL

RIVOLI
334 QUEEN
WEST

JUNE 1-4
9 PM
$6 WED THUR
$7 FRI SAT

R. PINNER / P. BELLINI

*K*ids in the Hall cast—clockwise from top left: Mark McKinney, Scott Thompson, Kevin McDonald, Bruce McCulloch, and Dave Foley.

*A*lternate Kids in the Hall cast shot.

*K*ids in the Hall: Brain Candy film cast photo.

In Living Color cast—clockwise from top left: Jim Carrey, Tommy David-son, Kelly Coffield-Park, Damon Wayans, David Alan Grier, Kim Wayans, T'Keyah Crystal Keymáh, Keenen Ivory Wayans, and Kim Coles.

The Fly Girls—left to right: Li-sa Marie Todd, Deidre Lang, Jennifer Lopez, and Lisa Joann Thompson.

Damon Wayans as Homey D. Clown.

Kim Wayans as Benita Butrell.

Damon Wayans as Oswald Bates.

Damon Wayans as Blaine Edwards and David Alan Grier as Antoine Merriweather in "Men on Film."

*T*he Ben Stiller Show cast—Janeane Garofalo, Bob Odenkirk, Ben Stiller, and Andy Dick.

*A*dditional cast member photos of Janeane Garofalo and Ben Stiller.

The State cast—clockwise from left: David Wain, Michael Showalter, Ken Marino, Thomas Lennon, Michael Ian Black, Michael Patrick Jann, Kerri Kenney-Silver, Kevin Allison, Robert Ben Garant, Joe Lo Truglio, and Todd Holoubek.

David Wain directing *Role Models*.

SNL cast photo (season 18). Top row from left: Adam Sandler, David Spade, Ellen Cleghorne, Kevin Nealon, Phil Hartman; middle: Chris Rock, Julie Sweeney, Dana Carvey, Rob Schneider; front: Chris Farley, Al Franken, Melanie Hutsell.

Dana Carvey as Enid Strict, "The Church Lady".

Molly Shannon as Mary Katherine Gallagher.

Chris Farley as Matt Foley, the motivational speaker, chastising David Spade and Christina Applegate.

Mike Myers as Linda Richman in "Coffee Talk," with Madonna as Liz Rosenberg (Madonna's longtime publicist at the time), and Roseanne Barr as Rosenberg's mother. Barbra Streisand ("like buttah") made a surprise appearance at the end of the sketch.

15

Gelatinous Cube Eats Village: Wayne's World

S *aturday Night Live*'s first seasons may have been the result of years of TV sketch experience in the person of Lorne Michaels, as well as the years of improv and sketch training of his actors and writers, but they were also an experiment. When Albert Brooks first signed on to do short films for the show, he wasn't yet an experienced director, so he worked alongside someone who was, namely: Penelope Spheeris. She had already worked with comedy legend Richard Pryor and started what is likely LA's first music video company, ROCK 'N REEL, in 1974. After *SNL*, Spheeris went on to direct several documentary and narrative features, including the landmark *The Decline of Western Civilization* and its sequels, intimately covering punk and metal music.

"In the late '80s I did the second *Decline* film, *The Metal Years*, so I guess I knew a bit about headbangers," Spheeris says. Like any director under consideration for a movie with a budget, there were obstacles. "I had to jump through hoops at Paramount and crawl on my belly like a reptile to impress those that needed to be impressed. I probably had to go to six different meetings before they finally gave me the gig. One time I sat in the hallway waiting for over two hours and the secretary came out and told me that the executives were too busy to meet with me. Fact of the matter is, they were jammed on time because the guys needed to be back in New York for *SNL*. They needed to hire somebody fast. My boyfriend at the time [the guitar player in the film's fictional band Crucial Taunt] called me 'the waitress that got lucky.' He's not my boyfriend anymore."

Spheeris was critical to wrangling a slew of creatives and trying to get a single cinematic voice onscreen. As with any other *SNL* creation, it wasn't clear if the "Wayne's World" sketches would be poised to become their own film at first. Wayne had existed since Mike Myers' days in Scarborough, a district of Toronto, and he adapted the character for *SNL*, giving him a best friend, Garth Algar. The first "Wayne's World" sketch, put up at the ten-to-one spot, didn't get a massive audience reaction, but it was enough to get eighteen more on the air while both Myers and Dana Carvey were still in the cast. Those bits could have been all there was for Wayne and Garth, too, especially since Lorne Michaels first pitched a different film to Myers.

"'Thank you, Mr. Gatsby, for inviting me. I'd always seen those lights across the lake and had wondered what was happening over here,'" Myers cheekily said to Michaels, the first time he visited his home in the Hamptons. "The next day he said, 'Do you want to make a remake of *The Graduate*?'" Myers says. Believing it to be a perfect film not in need of a remake, Myers was asked what he'd rather do instead; he believed Wayne was more a movie character than a TV character, anyway. So Michaels asked for more. "I brought my three by five cards with me. I put them out, and he was like, 'I don't want to hear three by five cards, what's your idea?'"

Michaels' first pitch to Paramount didn't hook them, but when former NBC president Brandon Tartikoff became the chairman of Paramount Pictures, they reconsidered. Tartikoff was apparently a big fan of the "Wayne's World" sketches. If they could keep it under a certain budget, they were good to go. The script would be by Myers and *SNL* writing duo Bonnie and Terry Turner. The movie just had to work around the schedules of their two stars, of course still under contract to *Saturday Night Live*. They also had to contend with the obvious: This was a sketch about two dudes on a couch in a basement. "The aspect that the studio and the writers and producers were most concerned about was whether or not it would be possible to turn a five minute skit into a feature film," Spheeris says. "They kept asking me if I thought it was possible and I kept assertively telling them that it was possible and I was positive I could do it. Fact is, I was not positive. I was just bluffing my way through." Once the film started moving forward, though, it was clear she was the director for the job.

"Very few people in both the music business and the film business know both areas well enough to make a good product," Spheeris says. "My experience in the music business really did help with a lot of the work in *Wayne's World*. Also, I believe I have a very good instinct for casting musicians. I fought very hard for Tia Carrere to be cast as Cassandra. I knew she was perfect because she was already a musician and I did not have to teach her that part." The '80s metal soundtrack—except for "Bohemian Rhapsody," already in the script—was all Spheeris.

To inflate five minutes into ninety, it had to be based on something real, or so Myers looked at it. The fictionalized version of Aurora, Illinois, then, would be based on Scarborough, where Myers had grown up. "One of the things that Del Close had said is, 'Don't invent, remember,'" Myers says. Truth in comedy was key, "'Speak the truth faster,' is what he would say. So for me, having [the metal club in *Wayne's* World] be The Gasworks was a love letter to Toronto." Anything that felt like Scarborough or Toronto in general would become part of the movie's Aurora, adding to the world-building. "All the language is stuff that people would say in Scarborough, you know, and certainly, there's a Scarborough accent. It's a heightened Toronto accent, and it's working class, which I am."

A fellow Canadian, Sean Sullivan, played Phil, the constantly inebriated and/or stoned member of the core *Wayne's World* crew who headbang in the back of The Mirthmobile. "The character is basically like a silent movie character in a talking film, except for when he's sober," Sullivan says. He was used to the marathon of four or five auditions before he'd get a small part. "It turned into an improv of Mike and I walking around the room . . . Phil in his natural state of nearly kneeling, you know, legless, and Mike walking me around and trying to make it okay for me, warning me when there was furniture to not run into . . . That literally was it, it was one audition."

Kurt Fuller, who plays Russell, assistant to Rob Lowe's Benjamin Kane in the film, had just quit the real estate business because *Ghostbusters II* had gotten him enough attention to boost his film career. Fuller was part of a reading of the *Wayne's World* script, which companies typically do to see how the film dialogue actually sounds, out loud. "I was a realtor, basically—still, very intimidated," Fuller says. He knew he was among comedy royalty, and he was making the king laugh. "I cracked Lorne Michaels up; I had no idea why. I didn't know why he was laughing. I certainly was just nervous and trying to get through the lines without screwing up." Fuller was cast based on the reading.

Plenty has been made of the reported difficulties during filming, but the final product and thirty years have leveled out most people's opinions of the shoot. "I loved making that film, and don't know why there was so much reporting of anything that was troublesome on set," Myers says. "I mean, we had to work shit out, but we all had a great time making that film." As a kid with blue collar roots, seeing a story unfold before his eyes as they made the film was something that stuck with him, and is the memory that seems to matter most. As for the people he was rumored to be tangling with the heaviest, "When I met Dana, you know, he just knew everything. I mean, that's how I felt . . . I lobbied very hard for Penelope, so I was thrilled with my choice."

"I know the urban myth has it that Mike and I did not get along on the set," Spheeris says. "That is absolutely not true. From my observation, really the only creative dissension that went on was between Mike and Dana. And it was a healthy disagreement usually.

Lorne teaches his players to 'compete with each other.' They constantly try one-upmanship to outdo each other. It's actually an edge that makes the comedy work better."

While on set, Michaels was always the one with the most power, which he exercised. He famously had Myers make his case when there was an attempt to replace "Bohemian Rhapsody" in the car scene with Guns N' Roses' "Welcome to the Jungle." "Lorne will challenge you," Myers says. "But if you're passionate and you make your case, Lorne goes with it." This was Myers' first film, so it couldn't have been an easy argument to make. Myers once told *Rolling Stone* that he was ready to quit over it, but eventually the older song won out: "I'm grateful to Dana, Penelope and Lorne for being as talented as they are and being patient with somebody who, not much earlier, was an idiot in Scarborough, Ontario."

"It kind of became a bonding thing because everyone got yelled at," remembers Sullivan. "Cast, crew, stars, day players—everyone. So it became this thing of like, 'Well, I got it yesterday. So it's probably not me, but I'm with you guys, whoever it's gonna be.'" Sullivan's first day on set was in Wayne's basement, the familiar setting of the *SNL* sketches. The props department had given him egg whites to help the scene play, because drool won't photograph well on its own. "I've never met Rob [Lowe], and I'm drooling egg whites that they put in my mouth, onto Rob Lowe, someone who in my mind was very famous." He recalls seeing Carvey and Myers get yelled at during this awkward moment.

"There was a lot of pressure because Mike and Dana had to wrap on time, because the next season of *SNL* was starting, and they literally flew back within the week of taping," Sullivan recalls. Over budget was one thing, but over schedule was impossible, and when producer Michaels was on set, it was never more clear that there was no nonsense in that department. "He was talking to me and just sort of joking, and I said something back to him, and then he looked at me, and he went, 'Don't ever speak to me.' I was like, 'Is this a bit?' . . . They say he is a trickster."

Breaking tension is always key on a set, even for a comedy. This is when you find the class clown among the class clowns. "We were filming outside the broadcast studio," recalls Spheeris. "It was an all-night gig and everybody was really tired. Mike would do impersonations of different people on the crew. For me, he would put my leather jacket on and my shades, then stick his ass out and run around yelling, 'Standby! Action! Cut! You screwed up, you idiot!' He was very generous, entertaining the crew that way."

"I've forgotten most of the things I've done, but I have not forgotten *Wayne's World*," Fuller says. "I had toiled for nine years selling houses and holding open houses; I'm tall, walking around the edge of the room, so I don't make the room look small, putting vanilla on a piece of tin and putting it into the oven, so it smells like baked bread. That was my life. So now, here I am at Paramount Studios." The guy playing the TV veteran was still relatively new to film, so the star power and the nerves were at their peak. Then there was the director. "Penelope Spheeris, she is a force of nature . . . I think she's one of the most genuine people I've ever known." Fuller describes the set as anarchy, at least compared to what he'd seen on *Ghostbusters II*, though he reiterates that Spheeris was approachable and "full of ideas."

Fuller also remembers being impressed by Carvey's range. "He could do anything, he could listen to you once and do [an impression of] you . . . I was delighted because it was like being in heaven for me. And I had no idea what I was doing." Sean Sullivan also recalled Carvey jumping from "impression to impression" between takes. To pass the time, Carvey also had his drum kit set up on a nearby soundstage, and the actors would occasionally play together. Many of them were amateur musicians, and clearly had similar musical influences.

"Bohemian Rhapsody" was released in 1975, when Sullivan was in high school. "My older brother and I would drive around listening to that song and singing to it," he says. So when he read the script to *Wayne's World* it was kismet. "It was just like, 'Oh my god, my life is on is on the page. It's gorgeous.'" Lee Tergesen, who plays Terry, one of the other members of the crew, told a similar story to *Rolling Stone*, even though he'd grown up in Connecticut. This otherwise disparate group of music lovers seemed built for being the guys in the back of a robin's egg blue AMC Pacer.

The headbanging scene, which would end up edited into a Grammy-winning music video for the song, was directly inspired by Myers' brother, Paul, who did hang out in a car singing along to the radio with his bandmates. In real life, the original Mirthmobile was his friend Michael Wojewoda's Dodge Dart Swinger. Becoming your own source of entertainment was part of growing up in Scarborough for the Myers family, and Mike Myers wanted to reflect that as part of Wayne's life.

"There's a law school in Toronto called Osgoode Hall, and it has a bridge between two buildings, and the way they've designed it is that it has a parabolic dome underneath the bridge, so it has this fantastic echo," Myers recalls. "Me and Paul and a group of his friends from various bands, we used to go there when the bars were closed in Toronto at one o'clock. They would just sing harmonies, in this beautiful echo. It was Beatles harmonies, and Everly Brothers and all that stuff. That's the sort of spirit I wanted to have for *Wayne's World*, which is no-money fun." Most of the iconic scenes that come from this part of Myers' life were shot in Los Angeles, but there were select shots where The Mirthmobile drives through Chicago and its suburbs, to get that Aurora-adjacent flavor. As usual, when anything came through Chicago that needed bodies on set, they reached out to Charna Halpern at iO.

Rich Fulcher had been put in a project that featured all the big names in Chicago improv at the time. "I was originally cast in a bigger role," Fulcher says. "Del had knocked me down a peg, just replaced [me] with somebody else." That's when the call came in that *Wayne's World* was in need of some local actors. "I guess they were looking for a body double that could do the Bohemian Rhapsody bit and the White Castle bit, so Charna recommended me." Rich was almost the right height and looked enough like Myers, though he'd be doing all back-of-the-head acting. "So I went in and I did what is called a look-see, walked around. [The casting director] said, 'Slump down a little bit, because you're a little bit taller than he is.' So I slumped down and then I got the job."

It was a lot of headbanging and pointing at stuff, all shot from a distance so you wouldn't know it wasn't the real Wayne Campbell. "I would actually sign autographs—I would sign it 'Wayne'—but people would come up to me and everything and I didn't know what to do, I didn't want to go, 'Get lost buddy!'" The fake Wayne and Garth were also accosted at a stoplight. "'Hey, man, we're in a heavy metal band. We love you guys. Would you come on over after the shoot and hang out with us?' and I thought, oh my god, half of me wants to go, the other half is saying 'they're gonna sacrifice me if they see my wig come off,' you know, take out my liver or something."

Wayne's World handily beat the other films playing its opening weekend, introducing the characters to a much bigger world outside of the *SNL* audience. Wayne and Garth were comedy icons, the first *SNL* had managed to squeeze out since The Blues Brothers, thirteen years before. After 1993, there would be nine more *SNL*-related films, and among the likes of *A Night at the Roxbury, Superstar, MacGruber,* even *Wayne's World 2,* none of them came close to grossing as much as *Wayne's World.* Someone left Lorne's cake out in the rain. "The success of *Wayne's World* is one of the unsolved mysteries of the universe," Spheeris says. "None of us who worked on it can really explain it. It was some sort of cosmic coming together of the right people, the right chemistry, all at the right time."

"It was one of those few movies that sort of defined a genera-tion," Fuller says. "A touchstone for that particular time." *Wayne's World*'s success, especially over what followed, has very little to do with happening upon the recipe for a successful film. It is—regard-less of whether you see it as a pile of catchphrases or a solid come-dic film—a pure collaboration between a few veterans and a couple scared newbies. The newbies just wanted it to go the best it could and the veterans had to snap everyone into shape. *Wayne's World* takes a seed of an idea and manages to grow from it fully-formed charac-ters—sure, the catchphrases were entirely intact, but now their use was justified. They were reverse-engineered in a way that didn't feel false. It's a pretty big-budget film about DIY, what money does to DIY, and how to get it all back on your own terms. *Wayne's World* ends on some "chimps in a davenport in a basement," who selec-tively break the fourth wall, and whom have found their little com-munity of people.

——— 16 ———
Cookin' with Gas:
The Groundlings

The Committee had started a wing in Los Angeles in the late '60s, bringing with it stage manager and occasional actor Gary Austin. "I don't think he was particularly treated well at The Committee," says Groundlings founding member Tracy Newman. He brought with him a wealth of knowledge about how improvisation theaters are run, even if performing wasn't his strong suit. "He wasn't a great improviser either, but he developed an environment that was conducive to people cutting loose." In 1972, he started a workshop to bring what he knew about improv to a town full of actors.

"I just walked into a class and I'd never done improv," Newman recalls. She was frightened of the whole situation, but wanted to try, though she describes some of her other classmates as scared but still fearless. Among that original class—often listed erroneously as members of The Groundlings—were Pat Morita, Craig T. Nelson, Jack Soo, and Tim Matheson. They left before the workshops became something more codified. In 1974, the group had a space at the Oxford Playhouse in Hollywood, and were calling themselves The Groundlings (historically the term for the ordinary folk who watched plays from the ground in Shakespeare's day).

Newman admits that, even this far in, she was still so afraid of performing improv that she eventually started teaching it. "I was real aware of how to do it, and why I couldn't do it very well," she says. This is a trait she shared with Austin. "Gary was helpless against that kind of fear. It's ego fear." She had a writer's instinct (she'd go on to write for *Cheers* and *The Nanny* and to create *According to Jim*), even with no experience at the time. "I could see when there was a good sketch, and I could really help them turn it into [one] with a beginning, middle and an end. But I couldn't be on stage doing it and help turn it into anything." Newman would also end up writing down the syllabus for The Groundlings, which was rooted in Viola Spolin, as well as whatever had passed through The Second City, then The Committee, down to Austin.

It was clear early on that not only did they have a solid group of improvisers, but The Groundlings also had sketches that were going to continue to work. "We developed some sketches at that very first class that made us decide we have a show." Most of the shows would still consist of improv, but the openings and sometimes the closing pieces would be sketches, though even within Groundlings sketches there would be room for improv. "We had a sketch called 'Blair House' that you could plug different people into if somebody dropped out of the company . . . So then we realized, 'Oh, let's just keep developing these pieces that you can plug new people into if somebody can't make the show.'" Like The Second City and other companies before them, The Groundlings developed their sketches through improv, transcribed and then performed them again if they worked.

Newman brought a number of people into The Groundlings, early on, like Archie Hahn, Valerie Curtin, and her sister, Laraine, who would often give the shows room to breathe. "Laraine was smart enough to write monologues. If everybody was busy changing their clothes, because ten people were in a sketch, sometimes Laraine would go out in a costume and do one of her characters. She developed all her characters that way." Necessity being the mother of invention, even for character development, sometimes scene elements would come from the exact opposite kind of moment. "I just remember times when I'd be teaching, and we'd be working on something for the show, and we didn't have an ending. We'd all be working on it and talking about it and trying things. Somebody would walk in for a second and watch what we're doing, standing there with a hammer, and they would say, 'Why don't you blah, blah, blah, blah, blah,' and then they'd leave. You'd realize, yeah, that's a good ending. Sometimes you can't come up with an ending, because you're too close to it, laboring too hard."

Everybody could pitch in, and just about anyone could get in; it was a question of whether or not you'd stick it out. "It used to be you could get in the Groundlings just if you wanted to," Newman says. "Then you had to audition, and all that audition was [was], let's find out if they're crazy." They also had to pay the monthly fee of around $40. Some people didn't pay and stuck around anyway, because they were skilled and poor. You either left because you didn't have the money or the skill or—and this started happening incredibly quickly—if someone snapped you up for TV.

In 1975, Lorne Michaels had recently produced a Lily Tomlin TV special featuring Christopher Guest, Second City alum Valri Bromfield, Doris Roberts, and Laraine Newman, among others. When he was casting for *SNL*, Tracy Newman recalls him offering spots to a number of people at The Groundlings, including Laraine, who was the only person to accept. "They just didn't take it seriously," Newman says. "Here they are in LA. They're being asked to move to New York to do a pilot, for a show that's going to be live and it's going to be on at midnight or something like that." Other people had offers for other shows at the time, as well, that made a move to New York even less feasible.

"I was thrilled to be around these people," Newman says. She recalls a time sitting around the office with Groundlings' future artistic director Tom Maxwell. "He said, 'I just hope all this is worth it. You know? I mean, sometimes I just feel like we're wasting our time.' And I said, 'I can't believe that you don't see that this is the future of show business and comedy in this town. First of all, what more do you need? They plucked Laraine out and she's a huge star, and she's just doing the same thing she was doing here. And that's what everybody here is doing.'" She recalls Phil Hartman popping up to play one night. "He came out of the audience and blew everybody off the stage who was already brilliant." The Groundlings was the place in LA that comedy minds gravitated to.

Theater people, though, don't typically flock to LA. You'll often hear that it's "not a theater town." Former Groundling George Mc-Grath sees it as a little more nuanced than that. "I think it's a theater town in the sense of small theater; a million small 99-seat houses and they're all doing plays." McGrath ended up in LA by accident, coming from off-off-Broadway productions and ending up in a couple of doomed traveling productions that he had to leave. Without enough money to return home to Brooklyn, he found himself stuck in LA. He tried out improv at LA Connection (started by former member of The Committee, Kent Skov), and in 1983 found himself at The Groundlings.

"I was kind of a hit, and I started writing sketches there because you have to write sketches to be in the show. It turned out to be something that I was pretty good at," McGrath says. He fairly quickly went from Groundling regular, to writing for *K.I.D.S Incorporated* and *Pee-Wee's Playhouse*. He also took part in a one-off video/possible sketch pilot that The Groundlings shot in 1984 called *Cheeseball Presents*. Along with McGrath, it features names like voice acting legend Tress MacNeille, John Paragon (Jambi on *Pee-Wee*), the famous billboard star Angelyne, Cassandra Petersen (Elvira), and Phil Hartman. It would be directed by writer and production designer Alfred Sole on seemingly no budget.

"We never had any permits to be on [Hollywood] Boulevard . . . This guy Alfred Sole was a fan of the Groundlings, and he asked me if I would write a couple of things." The group brought in their existing characters, including Pee-Wee Herman, Elvira, Angelyne sort of playing Angelyne, and McGrath brought in a nun character he'd been playing onstage at The Groundlings. The video was produced for ON TV, an early cable network, where it aired at least once, before moving to The Playboy Channel, where it aired a non-zero number of times. The latter venue makes the most sense, since you've never seen so many breasts on an American sketch show. Nor have you seen Phil Hartman with a yam sticking out of his pants, so if that's your deal, seek this out.

"Phil Hartman loved being Phil Hartman more than anything," McGrath says. "He loved being in show business. He loved every little thing he was doing." He recalls his early days in LA, scrounging for change with friends, and how Hartman would take them out to dinner, or to Palm Springs. In the middle of his time on *Saturday Night Live*, Hartman briefly joined McGrath on his sketch show *On the Television* to perform the TV version of a piece McGrath had written for him back at The Groundlings. The Groundlings are not as precious about keeping sketches or characters as company property. Historically, The Groundlings are about developing characters, and many people bring those with them to TV.

Phil LaMarr would eventually take Jaq, his high-energy UPS Guy, to *MADtv*, but he was getting praise for it at The Groundlings for some time before that happened. Like McGrath, LaMarr couldn't head to New York to pursue theater because of money; unlike him, LA was already home. "I started doing classes at The Groundlings not as part of my acting career; that was part of feeding my soul. *I need improv. I missed The Purple Crayon.*" The Groundlings started filling that void and, fairly soon, started getting him work. Wendy Cutler, part of Off the Wall Improv, a group that has been running since 1975, was hiring a loop group (a group of voice actors to add background voices to large scenes in films) for the movie *House Party 2*, starring Kid n' Play.

"So she called the Groundlings like, 'Hey, I need some improvisers. Got any Black folks?' And, of course, The Groundlings were like, 'Um . . .' There was nobody in the group. They had to go down to intermediate improv like, 'Yeah, we got one guy down here!'" There's usually no script for loop groups; they just need people who can hold conversations, to roughly match the actual background actors, or extras, in the shot. "Before improv was out there in the world, before *Whose Line,* this was one of the ways that improvisers could get paid, because nobody got paid for improv. I mean, Second City paid you, but Groundlings didn't." Eventually, this led to LaMarr getting to sit in with Off the Wall, which counts among former members and guests John Ritter, Robin Williams, and Chevy Chase.

In 1992, LaMarr was voted into the main company of The Groundlings, alongside Jennifer Coolidge. He was the first Black person voted into the company, despite the diversity of the early years. In almost fifty years, he notes, not a single person of Latin American background has been voted in. "And this is like LA's improv group. But before people got voted in, it was just funny people." LaMarr thinks it's possible that improv as an art form started out reaching more White people than anyone else. "At the time, improv was a very suburban art form. The vast majority of people of color didn't know about it . . . Also, most people of color, if they looked around and were funny, they didn't see improvisers, they saw stand-up comics. So, I think the pool of people that these improv groups were pulling from was pretty homogenous." Not that other companies have an ideal situation, either. "I think Second City had a little bit more diversity, just because Second City had slots. 'We're always gonna have a fat guy, we're always gonna have one pretty girl, somebody to play the mom.' So they would just constantly cast types. And I think at one point, they were like, 'Oh, let's, let's, let's make a . . . Black spot.'"

Stephanie Courtney has made appearances on *Mad Men* and *The Goldbergs,* and is probably best known as Flo, in the Progressive insurance commercials. She'd been acting and doing stand-up for some time before she checked out a beginner-level class at The Groundlings. "What I had going for me [was] I was comfortable performing. That was good, especially in the Groundlings, because it's really about emotions and character—behavior, as opposed to saying the most clever thing."

One of the early Groundlings shows she saw was with Mindy Sterling, who came into the scene hot, with a character ready to go. "What they teach at The Groundlings [is] you're going to start in the middle of a scene, you're not going to like ramp up nice and slow to get to something. If there's a fire, throw oil on it . . . When I taught it, I would tell my students that the good thing in life is don't assume and don't take things personally; in improv, assume and take things personally." It's a way to find conflict while also never denying anyone else's choices in a scene, or being too busy thinking about the joke you're going to make. Real human emotion is naturally silly and often stupid; the things we say to one another in the heat of the moment, when presented on a stage, are naturally funny. Eventually.

Among the mainstays of the theater-to-sketch-TV pipeline, The Groundlings remains a non-profit organization. Of the board members, three are actors in the Main Company. The organization no longer has a single artistic director, with the Main Company taking up that role as a group. Its legacy is well-cemented in the history of comedy, though Tracy Newman sums up where it stands pretty well: "The Groundlings were the cheap seats and they were the ones throwing tomatoes at the actors . . . The Groundlings is the dumb show. So yeah, we have costumes upstairs—you can't even imagine—and it's very character driven. It borders on slapstick, sometimes." Even the dumb show doesn't work without the right support onstage.

"The funny joke and the [denial] thing usually comes with nerves and ego. 'I want to look good, or I want to be funny—I need that laugh,'" Courtney says. Even veterans can fall victim to that. Courtney has been performing The Groundlings' long-form show *The Crazy Uncle Joe Show* for twenty-one years now, and she occasionally finds that old impulse creeping back in. "I used to do the show after therapy. I would be like, 'Today, I know myself, and I need a laugh in a gross way.' So what I would do to check my brain, I'd just be like, 'Just support the other person. Make them look good.' That's it, that's the only assignment. Then the attention's off me."

17

It's Your Fault for Watching: Late Night with Conan O'Brien

The O'Briens of Brookline, Massachusetts had a child in their attic in the early '80s. He lived up there probably to escape his five siblings and, as he told the Boston Globe in 1980 when he was just seventeen, "It's quiet there and nobody can shuffle my paper around." He'd just won a prize in a writing contest by the National Council of Teachers of English for a meta story about a young boy who has to choose between entering a writing contest and going into the family business. The story was entitled "To Bury the Living," something NBC would be considering doing to his show, *Late Night with Conan O'Brien,* thirteen years later.

In the same piece in the *Boston Globe,* he says he'll go to the best college that picks him. That ended up being Harvard (Harvard Driving School, if you ask him now), where he became editor, then president, of their humor publication, *The Harvard Lampoon.* There, he would meet future writing partner Greg Daniels, and they'd head to Hollywood for their first joint entertainment job, writing for *Not Necessarily the News.* When that gig ended for them, they worked on the short-lived replacement for Fox's poorly-planned *The Late Show,* entitled *The Wilton North Report. SNL* followed soon after, though it was cut temporarily short by a writers strike.

The strike meant that he couldn't write for TV, so he then traveled to Chicago with fellow *SNL* writers Robert Smigel and Bob Odenkirk, to put on a live sketch show called *Happy Happy Good Show,* with additional cast from Smigel's group All You Can Eat. They put together a revue of eighteen sketches, performed at Chicago's

Victory Gardens Studio Theatre. Not only was this a venting of pent-up, not-ready-for-*SNL* sketches, but it was a portent of things to come, which concluded w ith a portent of things that were likely not to.

"Take our very theatrical finale, where we make wacky predictions about the year 2000; it uses dark silhouettes and a deliberate pretentiousness that just wouldn't work on TV," Robert Smigel told the *Chicago Tribune* in July 1988. Beautifully ironic considering the bit entitled "In the Year 2000" was a staple of late-'90s *Conan*. It would eventually be called "In the Year 3000," after 2000 had passed. Perhaps my favorite, twenty-five years later:

"In the Year 2000 . . . Computers will be convinced
it is the year 1900. They will support President McKinley, grow
handlebar mustaches, and crack the heads of the filthy Irish."

Happy Happy Good Show planned to run in Chicago through August 7, the day the WGA strike ended. After Chicago, they took the show to Los Angeles for a four-week run, where the reviews were mixed. In October, they got back to New York to work on a new season of *SNL*. O'Brien left *SNL* in 1991 to work on *The Simpsons* for two seasons, penning among others the classic episode "Marge vs. the Monorail." He was under an essentially unbreakable four-year contract with Fox to work on *The Simpsons* when he got a call from former boss, Lorne Michaels, who proposed that O'Brien might be the head writer for the new version of *Late Night,* since Letterman was leaving. O'Brien made it clear that he thought no one could replace Letterman. "Dave had re-created the talk show," O'Brien said on the podcast *Inside Conan.* He considered the job for a bit, then decided against it.

After testing numerous comedians to host the show, Michaels and his producers had no one who met their standard, so Michaels proposed O'Brien to screen test for it. Not long after, using the set of *The Tonight Show*, O'Brien interviewed Mimi Rogers and Jason

Alexander as his audition. It was so last-minute he was writing his monologue down in the scant minutes before they had to roll the cameras and had to creatively hide an antifreeze stain on the white blazer he had chosen to wear. The audition shows an awkward twenty-nine-year-old kid trying his best, while still displaying a bit of his charm. From this moment on, O'Brien would continue to laugh at the idea that he was somehow on TV, which carried him through nearly thirty years of late-night talk shows.

Rumors started circulating, first on Washington, DC station WWDC's *Harris in the Morning*, that the young unknown had screen tested to take over *Late Night*. Even amongst rumors that Drew Carey and Jon Stewart had auditioned, and that Garry Shandling was the favorite to take over, O'Brien's name was now out there. Mike Sweeney, head writer on *Late Night*, was still doing stand-up when O'Brien was announced as the new host. "Most comedians hadn't heard of him, and they were all outraged." Five months later, O'Brien found himself on *The Tonight Show* and *Late Night* to get the public used to his white, white face, and on September 13, Yitzhak Rabin and Yasser Arafat signed the Oslo Accords. Hence the final line of the final joke of O'Brien's first monologue, that same night:

> "O'Brien, the day you get your own talk show is the day
> there's peace in the Middle East."

That first show opens with O'Brien gleefully going about his day as everyone around him tries to warn him not to screw up *Late Night*, including newsman Tom Brokaw, who violently crushes three saltine crackers in his hand, to show he means business. Whistling a little tune, behind a door that simply reads "New Host," O'Brien gleefully throws a noose over a beam and prepares to hang himself, before being asked to come out and start his first show. It's immediately clear that this late-night show is a production: It's not the anti-talk show of *Letterman*, and it's not the middle-of-the-road false ideal of Leno's *Tonight Show*. This show is going to try hard to hook you, because it knows it has to; the new *Late Night*, like O'Brien, isn't sure it even belongs on TV.

A lot of critics agreed with this assessment, of course, citing O'Brien's visible nerves and, in their opinion, lack of material. It was rough partially because before this, he had only performed at The Groundlings, and done some warm-ups before TV shows, and appeared as an extra on several *SNL* sketches. He was a weird choice, except for having the comedy chops. He was well known for cracking up a writers' room, which meant that with enough familiarity and looseness, he could probably have the audience in the studio and at home on his side. It just didn't look that way, at first.

"I used to say to Conan, 'I know that you need to get used to being on camera. I know you can get better, but to some degree, they have to just get used to you,'" Robert Smigel says. For the first year and a half of *Late Night*, Smigel was the head writer. "If you watch those early shows, he's pretty charming, even when he sucks. There's a part of him that's very lovable. Him and Andy were such neophytes and felt so in over their heads that when you watch it now, it's actually very endearing. I imagine there was an audience that found him endearing back then, and they understood he was taking risks, and they wanted to be there for the ride."

"The best job was starting up the *Conan* show . . . What was most fun about it was the Roman candle aspect of, 'Let's throw everything out there. Oh, my god, look at all these things we can do,' and then we figured it out and pared it down," Smigel says. From there, with competent writers, the show could deliver on bits the audience liked most. "The job is so overwhelming that you start becoming a manager, and you don't have time to just relax and let your mind go and free associate." Smigel was also a newlywed, so working constantly wasn't what he wanted. "It was one thing to be that kind of boyfriend, I [didn't] want to be that kind of husband." He left *Conan* in season 2, to work on the *Superfans* movie with Bob Odenkirk, returning occasionally for the "Clutch Cargo" sketches, where his lips replaced those of countless celebrities and political figures, and of course when he brought Triumph the Insult Comic Dog to TV.

"I was at University of Chicago, and [*Late Night*] asked me for material," Bill Odenkirk recalls. "I got to know Conan and Robert Smigel, and I sent packages of material to them because they were looking for writers, and I think I was close to getting hired there." He heard back, possibly from his brother Bob, who did write for *Late Night*, that they were constantly "on the bubble," or on the verge of being canceled/not renewed. They would only get orders of thirteen weeks of episodes at a time, at which point things had to be renegotiated. "They were being told, 'Don't put anything in your closets here, because you may be moving out literally in two weeks.' This was the way that show existed for a year." Just as he had with *SNL*, Bill hung out with Bob for the early days of *Late Night*, even if he was never on staff. "I was on the first show, and I was there subsequently a couple of times with Bob. I would just pitch in on sketches or monologue stuff."

Brian Stack started on *Late Night* in 1997, but the stories of the early days were legendary. One clear sign that things might turn around, early on in the run, was when David Letterman came on as a guest. "It gave kind of a stamp of approval from this legendary host to the new guard that was coming in," Stack says. "He had said, 'You guys are doing something really different and new, you're not doing my show' . . . that gave them some real wind in their sails." At one point, early on, the show had been canceled on a Friday, then un-canceled the following Monday. "I can't imagine living like that; when I got [there] it was much more stable and everything felt like we're okay. They did not have that luxury early on, and they were doing all new stuff every night."

That new stuff included anything from bits like "Actual Items," where early Photoshop allowed for all kinds of obvious bullshit to pass for "stuff we found in local papers," to scripted audience interruptions that O'Brien had to deal with for an entire segment—easy to stage and rarely involved more than a costume and a local actor who needed the work to be planted in the audience. "They saved us having to get, you know, real jobs like we had in Chicago, like I was a substitute teacher," recalls UCB's Matt Besser. Friendships that had formed in the Windy City, with the likes of O'Brien's co-host Andy Richter and many writers on staff, made the introduction of the Upright Citizen's Brigade pretty easy, and they ended up in innumerable sketches. "We did this thing called 'The Wussy Wagon,' which was like twelve dudes in suits and we're all in this giant, red wagon, being pulled around."

In one sketch, a few into the tenure of "The Wussy Wagon," these men in suits with briefcases are pulled through New York City, jumping and yelling at the sight or sound of anything even slightly upsetting. This particular episode took place during the New York Toy Fair, and the man pulling this large wagon apologizes for their tardiness to Studio 6A; the Wussies saw something at the Toy Fair that distracted them. We cut to them discovering a fifteen-foot-tall Radio Flyer wagon and beating on it with their briefcases as "Also sprach Zarathustra" plays, in maybe the dumbest take on the opening to *2001: A Space Odyssey* to date. "I remember I got a lot of 'Wussy Wagon' gigs . . . That's a good gig. I'd rather do that than substitute teach for a day."

Even if you didn't want to take Letterman's word for it, full-length sketches like this made it clear that this *Late Night* was a different animal. "Those early years for sure, it seemed like half the show was sketch," Besser says. "It was a talk show, but it definitely factors into the history of sketch comedy for sure. And to me, that was the innovative part, and what made that show so great, especially in that era." The show had its pick of local actors, especially helpful when the writers decided that the best way to exhibit their latest characters was in a segment called, appropriately, "New Characters." Here they'd debut "Robot on a Toilet," a visual gag that turns into an audio gag when you finally hear the sound of bolts hitting the bottom of the toilet bowl, and "The Interruptor," a character played by Brian Stack, whose sole purpose was to interrupt O'Brien in the middle of introducing "the next bit." Another robot, Pimpbot 5000, was exactly what you think he is. Brian McCann put a FedEx box on his head and became The FedEx Pope. Then there was Andy's little sister, Stacy, played by Amy Poehler in pigtails and orthodontic headgear.

"I was originally supposed to fill in for thirteen weeks at *Conan* and then go back to Chicago," Stack says. "I was filling in for a writer, Tommy Blacha, who'd broken his leg. I ended up staying eighteen years instead." He's pretty certain one of the reasons he stuck around (Blacha's leg presumably has since healed) is because of Poehler's performance as Stacy. "Amy kicked my 'Andy's Little Sister' sketch up to being memorable with her performance, which was so great . . . I'll always be grateful to her for that because I think it's one of the reasons I got kept on." It wasn't just Poehler, Roberts, Besser, and Matt Walsh, either: Their students starting getting called in to do sketches, once the UCB Theatre had been established. "They were always money in the bank. You could throw them into a sketch, and they would always make something better."

Andy Richter had come from Chicago, and success in *The Real Live Brady Bunch*, co-starred in a sketch pilot called *Head Cheese* with the *Brady Bunch* group, and ended up sitting next to another unknown, helping sell the show with his actual on-camera experience. "Andy, he kind of didn't care," says Mike Sweeney. "I don't think he ever cared that there's a red light coming on, and that he was on television, he was just always himself, in the best way possible." Richter's participation in the back-and-forth with O'Brien and co-interviewing the guests were critical to the audience reception. While he was certainly there to help O'Brien look funny when something did or didn't work, he was also there to help dig them out of a hole when a bit didn't go as planned.

As head writer, Sweeney would stand behind a podium off-camera as they shot the show, hoping as always for a positive hit-to-miss ratio as O'Brien delivered joke after joke. "Sometimes I think this made doing the show fun for him. If he added a joke to a bit, and his joke killed, he would stop and look over at me and just smile, and then keep doing the bit. It was just for my benefit, and I'd just be like, 'Uggh, you bastard.'" Sometimes a writer would insist on a dud of a joke. "You push back and go 'No, I think this is gonna do great.' And if it didn't do great, he'd stop, look over and just give a look of like, 'Thanks a lot. Thanks, guys.' But you know what? Never a look when we'd push back on something he didn't want to do and it did great."

Something that carried through till Richter left *Late Night* was O'Brien and Richter's interaction with sketches—sketches didn't exist without the two of them centering the whole experience. There was the normal back and forth of introducing and often "interviewing" a sketch character, the elevated stakes (sometimes), but there were also more opportunities for "what are we doing here" moments from O'Brien. Whether he and Richter were reacting to a failing prop, or if O'Brien was calling out someone fucking up a line, or—the absolute cream of the crop—if O'Brien could see something off camera that the at-home audience couldn't see, then the energy was immediately amped up to the point that it was eminently engaging. In one "New Characters" sketch, we are introduced to "Debbie Williams, Lois Lane's Lesbian Lover," the couple immediately interrupted by Superman. Superman isn't upset, and would prefer to watch while rubbing his nipples. Sophomoric, sure, but like many whiffs on *Late Night*, O'Brien's reaction as the actor playing Superman continues touching himself, off-camera, is perfection. He walks into the scene to physically stop the actor from rubbing his chest; there's no veil being dropped, because the reality of this sketch is that it's been introduced as a sketch.

Sometimes the sketch was mostly between O'Brien and Richter, like "The Staring Contest," where the two would stare at each other, O'Brien

cheating by bringing in increasingly weird characters or staging elabo-
rate scenes to get Richter to break eye contact. "It felt like old fashioned
TV," says UCB's Ian Roberts. "We were live to tape and . . . someone
would be dressed as a Roman soldier and someone's the Grim Reaper,
and someone's Abe Lincoln, because if they did one of those bits, like
'The Staring Contest,' where they run ten people through as different
characters, you'd have all these people in weird costumes and prosthetic
makeups. It's kind of what you imagine Hollywood being like."

The cheapest bit the show ever put on was often one of its most
successful. They're often referred to as the "Clutch Cargo" bits, from
the cheap '50s and '60s cartoon in which human mouths were super-
imposed over cartoon faces to save money on animation. Smigel's
occasional return to do these pieces was like returning to the parts he
loved about the first fifteen months of the show. "Having Conan interview a photograph just allowed us to be so much sillier and child-
ish. It was like the closest I came to the 10-year-old me and what I found
funny in a very pure way, when I was ten years old. [Conan] had a very
similar sense of humor, and we bonded a lot at *Saturday Night Live*, but
there was a limit to how silly we could be at that show."

Before submitting his packet to *Late Night* for a third time, Kevin
Dorff got some advice from Andy Richter: "Whatever you do,
make sure it's weirder than what you've seen and more you than
what you've seen yet. You just have to just decide that you're the
head writer for an hour." Dorff would end up writing for *Late Night*
for ten years, during which time O'Brien himself illustrated that
being a writer meant you were treated like one. "He never [said],
'Get out of here and never come back, I don't want to see you again,
go find another job that isn't a writer,'" Dorff says. "He didn't do
any of that. He talked to you like another writer." He would trust
that laughs in rehearsal meant it would probably work onscreen, so
he'd also trust his writers to make it work before the cameras rolled
for real. If it didn't . . .

"So many times I feel like that when things would go wrong, he was able to react to that, and enjoy the mistake and the humiliation and the shittiness . . . 'We wrote it at 11:30 today, this is what you get. It's your fault for watching, there's so many options right now. You could even be asleep. But you insist on watching so you're gonna get a masturbating bear.'" If things went poorly, O'Brien liked to keep score, but if the same idea came back to the table, he'd often try it again, and usually come in and try and help you rewrite it. Then the writers would have to gently kick him out so he'd eat and get ready for his show. "It was a two-way street. We really wanted him to do a great show every night and he loved to see us thrive; he loved it when we knocked one out of the park."

One of Dorff's most memorable characters on *Late Night* was the bartender, Joe, in "Joe's Place." O'Brien would often break out of a piece to say he just needed a little break, with friends who know the real O'Brien. Then they'd cut to an establishing shot of Chicago's Bucktown Pub; you can tell that's where it is because only the biggest of two signs in the shot is actually photoshopped to say "Joe's." Joe would berate O'Brien from the second he walked in the door, telling him he wasn't welcome because of all the stuff he'd done to mess up the bar before. A barfly, played by Brian McCann, would then pile it on from the sidelines until O'Brien cracked, screaming and throwing a bottle at Joe and leaving.

Dorff used to drink at a 4 AM bar called Marie's Riptide in Bucktown in Chicago, which is no longer open. One door let in so much sun that it would kill the buzz whenever anyone opened it to enter. "One time I was there with a friend and the door opened, but no sunshine came through. So we looked at the door and it was this huge mountain of a man, this really big guy. He's just getting into the bar and he's just shutting the door, and Marie, the bartender and owner goes 'Goddammit, Tank, you know you can't come in here.' And the guy [said], 'Marie, that was three years ago!' She says, 'Get the fuck out!' He turns around and he walks away and he leaves. Me and my friend were like, 'What the fuck did that guy do?' Nobody was 86'd from that place forever."

Dorff told the story to McCann and they came up with the idea that O'Brien should have his own local bar like Cheers and, like Marie to Tank, there'd be no love lost between the bartender and him. "That was just a dumb story until, again, the *Conan* formula: Let's try it and see what happens." Originally the sketches were written to show photos onscreen of all the things O'Brien had supposedly done at and to Joe's. When Dorff was stuck, McCann suggested the no-burn, hot start of the sketch instead of trying to make the photos work, and the sketch came together.

"That's as good an example as any of 'Good idea. Let's do it. Uh oh, I'm doing it wrong. Oh, and now this guy just bailed me out. And now Conan is doing it. And now we're bringing it back.'" The experimentation on *Late Night*, and on other iterations of O'Brien's idea of the talk show, never seemed to stop. The show and its host started out as underdogs, in terms of experience, who we watched grow up on TV. Deservedly so, he got a Carson-style sendoff, with Marc Shaiman—Bette Midler's pianist from her famous farewell song performance—accompanying the incomparable Nathan Lane in a slightly changed version of "My Way," called "Your Way." Shaiman had also played off Leno (both times) and would eventually also accompany Lane to send off Letterman at CBS. "I was like the Angel of Death," Shaiman says. "Your Way" ends thus:

> *Yes, NBC has filled your cup*
> *Replacing Jay, please don't screw up*
> *Jack Parr and Carson set the bar*
> *Go out and be just who you are*
> *Don't ever stop*
> *And if you flop*
> *You'll do it your way*

When O'Brien hosted *The Tonight Show*, he was given only a few months to fix his flagging ratings, and Jay Leno took the show back from him. O'Brien's final speech on *The Tonight Show* was heartfelt and sincere, and ended with a plea to his audience not to be cynical:

"I hate cynicism. For the record, it's my least favorite quality. It doesn't lead anywhere. Nobody in life gets exactly what they thought they were going to get, but if you work really hard and you're kind, amazing things will happen."

O'Brien's deal to leave NBC meant that part of his severance— $12 million—went to support his recently-uprooted staff while they figured out what was next. He then spent eleven years hosting his TBS follow-up, *Conan*, which seemingly meant less oversight, allowing him and his writers to experiment, since this was basic cable. Eventually, the show pared down to a half hour, with only a single guest and less-involved bits. At the time of writing, he has another show on the horizon at the streamer HBO Max, but there are scant details available. He's spending a lot of his time podcasting, now that he's sold his production company to SiriusXM for $150 million.

Late Night never looked expensive, regardless of the actual budget, but it was always working toward the best possible joke. Phoning it in was never an option. In a 1998 interview, O'Brien told *Playboy* magazine, "If the joke is that there is no joke, the writer gets no paycheck."

A failed joke is better than no joke at all, and very little could go wrong that they couldn't roll with, and that aesthetic gave the show life, sucking in young comedians-to-be, making some of us want to make comedy even more. As Brian Stack said, "I think about it like with bands like The Ramones. One of the reasons they're as important as they are, is because they made a lot of people say, 'Oh, they aren't that talented, and they can't play that great, but they're great. I love this, but they aren't intimidating' . . . It makes you feel like you could do it, and that's one of the most inspiring things in the world."

— 18 —

Performing for Snotty Rich Anglo Brats: House of Buggin'

John Leguizamo's first one-man show was entitled *Mambo Mouth* and consisted of him playing various characters, including an abusive punk, a lothario, a sex worker, and a rapper. If reviews weren't always kind to the show, Leguizamo was establishing a voice already, helping project his image beyond that of the bit parts he was getting in Hollywood already. David Bar Katz was the publicist for *Mambo Mouth*, but like a lot of people in PR, he really wanted to write. "That was my day job as I was trying to write, and then John and I sort of hit it off . . . we just sort of had ideas that we wanted to work on together. We started that process when I still was doing theater PR and trying to get people to come see *Mambo Mouth*."

As Leguizamo and Katz started collaborating, they found common ground and a way to showcase Leguizamo's character work, as he'd still be the big name on the bill, whatever the show. They were also interested in making the next piece be a sketch comedy revue with an extended cast, rather than another one-man show. "It was an interest in how to approach sketch comedy with Latinness as an agenda," Katz says. "It really wasn't just like, 'Alright, we're just going to kind of do whatever we think is the most funny.' We definitely wanted to do things that were making some kind of point, or speaking to that world in some way."

They threw some sketches at the wall, with Leguizamo's characters in mind, including a Latin character pretending to be Japanese (which oddly lost the Latin part of the character by the time it made it to TV). "At the time . . . we're very left people caring about all the proper things, still not having an idea of like, 'Oh, how could that be offensive?'" Katz recalls. He admits that a social shift eventually made him realize, 'Oh, yeah, that's so clearly offensive [in] 1,000 different ways.'" In 1993, they put the sketches onstage under the name *House of Buggin'* at the performance space P.S. 122 in the East Village in Manhattan, eventually moving to a venue called Downtown Art, and though they never advertised it, as such, there were announcements of "open rehearsals," so they could get audience reactions.

These rehearsals came with the typical bugs to work out, too, including getting the music right. Adam Schlesinger (Fountains of Wayne, *That Thing You Do!, Crazy Ex-Girlfriend*) and Katz had been college friends, so Schlesinger was brought on to do the sound design for the stage show (his first TV job would make him the music supervisor for *Buggin'*). Katz recalls Schlesinger and music partner Steven M. Gold working together in a very tiny booth at the already tiny space at P.S. 122. "They were like arguing the whole time . . . as the sketch was going on, the two Jews in the sound booth were fighting and smacking each other's hands, like 'You're hitting the wrong effects!'" Sound was critical to the show, even if longer sketches gave them more time to get it right.

"John and I were both huge fans of '50s sketch stuff, like *Show of Shows*, so we wanted to make it more theatrical sketches, ten, fifteen minute sketches that were more like theater." They would invite friends and colleagues to be their test audience in this 99-seat theater. Tickets were free, so they could work the kinks out and get feedback. It might be the longest development for a sketch pilot in TV history, perhaps because they weren't aiming for TV; they were still trying to perfect their stage show. "Then some HBO execs came and saw it, and they really loved it." By this point, the minimal press for the stage show was saying it was "aimed toward an HBO special."

"At first they were like, 'Oh, this would be a great HBO special,'" Katz says. They brought on writers Fax Bahr and Adam Small, who had come from *In Living Color*, and who would co-create *MADtv* right after *House of Buggin'*. "Then Fox was like, 'This can be our new *In Living Color*.' That's kind of how things then advanced." Even if that was part of the network perspective, the show itself wasn't influenced by *In Living Color* at all; if anything, this was a continuation of Leguizamo's other work, with seven other cast members. Creative influences and impulses are not what get shows on TV, though; executives are. *In Living Color* was a money-maker, and Fox was likely shooting for something they felt was "similar" to the show they were in all likelihood about to cancel. Fox could not have been expecting something expressly political, even if that was going to be hidden in amongst your typical fare, like another parody of *COPS*.

"Ironically, I feel like I was I was a little bit more political on these issues than John," Katz says. In 1994, a Republican assemblyman introduced Proposition 187, designed to deny illegal immigrants access to non-emergency healthcare, education, and more. "I wrote a sketch where John is playing Superman, who is injured from battle and shows up in California to a clinic, and they're like, 'Sorry, Superman, we can't help you, you're an illegal alien.'" Superman has been shot with a kryptonite bullet and can't save the earth from a meteor, and everyone dies. The intentionally over-acted sketch is called "Thinly Veiled Allegory Theatre." "It's a tough one, I think, for something to be funny and hit the political aspect without feeling like you're being lectured to."

Once *House of Buggin'* made its way to Fox, the concept of extended sketches was no longer a reality. More sketches meant they needed to pick additional brains, so the two-man writing staff grew to include a little over a dozen people. They bounced off of things Leguizamo wanted to see, and felt the writers out for solid sketch ideas. Leguizamo being there was critical, though, and not just because he was a writer and the face of the show. "I do not believe we had one Latin writer in the writers' room," Katz recalls. "Other than me, because everyone thought I was Latin because John and I worked together." Pretty soon it became clear that, even if the two creators knew what they wanted to see, they were technically outnumbered.

"It was pretty much almost every kind of cautionary tale when you hear these guys were doing this theater show and they made a television show of it, and then they bring in all the Hollywood writers and we're fighting for our thing." They were also dealing with network oversight for the first time—Katz says the network wanted them to be more conservative. Of all the funny, acceptable ideas pitched for sketches that could work, none of them were Latin enough. Sometimes, they'd hit a gem because it just worked. One sketch, entitled "Piñata Sanctuary," has Leguizamo satirizing charity ads, telling us how piñatas are hunted for sport, their lives "literally hanging by a thread." He gently introduces us to Benny, who lost his leg in a piñata trap, and gives us a number to call.

Writing was clearly one of the show's biggest hurdles so, by comparison, casting was a breeze. They pulled entirely from the stage show cast, including Jorge Luis Abreu, Tammi Cubilette, Yelba Osorio, and Luis Guzmán, save one newcomer: David Herman. Katz still remembers his audition vividly. "It was one of the greatest things I've ever seen . . . he just walked into the room, and instantly did like ten characters that were like, 'what the fuck,' I mean, everything he did was funny, real, true." They saw names like future *SNL* stars Chris Kattan and Jim Breuer before finding Herman, and these other actors brought characters with them we'd later see on *SNL*. "But then it's just a sketch. It's still just silly sketch at the end of the day, even if you're really, fully occupying it, but Herman came in, and it was like ridiculous characters, but it felt like you were seeing a great theater actor doing it, like the depth *and* the ridiculousness."

In one sketch, a parody of *The Ricki Lake Show*, a daytime trash talk show of the day, the subject is "My Dictator's a Jerk and I Want To Tell Him Off." Herman is only in the audience shots as Yelba Osorio plays Ricki Lake, introducing us to two men confronting the dictators who have abused them: Guzmán as Fidel Castro and Leguizamo as Manuel Noriega. There's great sketch stuff happening the entire time, but every time the camera cuts to the audience shot, Herman in the lower-right corner, you catch him looking skyward, clearly watching himself on a TV monitor without telegraphing a thing. When he finally gets up, asked to showboat and ask a question, half the time he's smiling because he's just caught himself in the monitor that we are now certain exists. He draws the eye without drawing attention.

In his autobiography, *Pimps, Hos, Playa Hatas, and All the Rest of My Hollywood Friends: My Life,* Leguizamo points out that he couldn't handle feeling upstaged by Herman, describing him as funnier and faster, something Leguizamo blames on his own surplus of duties as actor and producer. He recalls resorting to reducing Herman's parts in sketches, or cutting them out entirely, even trying to "scare him." "I exhausted myself," Leguizamo writes. "That's when I realized that jealousy and rivalry are destructive. You're just letting your insecurities get over on you, and it ruins your work."

The quality of the work was always a concern, especially as they fought to get their vision on the air. Even if the sketches were predominantly written by white writers, the show's cast was still an anchor. "Most comedic ideas are universal," Katz says. "So if someone comes up with it, and it's a good sketch idea, and you give it to Latin actors, it becomes Latin." Katz recalls little controversy over the show, and nothing made it to air that he or Leguizamo had a problem with. "The people that actually had issues were some people that were in comedy, and felt like, 'Oh, wait, that's our thing. Now you guys are taking it.'"

House of Buggin' included an introduction, interstitials and outro featuring Leguizamo, as well as plenty of the sketch comedy staples of the day: TV parodies, relationship sketches, and simple character bits, like the four kids in a movie theater talking about whatever movie they're watching, or the two nerds who are constantly asking "who would win" in a fight between two fictional characters, which we then see acted out in smoky, dramatic, boxing-movie-style footage. There were also big set pieces, in contrast to the smaller, cheaper-to-shoot stuff. "I'm a huge musical theater person," Katz says. "So the 'West Side Story' sketch I remember getting a big kick out of."

A 1990s gang (headed by Guzmán) heads off against The Sharks from *West Side Story* in one sketch. The bit has Leguizamo as Bernardo, looking like Adrian Zmed circa 1982, referencing malt shops and not messing with weed because, "it's illegal." The Sharks then end up circling the modern gang with a switchblade in a choreographed dance routine, and what you might guess happens next, does: Guzmán shoots one of The Sharks, and his gang busts out guns of various sizes, including a grenade launcher. Bernardo feigns a leg cramp and they run away: The modern gang have won. They are then accosted by a bunch of cats from *Cats*, Guzmán ending it with, "Man, I hate the theater district."

No TV sketch show had ever featured this many Latin actors in one cast. They dealt with the true root of the anti-immigration mentality in many different ways, including a fake documentary special called "Illegal Alien Makeovers," in which Leguizamo's Blaine Alexander offers people a service to "de-ethnify" them, or make them look White. Guzmán gets makeup swatches of varying lighter-than-his-skin-tone colors to try out, and is eventually convinced he now looks like Richard Gere. In one sketch, a group of mariachis perform for "snotty rich anglo brats," which you'd only know if you spoke Spanish or read the subtitles, which tell us all the ways in which these musicians-for-hire loathe their clientele.

Katz took pride in getting in a few jabs at anti-Semitism, as well, once with a game show satire that featured a speed round of questions at the end, entitled "It's the Jews." In thirty seconds, the contestants had to blame the most things on the Jews as they could. "In terms of being political, and funny at the time, I got a kick out of that, even though my grandmother was very angry. She's from a generation which didn't see it as 'Alright, you're making fun of something that exists.' It was more like 'You can't talk about that stuff, because now they're going to blame the Jews.' This sketch did not change anyone's minds."

As is typical with network TV, determinations of what would and wouldn't be allowed on air were, if not arbitrary, emanating from a mercurial source. Typically, a new show will get a showrunner, a producer who runs the whole game, or in the case of a show like *Buggin'*, they could expect an experienced, powerful producer who knows the business and knows how to go to bat for the creatives with the executives. "We had none of that," Katz says. "It was just me and John . . . So we didn't basically have anyone powerful enough to kind of watch out for us. That was why we never had a consistent [timeslot]." To make matters worse, Fox had brought in the former head of CBS, John Matoian, whose goal, Katz says, was to make Fox more family-friendly. There was an element of this show being adrift at sea, at the whims of the ocean. "We were just like, kind of two kids trying to put on a show."

Still, there was a budget—and a good one. There was money within each episode's budget to do a single-camera, filmed sketch. "We definitely had money to do what we wanted to do," Katz says, emphasizing that even the visiting directors commented on the budgets. "The problem was, we didn't have someone that would let us do the things we wanted to do in terms of subject matter. So that was the biggest battle on that show." Cue "Jewish Like Me: The Paco Vasquez Story."

Paco Vasquez (Leguizamo) discovers that, like many people of Latin heritage, he actually has Jewish heritage, too. The sketch, as aired, opens with a van pulling up on Paco, as a Hasidic man (played by Tim Blake Nelson) asks if he is, indeed, Paco. Paco is nabbed, told of his roots, and he converts. He doesn't just become Jewish, he becomes a walking stereotype. "Originally the sketch opened with kind of one of those sort of *Masterpiece Theater* voice-overs, 'In 1492, it was the Inquisition, Jews were forced to either convert or go underground in the Inquisition or die. That's why, to this day, you've got [Latin] people with Jewish Sephardic names.'" The sketch would have continued as written, including Paco/Moishe's surprise bris and adult circumcision. Standards and practices (S&P)—network censors, effectively—gave Katz a call.

"You can't do the sketch," S&P says.

"Why?"

"You can't make up this thing about Spanish people killing Jews." Katz tried to make sense of this in his head, but couldn't.

"Wait, I'm sorry. What do you mean?" he asked.

"This Inquisition thing that you're [talking] about, you can't just make stuff up like that."

It was now clear. "And I'm like, 'Okay. I'm going to just forward a few history books . . .' So yeah. Standards and practices thinking I made up the Inquisition was definitely one of my more favorite moments."

Another problem with having no producer authority backing them: they had no one to hit back at S&P for them in cases like this. "So what we just did, is horse trading. I always just added some wildly offensive things that I didn't even want in sketches." This gave them the chance to trade these moments for what they wanted to keep. Outside of these skirmishes, other collaborations were strong and lent to the show's artistic success. John Blanchard, who directed *SCTV, The Kids in the Hall* and *Codco,* and would go on to direct *MADtv,* directed some of *Buggin'* and brought with him a true cinematic aesthetic, as did John Fortenberry.

The theater group who had started this project were all brought together under the guidance of experienced TV artists, with little oversight and no choice but to still stay tight-knit, and as a result they—for the most part—let one another shine. Herman would go on to star on *MADtv*, voice innumerable animated characters, and play Michael Bolton in *Office Space*, and Luis Guzmán would go onto a huge film and TV career. "Discovering/revealing Luis Guzmán is a comic genius . . . That guy was just so unbelievable. Everything he does is totally grounded, he cannot *not* be grounded," Katz says. The show, though, never found its footing; bouncing around on the schedule took a toll on feeling like they actually had something of their own.

The *House of Buggin'* legacy is a weirdly mixed one, since it's hard to find, despite the cast. It might come up here and there when people are discussing supposed "forgotten shows." While hardly forgotten in a true sense, it doesn't have the physical media presence that has benefited some of these other sketch shows: It was never released on DVD. Videos you'll find online are from someone's old VHS tapes, filled with the typical artifacts and blips those rips will give you. The lack of a consistent airing schedule at the time is probably the reason there's no full collection of episodes uploaded by some kind soul.

"Back then, television viewing was about consistency. You knew something was going to be on at a time, and if you didn't know, that was what fucked you," Katz says. It's hard to argue for the reach of the show, but the careers it shepherded are undeniable, and the fan base is still out there.

"It never had the feeling of like, 'Oh, we're doing the show now . . . Oh great, now we've got a show on the air . . .' It just felt like a lot of work and upset, and joy, and hoping. Then all of a sudden it was like, oh shit, we're not really getting the thing we wanted to do. We're not getting an audience." Being the first of something doesn't mean you'll be the thing to change the landscape; it simply introduces a possibility, and mainstream media didn't seem interested in that possibility elsewhere. It might have been even easier to cancel because of that; there were no other Latin shows on the air, so they could have assumed there didn't need to be any. The show didn't even get your full, standard, thirteen-episode order. It was nominated for a single Emmy, for Outstanding Individual Achievement in Choreography.

As for the name: "That was all John, and no one quite ever understood it."

19

The Lighter Side: MADtv

M AD magazine started in 1952 (then technically a comic book), and once they became a magazine, famously didn't accept advertisers. William Gaines, the publisher of *MAD*, was also reticent to turn it into anything for TV. There were rumors of a TV special in 1961, and in 1973, Gaines indicated he'd softened, telling *The Long Beach Independent*, "I gave in a bit and agreed to let ABC do one *MAD* television special which I think will be aired in September. But it's only one." The special was entirely animated in the style of *MAD* artists like Mort Drucker and Jack Davis, and seems to have never aired. Gaines didn't experiment with bringing *MAD* to TV again, and it would be two years after Gaines' death in 1993 before Quincy Jones and producer David Salzman would purchase the rights to *MAD*, with the intention of bringing it to TV once more.

Jones and Salzman sought out *In Living Color* writers Fax Bahr and Adam Small to create a sketch show branded with the *MAD* name. The show would utilize a few pieces from the magazine itself, like a cartoon of "Spy vs. Spy," and the general format choice of going heavy on movie and advertising parodies, like the magazine. *SNL* was in yet another decline in ratings and general pelting from the press, so it seemed like the perfect time to bring in a new competitor. With no more *In Living Color* on the air, or any of Fox's other attempts to follow it and/or recreate that magic, there was a gap to fill. *MADtv* would be its own thing, though they planned to bring some of that bite that *In Living Color* became known for, especially in its final seasons.

"I remember that when we were writing the pilot, Fax and Adam really wanted to go after *SNL*," says writer Blaine Capatch. "The opening sketch, they wanted to do something where Lorne or some-body was out on a ledge, because *MADtv* was starting up." They were, appropriately, talked down from this idea. "David Cross was sort of taking the helm of this. Like, 'Why would we waste time on our show, talking about somebody else's show and reminding them that "Hey, we could be watching *Saturday Night Live* right now?"'" Eventually, Capatch says, the show leaned toward light over mean. In clear opposition to *SNL*, even as planned competition for it, *MADtv* would have no host, and in the beginning they had no mu-sical guests. The cast would come out and do bits between sketches, *a la Carol Burnett* and, later, *Key & Peele*.

The show debuted on October 14, 1995, at 11 PM, to cut into *SNL*'s 11:30 time slot over on NBC. The show decided against killing off Lorne Michaels; it chose instead to give itself a going over before we even knew what the show was. Two executives enter a bathroom at Fox, telling a higher-up in a stall that *MADtv* is ready to go, mer-chandising and all. When he asks about the cast, the executives pan-ic and rush out into the "Fox Casting" truck, driving around LA to find their actors amongst day laborers, sex workers, a non-commit-tal crossing guard whose charges get hit off screen, a suicidal wom-an who is lassoed into the truck, a postal employee on a rampage who needs the truck for escape, and a mentally disturbed unhoused person. In the case of the latter, it's clear that these shitty executives think his problems are hilarious quirks, so they grab him, too. They then consider the third most disturbing Alfred E. Neuman lookalike ever committed to video or film, before rejecting him.

With the actors presented as a cast of characters first and fore-most, the show establishes a very *MAD* magazine feel—different costumes, different story genres for each of them, and now they're going to be thrown into a pie together. Combined with some car-toony interstitials, the show was designed to be a buffer between young teens who might still read *MAD* and the just-slightly-older teens who may not have cared for *SNL*.

MADtv was also the first major sketch show since *In Living Color* to cast more than two African American actors from the beginning. The first cast consisted of Craig Anton, Brian Callen, David Herman, Orlando Jones, Phil LaMarr, Artie Lange, Mary Scheer, Nicole Sullivan, and Debra Wilson. Many of these actors did double-duty as writers, and they brought with them characters they'd been honing over years as performers. Unusually, the production allowed new actors to own to own their characters, even after they performed them on air. One such character was Jaq, the UPS guy (named the UBS guy for TV purposes) that Phil LaMarr had created at The Groundlings. When he got the call for the audition for *MADtv*, though, he was on a pilot that he felt was going to go places.

"Nah, I don't need it. I got the other thing," LaMarr recalls saying.

"No, we talked to somebody at Fox, they said, 'Go on. Audition.'" He held out hope for the new show, but took the hint and gave it a shot, though this was nothing like your typical audition where you've got a script to memorize, then have a chance to make it your own and maybe get a chance to polish your performance. Instead, they wanted him to have a stock of characters ready to perform, not unlike *SNL*.

"'Give us three minutes of your personal characters, impressions, whatever.' I remember being in the waiting room, there were people with bags of wigs, and props and stuff. Because I already had this other show in my pocket, and I knew this was second position, I went in there—I didn't give a shit." He had a legal pad with ideas written on it, like an alt comic in a bookstore, and just weaved in and out of those character ideas. He also did his Sidney Poitier impression and his Michael Jackson. He got through this first round, and had to do two more auditions. One of them was in front of producers David Salzman and Quincy Jones. First, the actors performed the characters they'd come up with again. Then they had to do something unusual: perform a scene with the other auditioning actors.

"We had to come back in and do scenes with two or three of us together. Which was a little weird, because you're working with people you're competing with." If you're acting well, you're giving room to everyone else on stage, but in an audition, typically, you're just supposed to show what you can do, on your own, in a vacuum. "There was some guy who was from Las Vegas or something, who didn't do what we were doing . . . the studio people had rehearsed us and coached us before we went into the network, and this guy just went off book and like, what do you do?" LaMarr just kept reminding himself that he was four feet away from Quincy Jones.

After writing for *The Ben Stiller Show* and a few other projects, Rob Cohen wrote for the first four episodes of *MADtv*. "They just asked a few people they knew from *Stiller*, and some people from elsewhere, who would come kind of get *MADtv* off the ground, just to have extra ammo." It wasn't a normal writers' room where a group of writers would punch up the sketch at hand, but then again, it wasn't a normal sketch show. It wasn't exactly sure what it was. "'If you remember *Mad* magazine, that might be the doorway to get you to watch this show, but it has nothing to do with *Mad* magazine.'" It would take the show some time to wiggle its way out of its namesake's roots entirely.

The writing staff was, as usual for most sketch shows, a mix of veteran writers and fresh ones. David Cross worked only on the pilot and used his Writer's Guild alias of "Sean Beam," in the end. Blaine Capatch remembers one particular moment that helped illustrate how certain standards were not a great fit at *MADtv*. "When he criticized Nicole Sullivan's 'Vancome Lady' character at the first table read by saying 'This isn't a character, it's a character trait,' he joined my Legion of Comedy Superheroes."

Patton Oswalt worked on the first two seasons; it was his first staff writer job after a brief stint writing "Small Doses," a sort of sketch show for *Comedy Central*. "My mouth had its own motor a lot because I was used to the role of stand-up when you're riffing and trying to, you know, outdo everybody," Oswalt says. "There were times I'm sure that I was very, very annoying to be around . . . a lot of times I was being the comedy Nazi and going, 'Well, that was already done on *Monty Python*,' but I didn't have a way to solve it. You can criticize things all you want, but then come with a solution afterward." He recalls the young writer's ego getting in the way, especially when another writer's joke or idea would elevate his existing idea.

"There's that weird instinct that will kick in like, 'Well, this is mine' . . . it is a group effort, and you can't be fuckin' Howard Roark in *The Fountainhead* if you're writing a goddamn sketch. If someone's got something that makes it funnier, fucking put it in." The creations you can own—at least spiritually—are lasting characters, catchphrases, or, in Oswalt's case, a fictional brand that the show could use to pretend to sell anything. "There was a fake company I made up, named after a friend I went to college with, called Spishak. It was just this great umbrella to write the worst products imaginable." These included the Omnibowl (which doubles as a pasta bowl *and* a cereal bowl), the Bris-O-Tine (a penile guillotine for brisses), and Spishak Margarine (works fine unless you're the guy in the sketch who is allergic to margarine). "Even after I left the show they would do Spishak ads, which made me feel really good."

The eponymous Spishak is one Steve Spishak, who was in fencing classes with Oswalt in college. He didn't know his name was being attached to a powdered animal protein substitute called "Meatbeaters" until a few years in. "What started happening was I would go to the post office and I'd slide the slip across the table and some guy would just start chuckling and he would go, 'Heh, Spishak Industries.' I was like, 'What?'" It took him some time, but he did the math—there was only one person who could've pulled this off. The same man who came up with the first season's most iconic parody.

It was an impossibly silly movie trailer mashup that was now—thanks to shows like *The Ben Stiller Show*—standard issue for TV sketch shows. It was a cross between *Forrest Gump* and *Pulp Fiction* called *Gump Fiction*. "I think I came up with the title while we were heading into the pitch," Oswalt recalls. "It was just this, 'Oh god, I gotta get a movie parody,' and those things were in the zeitgeist, and I slapped them together. And that's one of the reasons I got hired." It features a meta sketch moment that's hard to top, even if its commonplace now for celebrities to parody their character or movie now on *SNL*.

Since Phil LaMarr had played Marvin, the guy whose head gets shot off by accident by John Travolta in *Pulp Fiction*, they had a bit handed to them. "My thing was like, 'Okay, I want to play [the Jackson character] Jules,'" LaMarr says. "When I auditioned for *Pulp Fiction*, I read that scene—the Jules and Brett scene— with Quentin, where Quentin read Brett and I read Jules." Orlando Jones got the Jules/Bubba mashup, and instead LaMarr got to play Marvin again. His only line in the sketch is, "Not again!"

On the other side of the comedy pond, *Mr. Show with Bob and David* premiered about three weeks into *MADtv*'s run, and it was an obvious game changer; this wasn't unnoticed in the writers' room. "They were over on HBO getting, you know, no notes and really getting to explore stuff," Oswalt recalls. "And we were doing a sketch show where we had to consider 'Oh, who's this week's guest star? And what's this thing that we're trying to do that's in the news, or it's in pop culture?' And then of course, there were the network restrictions. So yeah, it was definitely frustrating." The writers and show-runners who would come to *MADtv* over the years included such notable comedy names as *SCTV*'s Dick Blasucci, Dino Stamatopoulos, David Wain, and Jordan Peele (also a cast member). There was also at least one uncredited writer who worked on *MADtv* partially because he wasn't allowed on air.

"*MADtv* wanted me and they tried to hire me right after *Whose Line*," recalls Wayne Brady. "Because of my contract with *Whose Line*, they wouldn't let me out to even do a sketch show. So for about two weeks, I was a writer on *MADtv*." For the same reason, he couldn't go to work on *The Martin Short Show*. For its part, *MADtv* was also notorious for exercising their contracts strictly, like when *Saturday Night Live* made an offer to Jordan Peele; his contract kept him under Fox's thumb. It so stained his experience that he didn't participate in the twentieth anniversary reunion special in 2016. Contract and pay issues ran rampant through the show's history.

By season three, David Herman was already getting a great deal of voice-over work. He told Entertainment Weekly in 2019 that he was doing whatever he could to leave *MADtv* before he finally left, but he was still under a seven year contract, and they wouldn't allow him to leave. "At the next table-read, I did every sketch screaming at the top of my lungs. They took me off the show." He was told he wouldn't work in Hollywood ever again, and a year later *Office Space* was released. His co-star Debra Wilson was the longest-running original cast member on *MADtv* when she left the show over a huge pay disparity she discovered as new White, male co-stars came in making more than her. According to Wilson on *The Comedy Hype News Show*, she was told there would be no discussion of her salary, so she walked.

Wilson was one great example of the kind of range the show's actors often displayed, and another reason why it might have felt like the show didn't know what it was, or didn't have a voice. Wilson's Whitney Houston will both impress and depress you (in a good way, through great acting), and in the next sketch she could be playing her mercurial meter maid, Bunifa. The show could be a great showcase for these characters and impressions, but *MADtv*, ironically, didn't have much of a brand. For that reason, though, they did continue to experiment, even as the show's budget began to wane.

In 2006, *MADtv's* producers saw the opportunity of a lifetime when cast member Nicole Parker became part of Martin Short's Broadway show *Fame Becomes Me*. It was her chance to live her Broadway dream, and showrunner Blasucci (a friend of Short's from their *SCTV* days) helped arrange to have her stay on while also doing the Broadway show. The experience was filled with positive surprises for Parker. "When you do something funny, and it gets a laugh—and then maybe it's something you pitch to him and it gets a laugh—he immediately stops and gives you the credit. It's wild," Parker says of Short. The Broadway show started a mini tour, heading to Chicago, Toronto and San Francisco, during Parker's spring hiatus from *MADtv*. The show would then open in August on Broadway, at which point most of the producers saw an opportunity to cross promote.

"The compromise [was] that it was going to be all on my dime, and I was privileged enough to be able to fund it, but it was insane . . . For six weeks, I would finish my Sunday matinee in New York, take a red eye back to LA, my mom would pick me up, drop me off at my apartment. We did camera blocking Monday, table read Tuesday. Tuesday night, I would take a red eye and go back and arrive two hours before my Wednesday matinee, do a Wednesday night [show] . . . Alternating weeks, I would then take another red eye back to shoot Thursday and Friday, or I would do the Thursday night show in New York and I would do the Friday Night Live tape. Prop guys were hiding lines in my props."

The compromise worked because they also got material out of it: specifically a sketch posing as a behind-the-scenes look at the Broadway show, hosted by Parker. In it, Short plays a lecherous version of himself, creeping on Parker while wearing only a robe, and insulting her skills as an impressionist. It was a nice boost for *MADtv* in terms of a cameo, and a bit of advertising for the Broadway show on national TV. As *MADtv's* budget decreased, it seems these were the kinds of deals the show needed to stay fresh. Especially as one of the show's key assets was no longer available.

"We lost our studios years in, and that was a bad time," Parker says. "They were just like, 'Can you guys pitch any shows that take place in a park or a parking lot?'" They still had their crew, so they could put sets together, just not on an actual studio lot. "I remember we shot some scenes in truly an abandoned warehouse in LA. They built an actual corner set that was supposed to be a bedroom . . . We're basically where all the *NCIS* shows shoot, when they find dead bodies. It was bleak." There were even times when the production was so disorganized that they found themselves scriptless.

Parker played Rachael Ray in a parody of Ray's reality show *$40 a Day*, where she sees how well she can live on $40 over a single day; in the sketch, Parker burns it up fast, mostly by buying alcohol. "It was just the kind of thing where I pitched it, and I think no one knew who was writing it. We literally get to the day before, and it's like, 'Is there a script?'" She had already decided Peele would be her co-star, playing the waiter, because they had a comedy history and chemistry, so they went with an outline in place of a script, and improvised the whole thing. Even with some of the equipment failing them—and with an hour (as opposed to three) to shoot the whole thing—they kill it. "It's one of my favorite sketches. I actually think it turned out great, and makes me laugh every time, but I couldn't have done it without Jordan."

Over fourteen seasons, *MADtv* would have sixty-six credited players, including Keegan-Michael Key, Michael McDonald, Will Sasso, Arden Myrin, Simon Helberg, Andy Daly, Mo Collins, Ike Barinholtz, Matt Braunger, and Taran Killam, who was there a single season before bouncing around TV, ending up on *SNL* in 2010. Fox had a legacy show on its hands, but it was purportedly too expensive to produce, and had escaped the axe a few times before the final season. In 2016, the CW put on a 20th anniversary special, followed by a truncated 15th season of only eight episodes.

Nearly every other sketch show that started in the '90s ended in that decade, too. *MADtv* couldn't compete with *SNL*'s topicality or use guest stars to bump its ratings to the same effect, but it had an impressive run. It illustrates the harsh reality of sketch TV: For the most part, it can't last. Sketch shows being live gives them urgency, even when the material isn't there. The *art* of sketch writing thrives in timeless sketches; even some of the broader stuff on *MADtv* has undeniable mass appeal. Those sketches have longevity, but that doesn't equal what we've come to value most on TV: engagement. Butts in seats. Hard to fill seats when you've gotten rid of the studio.

20

Don't Do Your Act:
LA's Alternative Comedy Scene

In the late twentieth century, there were at least four movements called "alternative comedy," or "alt comedy." Both set the crosshairs on the live comedy status quo, with very different goals. The UK alternative comedy scene of the early '80s was started and peopled by the likes of Nigel Planer, Alexei Sayle and Rik Mayall, with the noble goal of putting together comedy without the bigotry—specifically racism and sexism—that cheapened a lot of the UK comedy club fare. Some of the greatest minds of UK comedy came out of this era, who would go on to create countless sketch shows that most of us in the United States didn't have access to.

In the US, alternative comedy came about in the late '80s and early '90s, with a goal aimed equally at the comedy everyone else was used to, but perhaps with less of a fine blade. Tired jokes, tired concepts, blazers rolled up to your elbows, brick walls and anything else that looked and felt like the comedy of a bygone era was passé in this movement. Indeed, so was your existing act, at least at The Diamond Club, where you might find Patton Oswalt reading from his list of half-finished joke ideas, none of which are ready for the stage. You could be witness to Rick Overton telling you about his time as a road comic, warts and all. You might see Will Ferrell in a skintight leotard as a Canadian mime.

The LA alt movement started to happen because many of these comedians were, for the most part, not getting booked into traditional clubs like The Comedy Store, so they started finding and making their own venues. At the time, the alternative scene was growing outward from a small space in the LA bookstore Big & Tall Books. Entertainment manager and comedy lover Dave Rath sagaciously sought out a club for the underserved great comedy minds of their generation, and settled on The Diamond Club, a disco joint where he could set up weekly alternative comedy shows, in a spot mostly away from the disco music. "They have this back room that was past where the disco shit was . . . We were just entertaining ourselves and having a great time doing it," David Cross says.

Dave Rath had worked in comedy clubs, making friends throughout the world of comedy, a position which eventually led to him booking and segment producing the Comedy Central show *Comics Only!* This led to MTV's *Comikaze*, a mix of stand-up and sketches, for which Rath booked a group of San Francisco comics including Margaret Cho, Patton Oswalt, Brian Posehn, and Blaine Capatch. "At the time, I was kind of dabbling between managing and producing . . . Between jobs, I had some friends' headshots and tapes, and I had a phone and I was trying to hustle auditions or stand-up work or commercials or whatever, as a kind of a DIY manager."

When Rath eventually joined a management company, he brought in those San Francisco comics, and also worked with Janeane Garofalo, who was already with this company. "Patton and Blaine moved down from San Francisco, and they weren't getting stage time, and I couldn't break them through Laugh Factory." Within a decade, many of the names who performed here, like Ben Stiller, Will Ferrell (with his fake mime troupe "Simpatico"), Janeane Garofalo, Dana Gould, and Jack Black, would be taking over Hollywood.

You'd find these names everywhere, like in the long-standing Diamond Club show called *Tantrum*, where Laura Milligan (another San Francisco transplant) played her character Tawny Port, a former child star. Milligan had published an entire book of poetry in character, called *My Higher Power 'n' Me*, and based *Tantrum* on the world Tawny inhabited as she tried to get sober and get her life together. "This room [where] we were doing comedy, you could barely hear. It was just awful, so that was perfect, because the whole premise of the show was that everything was supposed to fall apart," Milligan says.

"One night the club had been 'taken over' by a medical-themed sort of TGI Fridays. So every time someone would get up on stage to do a straight stand-up act, like Bobcat, or Janeane, we had a wall of, I think, sixty blenders. We just got everyone that had a blender, come and push the blender buttons at the same time, so you couldn't hear a word." She also recalls bringing in some new musical blood to her show. "One night, the show got canceled, and David Cross and I went downtown. We saw these two guys that were hilarious, and we asked them to come do the show, and that was Tenacious D."

"Jack and Kyle had done one or two shows, and were messing around with stuff, literally got into an argument at our club," Rath says. "They came back the following week and performed their entire break-up and reconciliation suite to the Diamond Club audience. As scenes do, the alt scene in LA expanded, eventually to a show called *Un-Cabaret* at the club Luna Park, and Kathy Griffin's *Hot Cup of Talk* at The Groundlings. "Now it's considered 'alternative comedy,' but it was kind of just a transitional place for these people."

In the one surviving video of a full Diamond Club show, Patton Oswalt tries to work out a bit called "Mad Libs Wills," and Laura Kightlinger does a full fresh set about her mom and her personal life, while later David Cross improvises a story about losing his virginity at thirty. At one point, Greg Behrendt runs out in a gingham dress, dancing and lip syncing to Motorhead's "Ace of Spades." This is most of the bit, and then he grabs the mic, out of breath.

"This is the fifth 'space' that I've been invited to perform at for the past couple weeks. I think you know what I'm talkin' about: the Un-Caba-ret, Lava Lounge . . . 'Hey buddy, come on down! Don't do your act! No, bring me something new. Why don't you talk about your life or do something

weird? It's not like you fucking moved down here to do your stand-up act that you've been honing for fifty years. So come on down, do somethin' different.' Well you know what people, I'm at the end of my fuckin' rope! Thank you very much."

Another act did The Diamond Club two or three times: The Three Goofballz. They were Bob Odenkirk, David Cross, and the third Goofball—a different person at every performance. "I'm going to guess maybe, grand total, 170 people saw those shows," Cross says. In one show, Bob and David came out of giant boxes on stage, while the third remained empty, because that Goofball was dead. The alt scene, specifically The Diamond Club, was where *Mr. Show* was, if not born, aggressively conceived.

21

Devour Cowards Every Hour: Mr. Show with Bob and David

"The first comedy sketch that I typed out on my mom's typewriter was for a fake commercial for 'Tasty Paste.' It was some kind of like glue that you ate. I was probably 10." Bob Odenkirk got the commercial parodies out of his system early. He spent $30 on a cassette recorder, taping sketches with his brother, Bill, and they both listened to comedy albums by The Firesign Theatre together. Firesign was especially notable for their sketches weaving together seamlessly throughout these 40-minute epics. "I think that Firesign Theatre was great. Fucking great . . . It's wonderful and it can be fantastic and it can be as funny as anything, but it can be a more delicate thing. And it can be a softer kind of funny, and I don't think there's anything wrong with that." On the other end of the spectrum, from the same era, the Odenkirks also grew up watching *Python*.

"*Python* is as clever and absurd as anything. And sometimes it can slip into a self-congratulatory, absurdist disconnect that really is about playing with form only. But very often, mostly *Python* is *funny* funny. Make-you-laugh funny." If there's a show that mixed the *Python* sensibility with Firesign's obsession with flow and subversive satire better than *Mr. Show with Bob and David*, you won't find it in this book.

"I think the first time I met Bob Odenkirk was a situation where Dave Cross had his car stolen," remembers *Mr. Show* composer Eban Schletter. "He bought a new car and then he had a little party at Laura Milligan's house, where people would gather and paint his car. He ended up driving this funky car that had murals all over it because he figured if that gets stolen, anyone can describe it so quickly and easily . . . I didn't know Dave Cross all that well, and yet somehow I got the prime spot of the back trunk, perfect canvas, and I was drawing this weird kind of Don-Martin-ish guy with clouds behind him and stuff. And I thought I was doing a good job. And Bob Odenkirk is standing there . . .'"

"'You know what that needs? Little flying saucer going by in that cloud.'"

"And my first [thought] was like, 'Who is this guy telling me what to paint? What the-?' And then I looked at it and I go, 'Oh my god, he's right, that would totally make it.' So I did do that, and that's the thing that made it worth looking at. And I'm like, okay, all right. This guy was kind of butting in, but he obviously has good taste. And that was my very first meeting of Bob Odenkirk." Bob also famously blew off David Cross when Janeane Garofalo tried to introduce them, because he had a sandwich to eat.

"Bob and I . . . did not get along at first. He was pretty brusque and not friendly, but we had all these mutual friends and eventually kind of warmed up to each other," says David Cross. "We were at a party at Laura Milligan's . . . we're in the kitchen, and we end up riffing what became the infomercial with [the line] 'Kiss the pan.'" They wrote the "Super Pan" sketch up right away, an anxious meditation on abuse within the framework of an infomercial. Or, it's an excuse for Bob's British infomercial host to fly out a window, declaring "Only British people can fly." Maybe it's both. This started an immediate effort by the pair to write up material for each of their individual shows, outside of kitchens in other peoples' homes.

"We were at Bob's then apartment, on Sierra Bonita I want to say, and we had these other ideas, and we went to write them out . . . It was this effortless communication, where we were just building on this sketch idea in a symbiotic way that I just haven't experienced, and

I think very few people have that connection." They quickly knocked out "Third Wheel Legend," "Thirteenth Apostle," and "Racist in the Year 3000." "Bob did his show. He had a whole bunch of stuff, I did like two sketches on that. Next week, I had my show, did a bunch of stuff, and Bob and I did two sketches in that. Both weeks, it was not even close—they were the most well-received sketches." This is what made them decide to do a show together, and thus was born "The Three Goofballz," out of which grew a bigger concept, which slowly but surely became the stage version of "Mr. Show," sometimes called "The Cross/Odenkirk Problem."

"Bob was much more savvy and driven about this stuff then I was," Cross says. By this time, Bob had written on at least five shows, Cross just two, and only briefly. Still relatively fresh from the Boston comedy scene, for Cross, it was more about the pure joy of making comedy together; getting something on TV was the last thing on his mind. "It was an extension of [my time in] Boston, which was not particularly responsible. But it was fun and I guess I had some subconscious idea of like, why rock the boat? We're having fun, who cares about making money?" Meanwhile, fortunately for them both, Bob was thinking of where the show could go, but quickly realized it was an unpitchable concept: It wouldn't translate in an obvious way to TV, so they had to develop it further. Cross estimates they spent $12,000 of their own money (about $24,000 in 2023 money) to shoot and edit video elements for the live show—sketches and transitions—just like they'd end up having on their TV show.

Bob wanted to tweak the shows and invite audiences, making it clear that this could work on TV. They put on this new version of it at the UpFront Comedy Theater in Santa Monica. "There was an undeniable energy to it," Cross says. "It became a kind of a hot ticket in town to go to one of these shows . . . We probably did a different one each month." The UpFront was a substantial change from The Diamond Club; for one, there were lights, and people could be treated to something that "felt more like a show." At some point during this run, HBO's Carolyn Strauss (who had seen them perform at The Diamond Club) saw the new show, which would lead to her bringing *Mr. Show* to HBO's president of original programming, Chris Albrecht.

While HBO wasn't specifically looking for sketch comedy shows at the time, Odenkirk and Cross eventually got some development money from the cable network to turn what they had into a more streamlined live show, even before it would become a TV script. They took the new version of the show to the brand-new US Comedy Arts Festival at Aspen, performing on the first night, where Bernie Brillstein was in attendance. By all accounts, in their first performance, they kinda sorta shit the bed. In Naomi Odenkirk's great book *Mr. Show: What Happened?!*, Bernie Brillstein says that he told the guys to introduce themselves before their show, rather than go guns blazing, right into the sketch comedy from the top.

Brillstein's advice worked, though not enough to get them a series order from HBO, who afterward requested some more material. Odenkirk and Cross soon delivered, and to their surprise (and possibly HBO's) they got a four episode order—sort of; they were only given the budget for two. The only running theme or real bridging material between episodes was intended to be the perspective of Bob and David. Their style would inform what the show was and how it felt, which they intended to make up the gap that would be left by avoiding the typical sketch fair of recurring characters. "Chris [Albrecht] said, 'Yeah, we'll do the show, but we can only afford two,'" recalls Troy Miller, director of the *Mr. Show* pre-taped segments. "'And it has to look like what I saw; it has to be shot in a club.'" Miller found a club called Hollywood Moguls that was too small to shoot in once the lights were hung. He worked the magic he'd honed back on his *Not Necessarily the News* days, first by making the club shootable, knocking out a wall (that they'd later have to replace).

"They had put risers and floor space in for the audience," recalls Bill Odenkirk, an uncredited writer for some of the season one material. "We're not on a soundstage, so we often had to go around looking for crickets. Because there'd be crickets in this nightclub, and we had to silence them while we're shooting scenes and whatnot. So it was really tough. But then shortly after that, Bob and David got an order for six." This meant more money, more writers and, presumably, no more six-legged comedy metaphors to take out.

Among the new writers for season two were Paul F. Tompkins, Brian Posehn, Dino Stamatopoulos, Jay Johnston and Bill Odenkirk, who recalls writing with his brother to be a great process, even if it could be contentious. "We actually kind of butted heads a lot on the show, but he really would try to find what it was that was so compelling about a particular idea. If it might fall flat, as they often did when we read them in the room, he would try to dig deeper and find out what it was that you thought was funny originally about it, and tried to bring it out and nail it down, and saved a lot of sketches that way." Maybe because he'd seen the worst sketch comedy has to offer, Bob wasn't dictatorial. Final say on a sketch also didn't mean the only say; some sketches also had to pass the audience test, even before they were shot for TV.

"HBO had a tiny theater on Seward," Bill recalls. "We would have a collection of scenes that we wanted to present before an audience. As I recall, there were scenes that we really loved, but we're not sure if a larger group than this group of writers is going to love it." This also happened if the room was split, or even if a sketch didn't work on paper, but might on stage. The biggest struggle, though, were the "links," which is what they called transitional sketches, which made everything flow seamlessly from piece to piece.

Bob explains that he and Cross wanted each link to work for the sketch they were leaving *and* the one they were transitioning into, and if they could, the link should be funny on its own. "Well, that is just ridiculous. And we would get stumped up trying to link up two sketches. I would say the most we spent was two full days on one stupid link." It eventually was made clear to them that the audience loved the act of linking the sketches, but didn't necessarily care about the nuance the writers were losing forty-eight hours of their lives to. "Somewhere around the third season, we really wised up. We stopped trying as hard because the audience just didn't notice that we even tried so hard. They didn't give a shit."

"I think Bob and David really sweated it," Bill says. "We didn't want to do a lot of those connections where you were on one scene, and that finished and then you pulled into a TV and then you pulled out to some other place." They *would* do the TV thing on occasion, but it wasn't preferable, and either way, it was all an experiment in what sketch comedy could be, while also still being funny.

"We had a very, very capable director, Troy Miller, who helped see these things through on a miniscule budget," Cross says. "Like 'Coupon: The Movie,' where even though we had a budget of $1,000, Troy was like, 'Oh, we're gonna use this camera, we're gonna do this, we're gonna do that, we're gonna shoot a plate.' All of a sudden, you've got this cool thing that you didn't think was going to look that cool or interesting." The joy of discovery on shows with small budgets can sometimes overshadow the stress of making it work in the writers' room. "Outside of the arguments and stuff, when you're doing the actual scenes, they're fucking funny."

Actor Brett Paesel recalls that, like a lot of shows in this period, Mr. Show's on-location shoots could be pretty run-and-gun. "It was like stealing shots, like literally driving around in a van . . . running out, getting the shot and coming back. A lot of things in Troy's back yard. I mean, it was really, really, really bare bones." While it was a young show, she found it to be mostly supportive once she established herself. "The group very quickly split into those guys who would talk to me since I was married and those who wouldn't, and who would just sort of simply look over my head, like, 'Who's next?' So socially, that was very interesting because there was one group of guys who were pretty sort of straightforward and dealt with you like a person and then the others who just sort of ignored you because you were in the way."

Jerry Minor, who would go on to *SNL* and VH1's *Random Play*, among a number of other shows, got his start on *Mr. Show* while he lived in Detroit. Bob and David were working on their stage show and hoping to shoot a sketch called "The Recruiters," about two basketball recruiters who start scouting before their future players are even in school. Minor's Second City director was Tom Gianas, who would go on to write for *SNL*. "He introduced me to Bob and David . . . They came to Detroit to shoot some stuff just because they were friends with Tom and he directed this sketch . . . they wanted to use the backdrop, and they used some of the people that were there." Minor plays the father of one of the young future basketball players. A few years later, he'd run into Bob once more, in time to be cast in the final season.

Brian Posehn started writing on season 2, after Bob had seen him put on a sketch show of his own. "I wrote a sketch for Bob to be in where he played a boss . . . I was a guy who passed out when he lied. It's the traditional, 'We're having the boss over for dinner, and I hope nothing goes wrong.' He would say things to me, and I would lie and then I pass out and fall on things." Brian's handle on the format and his ability to be meta, he says, got him in the circle. In an era where anti-comedy and alternative comedy cohabitated with a sincere desire to make something funny, they needed people who could strike that balance well.

Mr. Show became well known for taking chances, too, without the sort of cynical "take no prisoners" attitude of other sketch shows that weren't sure what they were about, so chose instead to push the envelope. A lot of *Mr. Show*'s big swings were directed with such biting irony that the content alone would've kept them off of network TV. One such sketch is *Larry Kleist: Rapist,* which shows a world where saving money on incarcerating criminals means following them with a sandwich board that says "Rapist," and that every introduction to every other human must begin with a similar verbal introduction. The sketch simply explores an idea, but you can imagine letters coming from people of all stripes who don't understand it.

"That's what our standup was, too," Posehn says. "I mean, that's already what Patton and I were doing in San Francisco. We just didn't want to be like brick wall stand-up, and we also didn't want to be *SNL*; we didn't want to do exactly what those guys had already done. We were inspired by what they had done, and we weren't saying that what they had done was wrong or not funny . . . I was always going to do my own thing." To accomplish this, *Mr. Show* had some simple guidelines—no parodies or impressions—it wasn't going to be *The Ben Stiller Show.* This seems to be the case with the actors, too. They could all pull off typical "sketch acting"—two of them had to do that on *The Edge* not long before— but they also knew plenty about committing to the reality of a piece, no matter how stupid the premise.

John Ennis, Jill Talley and Tom Kenny acted on all four seasons, but didn't write. Their investment in these sketches is visible onscreen but doesn't come with the weight of having created the shows from scratch. Ennis was a college friend of Cross from Emerson, who followed him to LA when the big move came. Talley was at Second City and in *All You Can Eat,* then *Happy Happy Good Show.* While there weren't a ton of parts for women on *Mr. Show,* Talley has since said that she was given a lot of room to make the parts her own. *Mr. Show* demanded commitment from apparent utility players in sketches so tightly written that it became clear that there weren't any incidental parts, especially for Talley, whom it took a few actors to replace.

"The main moment for me was when Jill Talley got pregnant," recalls Brett Paesel. "They sort of split Jill's roles up with two or three other women who handled them for the most part." Some of the other roles went to Stephanie Courtney, who—though they're in the same age range—felt like Bob and Naomi Odenkirk were her "second parents." "I was clueless, I was twenty-eight, but I was a young twenty-eight . . . [Naomi] gave me the best advice. She was just like, 'You are either watching or doing comedy every night. That is the deal.' And that got me meeting people, which normally I would be in a fetal position, I think, at home." She was a waitress, a nurse in a hospital, a few small roles that would help her join the union. "I think my first part was, I was a sex worker about to be murdered by Brian Posehn."

The first season of *Mr. Show* was a magic trick of turning two shows into four, and season two was a reasonable, six-episode order. Both seasons three and four were to be ten episodes each, but they were given the same amount of time in which to make them. Piling it on, Bob and David were also producing and co-writing the *Tenacious D* shorts for HBO. "We worked straight thirty-eight days, and those are long days," recalls Cross. "Let's say you're shooting episode two, but you're rehearsing episode three, which you're going to shoot in five days, and then doing the post on the first show, and figuring out music . . . then when you're getting the latter half, then you're also starting to promote the show that's going to air even though you're still working on the back half and trying to do *Tenacious D*." Cross wasn't sure if he could do a season four, but with a little rest, he was ready to try it again. That season, though, sealed the deal. "By the end of season four, I was done. And I would have said no to a season five if HBO didn't say no for us. It stopped being that much fun." HBO had pushed them to midnight on Mondays, away from their "Comedy Block," and into a no-man's-land where shows go to die.

Scott Aukerman (*Comedy Bang! Bang!*) and his writing partner B.J. Porter both worked on season four, and afterward worked with

Bob on several movie scripts, one which nearly got made. Auker-man recalls a conversation with Bob about a possible season five. "At one point, he was like, 'Well, we're thinking, we're going to do more *Mr. Shows* and more *Tenacious Ds*, we're going to do ten episodes of each. We want you to produce the *Tenacious D* show, and . . . you guys just want to like host *Mr. Show* instead of us, or whatever? Because I think it's too much work for us.'" This proposed iteration would've been less about sketch "links" and Bob and David wouldn't have to be in everything. "'Sketch should be fun and easy, why are we wasting our fucking time doing these?' The links were a big problem. They're what made the show kind of special and arty in a way, but in terms of the writing, they had so many rules about them."

Bob recalls some of the thought process behind a proposed shift in the *Mr. Show* operations. "I'm sure we talked about the second one. Doing *Mr. Show Without Bob and David*. Because isn't that something you should be able to do if you get a couple of good comedy writers together? Do some version of that show? But of course it's kind of ludicrous, too, because what was great about *Mr. Show* was it wasn't some generic framework. It was our point of view on the world. It's why that show is still, for me, the strongest expression of my outlook on life."

Run Ronnie Run

Almost every sketch show of the '90s found a way to parody the reality TV show *COPS*. Not only was it one of the first reality shows on *TV*, but for people with a comic sensibility, it was the exploit-ative death knell of TV as a medium. Ironically enough, reality TV becoming the cheapest thing on TV may have also signaled the death of sketch. Only one show managed to take on *COPS* in a way that made it something else, and that was *Mr. Show*, when it created Ronnie Dobbs, a character who goes on to star in his own reality show where he specializes at getting arrested and, in perfect *Mr. Show* form, also gets his own hit song, "Y'all Are Brutalizing Me." If you haven't heard David Cross' ridiculously beautiful voice singing it, you're missing something. Ronnie Dobbs was already such a fleshed-out story and character, he had the edge for the best possible film adaptation.

"Season Four just felt silly and fun," recalls Aukerman. "The spotlight was sort of taken off of them. They brought other people in like Scott Adsit and Jerry Minor. So they were like, 'We want to do a movie, but we want to do it like we did season four, where it's silly and fun.'" Cross recalls the promise of a *Mr. Show* movie feeling like a sign of a significant shift for the group. "I think there was an unspoken understanding like, 'Okay, we're in this part of our careers . . . we get to keep making films, and then we're going to get to do whatever we want. This is going to be great. And we've got all these ideas for the next film after this.'" The film was going to be written quickly, to get the ideas out: a six-week process to make what was to be the first of several *Mr. Show* movies.

Aukerman remembers the first day of writing was a simple brainstorming session, as you'd expect. "We all started spitballing ideas for stuff that we wanted to have happen, and we knew Ronnie Dobbs was the movie." The film would've used Ronnie as a structural element, carrying the audience through to other sketches that didn't relate directly to the story. It would've been the first sketch feature film to hit theaters in over a decade. "The structure of it was essentially Ronnie Dobbs was going to travel to England, wrestle the Loch Ness monster, and have sex with the queen, in a real Cinemax-style sex scene with dissolves and fades and soft focus and everything." Some of the memories of this film's creation vary, but not this. As David Cross explains, "In the original story, Ronnie fucks the queen."

"So that's what we planned out and it was going to be great," Aukerman says. "And then Bob went away for three days . . . We wrote the first forty pages, I feel like in three days, and it was silly. It was super funny, and we really, really liked it. And then Bob came back and read it and was not incredibly pleased with it." Bob tried to relay the importance of finding a focus for Ronnie. "He kept mentioning *Happy Gilmore* and how *Happy Gilmore* loves his grandma, and is doing it all for his grandma. And that was very important. We needed to figure out what Ronnie was doing it for and what emotional stakes are there."

David Cross says the notes from the production company, New Line Cinema, started picking apart what they'd come up with pretty heavily, perhaps the reason for these new concerns. "The notes would, in a nutshell, be 'pull back on the sketchy stuff and do more Ronnie Dobbs.' We did several versions of the script, and by the time we got to the last one, there was barely any sketch type element to it."

"The sketches in it were very funny. Some of them were super, super funny. They were filmic. I wish we would have made that," Bob Odenkirk says. "I fucked up by convincing everyone not to make it. But I think Troy would have maybe pulled that off better." Odenkirk admits that the sketches would have played on the strengths of director Troy Miller to pull off style pastiches. "It would have been something people loved, I'm telling you. All the sketches wouldn't have been great, but two of them would have been fucking amazing."

From a three-day writing binge, the five writers then took a year to write the new version. When it finally came time to make it, they went to Miller. "I said, 'I'll direct this movie. No matter what, we've got to get it made.'"

"We eventually got a green light to shoot it," Cross remembers. "And we did, and then it got really bad because of Troy and the other guy, I want to say Richard Brener, at New Line." The budget was insubstantial, and though Miller was used to this, it was his first feature film and, as Aukerman says, the shooting was inflexible. "Because we only had like two takes and no time to fuck around and stuff, the movie was shot as written." There was a feeling that Miller was prioritizing the look of the film over the actual content: comedy. "Also, I had an agreement that I was going to shadow him to learn how to direct, and I flew out for the first week of shooting, and within half an hour, I was banned from the set," Aukerman says.

From the shitty notes to the weird shooting environment, the writers understandably hoped that the editing room for *Run Ronnie Run* would be at least somewhat like it had been at HBO. "Everyone had assumed that it was going to be like the TV show, which was a collaboration between everybody, you know: Director, Bob and David, the writers, everyone. We were all going to just sit there in an editing room and get it to the best shape it could be," Aukerman says. Bob and David put together their own notes, as the creative minds behind the film, to help shape it into its next form. "They had so many notes that Troy basically said, 'Hey, you guys are banned from the editing room.'"

"We were booted out of editing, Bob and Troy were really, really, really not getting along and it was a shock, because it was the opposite of the approach that we had at *Mr. Show* that was so successful that got us that movie in the first place," Cross says. "I think it was just a matter of like 'These kids don't know what they're doing.'" Miller says that the blame shouldn't be on his shoulders for not letting anyone re-edit the film. "I don't have control over letting you change it; I have control over the edit bay that we have no money to pay for. And we'd already finished the film like three times."

"I produced it, and I funded it. I had to mortgage my house, I had to basically put up everything I own to make this movie because they wouldn't fund us until a certain milestone had [been met]," Miller says. He says the post-production budget was in the red. "We went way, way over and we just kept posting and posting until we were running out of money and I'm like seeing how I can get out of this financially. Because they don't pay until you finish the movie."

"I knew the movie was not going to make anyone happy," Bob Odenkirk recalls, while echoing the perspective of the other writers. "He absolutely locked us out of the editing room. We begged, I wrote letters and dropped them off that said, 'Whatever we've done that has insulted you or hurt your feelings, I apologize.'" The letters pled for the opportunity to make the film a joint effort, but Odenkirk says they never heard back. "I waited for the phone to ring every day for months. I was sure he was going to call and say 'I just needed to get it this far on my own. Please come in. I want to hear what you have to say' or 'Look, I was wrong. I know you're upset. Please come in. I owe it to you to give you a shot.'" Instead, they got one screening, and their notes reflected how unhappy they were with the direction the film was taking.

As for the mortgaging of Miller's house, that's news to Odenkirk. "I've never heard that. And I hope that's not true. And I certainly would never have allowed him to do that. If he'd said, 'I'm going to mortgage my house,' I would have said, 'No, no, you're not.' . . . If I knew that he had done that and then I was cavalier or rude or uncooperative, that would be something to talk about. But the fact that the first time I'm hearing about it is you telling me, it's not a selfless thing." Cross and the other writers still feel like the film's editing could have done more to make the film serviceable. "I think there's some funny stuff in there. It's okay, but it's not really even close. You make a movie in editing, and we would have made a lot of different choices," Cross says.

On top of the editing room debacle, there were other concerns the writers had with the whole production. "There also was like weird shit like the director sending us contracts to sign saying everyone else had signed them already," Aukerman remembers. "Then you call around and no one had [signed them] and you read them and it's selling the rights to the songs you wrote for the movie to him for one dollar, and stuff like that." Cross says that his own suspicions about some of the things they were signing were later confirmed. "Because of our naiveté, we shouldn't have been allowed to sign off on certain things. There were little lies and big lies and the things that we couldn't prove . . . and then they were proved to us by Troy's old assistant."

Run Ronnie Run played at Sundance, though it was a shadow of what the writers had envisioned. "It was a massive disappointment, especially because it didn't fail on our own terms," Cross says. He believes that New Line may have wanted something along the lines of *Joe Dirt*, another hillbilly-caricature-centered comedy. *Run Ronnie Run* was bumped from theaters in favor of the release of *Jason Vs. Freddie*, and then only released on DVD. Miller claims that Odenkirk "released executives email addresses to his fan base" and that the servers at New Line were clogged. "So, Bob pretty much shut us down, sent it straight to video."

Bob and David did post something on their site, which was later reposted elsewhere online:

> *Bob and David here. Apparently the release of Run Ronnie Run is being moved from the much-mentioned date of April 12th, to sometime in August, September, October, Winter, or Never. While we can't verify when exactly (simply because no-one at New Line will call us back, or for that matter, knows) we can look at the track record of RRR's continual postponement as cause for concern.*
>
> *While we have very little recourse, we can encourage you to let your voice be heard. Through the miracle of e-mail, you can contact the people at New Line and tell them, simply "We wanna see the movie." We've always felt that everyone down the line has severely under-estimated our fans, both in numbers and sincerity. Don't be dicks about it, but just let them know that there's an audience waiting out there.*

It remains to be seen if this had anything to do with the film going straight to DVD. Its one potential moment in the sun was at Sundance, where everyone was invited to screen the film. Troy Miller recalls the screening fondly. "When we premiered, we sold out in one theater and there was so many I think we had two more the same night at the same time in Sundance. So it really did well." Scott Aukerman recalls a few less-than-satisfied people in the crowd that night. "Unfortunately, by the time it aired at Sundance, Bob and David were not even allowed to speak before the film by the director."

There was also an incident with one of the film's producers. "We were all picked up in RVs and taken to a bar," Aukerman says. "I get into this RV with Brian Posehn, and there's this producer that I'd never met before, who had never come to the set or anything, and he decides to yell at us, because we didn't applaud when the director's name came on screen. And he's like, 'You should suck his dick every day for what he did for that film!'"

Miller says he did make another attempt to get *Run Ronnie Run* a theatrical release, even if it wasn't the film the guys wanted. "New Line approached me to do *Dumb and Dumberer*. In exchange, if it hit a certain box office number they would release *Run Ronnie Run* theatrically, so I made a side deal that no one really knew about." It's not likely this information would change Cross' mind about things, however. "Troy and that guy—Richard Brener, I want to say his name is—at New Line, went on to write and produce and direct *Dumb and Dumberer*, and that's a just a fetid piece of garbage. It would be like if there was a big pile of shit, and then he threw up on the pile of shit, and then took another shit on that. In fact, I'd rather watch *that* than that other [film] . . . That's what those geniuses went on to do."

"Troy did his best, but the idea of the making that film as though the script were amazing and all you have to do is shoot it and you'll be golden is crazy," Odenkirk says. "The script was hinky and had all kinds of overwritten things, and it needed pacing, and it needed a stronger sense of tone, and it just needed so much. That's true of a lot of movie scripts, by the way, but in this one in particular, I can't pretend or sell to anyone that the script was great and Troy fucked it up. That's just not true."

Inarguably, *Run Ronnie Run* is a rough watch. There are great pieces in it, but we can all agree that wrestling a cryptid and making love to a monarch would have been better. Still, Posehn is fond of it. "Looking back on all that stuff. It's like, now I have a funny movie and the right people love it. It's not what we wanted. Some shit went down with us and the director. He took a movie away from us at one point, New Line fucked us. Bob and David, and the other three writers, you know, we didn't get respected at all." Still, some good bits.

The guys would go on to do a live tour called *Bob and David in "Hooray for America,"* that was all them. Something they had control over. It was Bob, David, Posehn and Ennis, putting on a live show for the first time since their show tapings, as always mixed with pre-taped bits. "That was going to be a movie at some point, too," Posehn points out.

In 2015, the *Bob and David* cast and writers got together to create four new episodes of sketch comedy very much in line with the old stuff. Twenty years down the line, they remained relevant and, as you'd imagine, as full of Gen-x angst turned into lively satire. They were the first American sketch comedy series to successfully revive their own show successfully, and certainly the first time it happened with a show where there was a core unit of creatives. It would be impossible to sum up everything they've done since *Mr. Show* ended, but Scott Aukerman puts it pretty succinctly:

"Some people wrote histories of *Mr. Show* right after *Run Ronnie Run*—it really does feel like a tragedy, like *Macbeth* or *King Lear* or something like that, where it ends in pain for everyone. But thankfully, for most of us, it ends with these redemptive third act scenes where Bob is one of the greatest actors on one of the greatest TV shows, and David is selling out all of his concerts, and I get my own TV show, and one of us is arrested storming the Capitol. So if you're making the biopic of *Mr. Show,* it's got a really interesting third act now, and feels more like a normal biopic like *What's Love Got to Do With It,* where we rise up out of adversity."

22

Too Many Nipples: The Dana Carvey Show

After the success of *Wayne's World* and the promise of more film work on the horizon, including *Wayne's World 2*, Dana Carvey left *SNL* in 1993. By the end of 1994, Robert Smigel had left *Late Night* to write more screenplays. Sometime in 1995, Carvey was throwing around the idea of returning to TV, in sketch form. Smigel discussed possibilities with Carvey over the phone, and it was clear this was the perfect confluence of opportunities for each of them. "Dana called and started daydreaming about, you know, 'I'm getting opportunities, people are interested in me hosting a primetime show.' And I'm always interested in like, reinventing a format. So in this case, what attracted me to it was we're gonna have a late-night sensibility in primetime. That felt new at the time."

Whether Carvey was invested in reinventing anything is not entirely clear, but he definitely wanted— maybe needed—to be back on TV. Still, the opportunity was there; no one had successfully pulled off prime time sketch comedy on one of the three original major networks in some time. That very year, *The State* would go on to be too much for CBS to handle, in fact. Instead of an unknown quantity in terms of network TV, Carvey was well-known, associated with a major network, and had a successful stand-up career. Mathematically, this all made sense, and it was technically years in the making.

Smigel had been wanting to try this experiment since his days at *SNL*, using the biggest sandbox on TV. "I would sometimes float to Lorne, 'Do you think the show should stay on at 11:30 on Saturday night? It's so great and like, it feels like you're older and the cast is a little older than it was when the show started, and the audience is a little older. Maybe it should be on at 10 o'clock on a weeknight.' And he had no interest in fucking with a good thing. And he was right." It wouldn't be ninety minutes or with a cast of current movie stars, but Carvey wanted to try to do a sketch show. "[It] was the opportunity I saw to give that a try. Like, let's put really silly and edgy stuff on in primetime. It had never really been attempted," Smigel says.

By the time ABC agreed to do *The Dana Carvey Show*, Smigel and Carvey had only a couple of months to get it ready before their planned March premiere. They were trying out the best comedy actors in the country, and writing up pre-filmed sketches that wouldn't depend on timeliness, like some of the studio audience pieces would. In January 1996, Carvey said, "I'm getting the very best people I possibly can. And if they upstage me, that'd be great." It was a positive note to start on, even if every interview from around this same time left journalists not quite knowing what to expect. Carvey would try not to pigeonhole the show into a particular style of sketch comedy, perhaps because there would be no way to know the show's vibe until it was shot and edited. "Sketch comedy, when it's bad, is probably the worst thing a human being can see or endure. And I've been in plenty of that," Carvey told the press. "It's a dicey game. We'll see. I don't know."

At the same time, ABC was actively placing this new sketch show amongst its other safe fare, placing it in the "family hour" of 8–9, where some networks were purportedly taking chances with edgier sitcoms and losing viewers. Ted Harbert, then president of ABC, claimed his greatest difficulty at the time was finding another show like *Home Improvement*, and the same article listed Carvey's show as part of "ABC's new midseason family shows," along with *Muppets Live* (which became *Muppets Tonight*), and a sitcom called *Second Noah*, "an *Eight is Enough*-style show about a couple with eight adopted children of various ethnic backgrounds and dozens of animals."

Animals with, we can safely assume, at least a gross of nipples among them.

"When I was in college I had a Dana Carvey poster on my wall," recalls cast member Bill Chott. Getting an audition for the show was a dream, even though he didn't have the typical sketch show audition bag of tricks. "You could either do some characters and impressions, or you could read this monologue through three different times as three different characters. But instead, I did it one time through as like thirty-two different characters." Some of these, Chott admits, were accents, or hints of characters. He did have one fully-formed bit he could have done, but he refused when Smigel personally requested it. "I was like 'No way, that tanked my *SNL* audition.'" On Smigel's insistence that Dana would get the bit, he performed the piece: his impression of Jackie Gleason taking a difficult shit. "Which I guess sealed the deal, because they wanted me in the next round of auditions."

"I certainly was brought in on every sketch show that was going," recalls Deborah Theaker. "I did audition for *The Dana Carvey Show*. I remember sitting out by the dumpster with Steve Colbert, and it was really hot. And it was this comedy club, Igby's, and we're out in the parking lot going, 'How long is this gonna go on?' Because it was like a big bake off. You'd go in and do your stuff and then they'd [say], 'Come back and let's see that again.'" The core cast of the show was promisingly small: Heather Morgan, Bill Chott, Stephen Colbert and Steve Carell. The characters would be coming from their own backlogs, like the "Waiters Who are Nauseated by Food," a combination of similar characters in the quivers of both Carell and Colbert. Carvey was also going to bring his character The Church Lady with him, somehow, despite NBC's notorious litigiousness regarding "intellectual property."

"One of the things that attracted me to it was Dana said, 'You can put yourself in scenes,' so I did," Smigel says. "I'll only do something if I think I'm the best person for it, or if I look the most like [them]. So I played Ringo Starr, and I had already done Bob Dole on Conan for years." This was another idea that took a long time to come to fruition. Like many people who started at *SNL*, Smigel had auditioned to act as well, but was happy as a writer. "That first year [at *SNL*], the show was very rocky, there was a little part of me saying, 'Maybe you should pursue this more, because these people aren't that good.' Then they brought in Dana and Phil, and I was like, 'Ah, right, you have to be *that* good.'"

The Dana Carvey Show premiered on March 12, 1996, running right after *Home Improvement*, the stable, successful family sitcom that had been a reliable workhorse for ABC for five years already. Echoing variety shows of years past, *The Dana Carvey Show* would not only have commercial breaks but episode-wide sponsors that each show was officially "brought to you by": Taco Bell, Mug Root Beer, Mountain Dew, Diet Mug Root Beer, Pepsi Stuff, the list almost went on and on. The first episode was introduced as *The Taco Bell Dana Carvey Show* and opened with a big musical number, a tongue-in-cheek celebration of Taco Bell, featuring a dancing bell mascot, the "clapper" of which was placed on the crotch of the dancer.

The actors were all credited writers, as well, working alongside people like Charlie Kaufman, Jon Glaser, and Robert Carlock. Chott's sketches never made it to air, though he wasn't paired up with another writer the same way everyone else on the staff had been. "I would improvise things that would make their way into the show, but never any of the things that I had written down. In fact, I think I almost got fired at one point." He was called into the head writer's office, at which point he pitched some stuff he'd had in his back pocket that he'd avoided submitting. "A parody of a sitcom that's about the early works of St. Thomas Aquinas . . . I work so much better when I'm paired up with somebody and I wasn't. I didn't have somebody else to write with."

There would also be some additional material from Bob Oden-kirk and Greg Daniels, who weren't on staff. "When *Dana Carvey* started up I went out there for I think three weeks," Odenkirk recalls. "I tried to help and be a part of it. I wasn't much help. I'm not sure what I wrote there. I kind of lost the plot with that show pretty quickly . . . In the end, I think it was more Robert's show than it was Dana's but I think Robert should have his own show. So that doesn't bother me." The show shot in New York, since Carvey was still on the East Coast. Director John Fortenberry handled both the live aspects and the pre-taped shoots for the show. "*Dana Carvey* was a blast, because it was a mix of doing little short films and doing pieces where it's a guy at a desk, so it's not so stressful, as a director."

Among the varied sketch ideas would be simple news parodies, press conferences and other opportunities for impressions of George H.W. Bush, Ross Perot and Bob Dole. There were also "The Stupid Pranksters," a series of sketches starring Carvey and Carell as two guys who are the victims of their own pranks, like trading in one of each of their shoes for bowling shoes, and running off with no intent of ever bowling, losing one of their personal shoes in the exchange. The committed laughter of Carell at the end of each of these sketches sells an already elegantly simple idea, which is the kind of material where the *Carvey* show shines. There are other pieces that, if not exactly edgy, would have been perfectly at home on *Late Night with Conan O'Brien*, where the experimentation would've been appreciated, like "Grandma the Clown" or even the famous opening sketch with Bill Clinton breastfeeding animals and a baby.

"Sketch comedy and primetime had always been kind of like, the most edgy stuff was just innuendo, like, *Match Game* kind of humor," Smigel recalls. He had assumed America was ready for *SNL* at prime time, and admitted he knew nothing about their lead-in, *Home Improvement*. "Pamela Anderson was on it. I just assumed like, 'Okay, so there's got to be some sort of like *Three's Company* kind of sexual innuendo on the show.' And then, I had heard that Tim Allen had dealt cocaine, so I think, 'Okay. He's an ex-coke dealer, so he's got to have some kind of edge to him . . .' could not have been a dumber Kamikaze."

The reviews were not kind early on, though they eventually started to turn around, if not in time to save the show. Two separate readers wrote into the Fort Worth Star Telegram to complain about things like "this totally unnecessary display of profanity." ABC had ordered a full slate of thirteen episodes before the season began, but they only shot eight, and only seven of those would end up airing during the original time slot; the eighth aired sometime after sweeps. "I disagreed with the decision to open the show with Bill Clinton breastfeeding puppies," Chott says. "I was kind of upset with it. After that point, I realized okay, well, that's the focus of the show. That's what we're trying to do." Onscreen, he wasn't used nearly as much as the other core actors, either. "The final episode didn't air. We had a screening at a bar somewhere. And I was like, wow, the one episode that I was pretty heavy in, that's the one that didn't air."

"It was just a crazy clash of just bad decisions," remembers Fortenberry. "Not that it was bad comedy, but where it went on the schedule, and the night." The atmosphere behind the scenes also contributed to where the show ended up. "I must admit, at the time, there was this sort of rebel attitude that we all had." Fortenberry says that there was a great deal of tension between Smigel and the Brillstein-Grey producers, while Carvey avoided conflict whenever he could.

"[There was a], 'Trust us on this. You'll be thanking us in the end,' kind of attitude," from the production side, Fortenberry says. Smigel sees the approach now for what it was. "I didn't really understand how wrongheaded it was. We just wasted an opportunity, basically. Either we should have gotten rid of the edgiest stuff, and just made the show smart—which was eminently doable—or we should have done the show on HBO or something and it would have been on for ten years.

"When I was a stand-up in 1981, I remember I used to start my act like this crazy thing where I was dressed as an orthodox rabbi, and I wouldn't say anything. I just came out with a prayer book, and I would just turn the pages with my tongue." He also had a cotton candy beard that he would take little bites from throughout his act; Andy Kaufman was one of his '70s heroes, so this was his attempt at that sort of humor. "It would get funnier and funnier, and then it would stop getting funny. And then I would do it a little bit longer till it was funny again, and then I would stop . . . some nights it was just alienating and one comedian was just like, 'Just ease into that, you know, just let them feel safe with you first and then go crazy.' I was like, 'I don't think there's any way of getting laughs with that unless you just come out with it,' which was true. With Dana Carvey's career in my hands—his sketch comedy career, anyway—I probably should have taken that to heart once again."

The Dana Carvey Show was a throwback in its apparent execution—the sponsorship bit, the simple presentation without linking material—but it was loaded with skilled writers and performers. Its genius was simple premises you hadn't seen before, and a small cast asked to do a lot of heavy lifting. It was centered around one name, but it was a name who liked sharing the spotlight. The experiment was putting late night into network prime time TV: It was impossible, but for the comedy obsessives like myself who tuned in because it felt like the next big thing, it was worth watching thirty minutes of big swings and awkward audience reactions.

"A year and a half ago, I actually did go back to sketch comedy," Smigel says. "I was offered to produce what I thought was an awful idea at the time." It was a topical sketch comedy show with puppets, similar to *Spitting Image*. He ended up excited at the idea of developing

it, having caricature (non-Muppet) puppets interact with real people—something he hadn't seen on TV before. "I took the job and
you know, no one saw it. It was on after Tim Allen's show [*Last Man
Standing*], which was a cruel irony . . . like a twenty-five-year anniversary practical joke." Smigel says no one saw his political puppet show.
"We didn't even have a chance to ruin it."

23

When Improv was Illegal: Theatresports and ComedySportz

If a Princess hadn't been stuffed up, twentieth century improvisation would've been quite different. In 1961, Keith Johnstone was about to open a new theater in London's West End. "Princess Margaret had a cold—a sniffle—so she couldn't open the Jeanetta Cochrane Theatre," Johnstone recalls. Anywhere else in the world, this might be a minor hiccup. "She didn't have another date in her book for two years, so the theater was standing empty, for two years." No public performances were allowed: Princess Margaret herself would have had to sign off on any such shows before the official opening, and that wasn't going to happen.

Three years before this attempted opening, in 1958, Keith Johnstone began slowly falling, quite by accident, into the world of theater. *The Observer*, a London paper, ran a contest that March offering £1,000 in prizes for a short story called "The Return." The winners were announced that December, but word must have gotten out beforehand, because by June, the Royal Court Theatre was putting on Johnstone's first one-act play, entitled *Brixham Regatta*. "I had never been a playwright," Johnstone says. He had been teaching in Battersea when he submitted the story. Once it had been published, word got out to director and writer Lindsay Anderson, who recommended that the Royal Court Theatre stop making "safe choices," when choosing writers and material, so Johnstone was picked to appease him. "I'd written hardly anything . . . it was a sort of scandal. Playwright Ronald Duncan insisted on interviewing me, because they were paying money to this school teacher from Battersea to write plays, and they weren't commissioning *him*." Three years on, Johnstone remained in the theater.

While no public performances were allowed at the temporarily shuttered Jeanetta Cochrane Theatre, Johnstone and teacher/director George Devine could put on workshops there for students. The directors of the theater would have to teach the classes, however, since they didn't employ any teachers: This was an experiment, born out of necessity. As before, Johnstone was out of his element: He'd never directed, or worked with actors; he was just freshly a playwright. "But I like to find stuff out."

"Starting with a group of actors and just an empty building meant we had to start with doing improvisations of some kind from the very beginning. I became obsessed with making actors look like human beings on the stage." He may not have been certain what caused this at first, but he admits he didn't realize how prevalent stage fright was amongst experienced actors. "I had the belief that actors weren't scared for some stupid reason . . . 'They can't go through their working life scared, can they?' Yes, they can. I didn't realize that." He felt that actors often looked like "very cleverly-made robots," and noted that they often shook off the tension when they exited the stage, which felt wrong to him. "I didn't think they should be afraid when they were in front of the audience." He made his goal to find a way for actors not to *hide* fear, but to get rid of it. "The quality of not caring is really important."

By the time Johnstone and his colleagues were having their students improvise, The Second City had been open for two years in Chicago. These were only exercises, to be sure, but there was also no way they could ever go beyond the confines of these classes. "We couldn't open up to the public. It was illegal to improvise," recalls Johnstone. "There was a special censorship in the theater, which had been there for 200 years. Every significant gesture or whatever, anything important in mime, and all the text had to be seen by the Lord Chamberlain's office." This practice ended seven years later, in 1968, but it meant that, until then—technically—the Lord Chamberlain could have you shut down if you asked for an occupation or a word from the audience.

"But I ignored that. I thought, 'Well, let the Lord Chamberlain do what he wants to do . . .' I was worried about whether we were a self-admiration group, because we were laughing hysterically the whole time of the class. So I had to test it, and the only way to test it is to go in front of real people." He wrote to six different colleges for teachers, to see if they'd like to see his group's techniques, and they all said they would. "And then, to kill the feeling of it being academic, the improvisers would be as disrespectful as possible. When things weren't going well in a show years later, I would often say a couple of words in private to the improviser and it would all get a little better . . . nobody ever knew what I said, but I'd just go over and say, 'Make my life difficult, fuck about,' and that would cheer them up. They'd come on the stage to fuck about, and fuck me up, and that could get rid of a lot of fear."

One of the games that really got the audience invested in their shows was "The Hat Game," an improv game in which one performer's goal is to get the hat off of the other's head; the game is designed to get you out of your own head and invested in the action. "They don't care what they say. They're worried about the hat, which is a very good thing." For his version of The Hat Game, Johnstone split the audience into teams, who would each cheer for one of the players on stage. The shift in the studious academic audience was immediate. "They're suddenly all screaming and howling and jumping up and down. So that was my first understanding that there's something here which is much more potent." Those free shows got such a tremendous reaction that Johnstone realized he had something.

From there, he slowly built up a group of fearless actors who were called "The Theatre Machine." In 1967, they were invited to perform in Montreal for Expo 67, putting on a show called *Caught in the Act*.

He would come to Victoria, British Columbia, the following year to direct a modernized version of *The Wakefield Cycle*, and to be a visiting lecturer at the University of Victoria, during which time he also put on improvisation workshops. He eventually settled in Calgary and, after seeing a wrestling show with two friends—noting how fun, clean and friendly Canadian wrestling was—they discussed the idea of something like a wrestling show with improvisers instead of wrestlers. In the late '70s, he started the improv-centric Loose Moose Theatre Company in Calgary. Around the same time, he told the *Edmonton Journal*, "Theatre was originally a spectator sport."

Theatresports started at the Loose Moose to teach everything Johnstone had learned since those early years in an unopened theater, concentrating on the team part of team sports rather than the competition. In 1987 he published the book *Impro: Improvisation and the Theatre*, which still informs how Theatresports locations around the world teach improv and put on their unique brand of competitive improvisation. Theatresports would eventually help launch the careers of people like Dan Harmon, Colin Mochrie, Ryan Stiles and Joel McHale. In the '90s, Wayne Brady found himself performing at SAK Comedy Lab in Orlando, eighteen shows every week. He also found himself closely following the teachings of Johnstone. "Once I started doing Theatresports in Orlando, that's when my life really changed. That blew my mind. I went, 'Oh, shit, this is amazing.'"

"The thing that I loved about Theatresports, and about improv, and sketch is it was a team sport. I liked playing my role," Brady says. His Orlando team won the 1991 International Theatresports competition, beating out the Los Angeles team. While Brady became well-known for his skilled improv on *Whose Line is it Anyway?* a few years later, he always treated improv as an immersive educational experience. He read Johnstone's work and gravitated toward the use of one's own personal skill as an element of improv—dancing, singing, etc.—rather than fixation on finding funny moments. "I didn't think I was funny. I was like, 'I'm the wrong choice to put on *Whose Line*. Are you guys shitting me? Why are you casting me for this? I am wrong, don't you get it?' Because I'm just an actor."

Once he realized he could use his own singing ability, especially, he found his way into the comedy of it. "I call it 'stupidity in cursive.' You always want the most elevated version of what the thing is, and that allows you to be as silly as you want to be . . . [Johnstone] changed my life. Reading his book changed my life, because I use everything that I learned from Theatresports, and from his school of improv every day . . . Try to be truthful to the art and the funny will come."

To a similar end, Johnstone's work has also had a heavy influence on The Kids in the Hall. "He was about not being funny," Bruce McCulloch says. "It was about creating something on the spot, and not saying no, and exploring your mind. And in that form, it's beautiful. I'd just get on stage with Mark, we'd open up a thesaurus, we'd point at a word and we'd just start doing a scene for ten minutes." That same attitude has carried through to his writing, for *Kids in the Hall* and the many shows he's worked on since. "I think *The Kids in the Hall* will write faster than anyone, throw away shit faster than anyone . . . but it's just like, 'Oh, we have nothing. Let's just talk. Let's just do a thing.' So we're the opposite of all the rooms we've been in, and all the *SNL*s, or when I when I run my own rooms. People bring in their pitches, and it's like, no, no, you're allowed to just go, 'What if a guy got his tie caught in a bank machine?' Or not even that, just go 'bank machine.' And then let's stare at each other. So I think that fearless thing we still have comes from Theatresports."

Kentucky Fried Improv: ComedySportz

"I think it was just somebody who didn't want to pay any money," Johnstone says of Dick Chudnow, creator of ComedySportz.

"I think the fee was $25 to use the name at that time," Chudnow says. "I saw Theatresports in Seattle, and I thought, 'This isn't a show.'" Chudnow saw no beginning, middle and end, and instead saw improv game demonstrations, followed by thirty minutes of competitive improv, with scenes that were too long. "We decided to make it an actual sport." Chudnow took the Theatresports concept with him, back home, to Milwaukee, which in 1984 didn't have a comedy scene beyond a single monthly stand-up night at a club. "So when we started, we were the only thing. And again, we were sold out, from like the second day that we started." The first time Chudnow had blown the doors off of the Wisconsin comedy scene was in Madison, with the co-creators of *Airplane!*

Inspired by the sketch movie *The Groove Tube*, Chudnow, Jim Abrahams, and Jerry and David Zucker decided to stage a live show comprised of video pieces, improv and original sketches called *Kentucky Fried Theater* in Wisconsin. They did a little guerilla marketing, like painting their logo on a construction fence, and took out a small ad in a college paper, and ended up sold out for nearly their entire run. Chudnow took the show to LA with the Zuckers and Abrahams, but eventually moved back to Milwaukee after being bought out of his piece of the show, before *Kentucky Fried Movie* was created. A few years later, Chudnow saw Theatresports, and eventually changed the name to ComedySportz, which itself now has over two dozen spaces in the US and the UK. Actor Mike Rock was one of Chudnow's first students.

"For the first year in Milwaukee, he called his show Theatresports, and he did basically the rules that they did. And then he came to Madison, where he had gone to college." Rock was in a play at the time, and was invited to try this new thing out. He was joined by the cast of his play to become part of the first cast at Madison Theatresports, which six months later changed its name to ComedySportz. "In all due respect to Dick," Rock says, "He just didn't want anything to do with the international Theatresports organization. He didn't want to pay royalties; he also didn't want to follow the rules that they had set up for how the show should go. So he kind of built a better mousetrap in his view." Competition was part of every ComedySportz show, so much so that there was a referee, and the teams wore sports jerseys.

Upright Citizens Brigade co-founder Ian Roberts found himself in Milwaukee after following a girlfriend there at the beginning of his theater career. He checked out all the improv that was available locally, and settled on ComedySportz who, in a change of pace from everywhere else, actually paid you for performances. They also, not unlike iO in Chicago, found outside gigs for their improvisers. "They were introducing the lottery to Milwaukee, and they got a bunch of us guys from ComedySportz to go out and improvise these scenes at fast food restaurants and Seven Elevens," Roberts recalls. They were hired by the lottery to get the word out. "I think the law didn't allow them to advertise, so they wanted us to do some kind of weird grassroots thing. And I remember people getting angry at us, because I played my guy like a dumb hick, and some guy stood up and said, 'You think we're a bunch of idiots?!'" This was only the beginning.

One year, Roberts was hired to play a mummy at a rich person's Halloween party. "Their mummy costume was a freakin' wet suit with bandages around it. So imagine how hot that was." The place was decked out, filled with great food, all of which was served out of coffins. Coffin food was for guests only. "They put us in the basement and gave us weird white bread sandwiches in wax paper and we sat down there and ate." He was then asked to wander around the backyard as a curiosity for guests to point at, and afterwards asked to climb their garage, get onto their roof, and hang over their skylight. "So I get up there, and I'm just laying down on a skylight, in a wetsuit . . . and it was such a surreal moment of realizing what a dirtbag I was in the hierarchy of the world that I was, for a hundred bucks, on someone's roof, laying down on a skylight so rich people could point up and laugh at me."

For others, ComedySportz was either their first job or their only outlet for theater kid energy. Mike Rock became "Artistic Director" not long after the launch, at twenty-one years old. His future cohort in the sketch group "The Bert Fershners," Chris Tallman, joined up when he was about fourteen. "[I'd] never been to like a live comedy show, so already that energy is kind of fun and exciting. And then it was my first experience with improv, so just seeing people go up on stage, and you know, the audience shouts fucking, I don't know, 'turkey baster' and then they do a scene and they get laughs. To my little brain, I was like, 'I'm running away and joining the improv circus. That's it.'" Even better: he could join whenever he wanted. ComedySportz shows are clean, intended for all ages; there are foul cards in the shows for swearing, as well as for terrible jokes (groaners). "When you're fourteen, you want to start leaving the house, but you can't really go to bars. So ComedySportz, all of a sudden, on Fridays and Saturday nights, starting around my sophomore year of high school, that's where I went. Every fucking weekend I was there."

Matt Gourley, co-creator of the improv group/podcast *Superego*, actually brought ComedySportz to his California high school, where he managed to reel in future *Whose Line* improviser Jeff B. Davis. "They'd kind of treat it as a varsity sport, where you could start a ComedySportz team at your school and you would play other schools, and people from the professional show in Hollywood would come and ref." Gourley had met James Bailey, the founder of ComedySportz LA, at a theater festival, and fell in love with improv immediately. Right out of high school, Bailey called him to join the professional show in Hollywood, which would stage itself in the theater that later became UCB's first LA theater, on Franklin Avenue, often performing on the set for whatever other shows were booked there, like a café or the inside of someone's personal anatomy.

ComedySportz competitions don't stop at the local level, either; they have national competitions. If it weren't for those, Gourley wouldn't have met his *Superego* podcast co-creator Jeremy Carter, who was part of Kansas City ComedySportz. They have a particular shared sensibility that comes both from a few decades of friendship, as well as a brand of improvisation that feels unique to *Superego*, which has seen Jeff Davis, Chris Tallman, and Mike Rock as guests over the years. Guest actors tend to fall into the patterns and stylistic habits of the core Superego group of Gourley, Carter, Mark McConville, and *Mr. Show's* Paul F. Tompkins. It's a thing to behold: people from every type of improv background coming together to make absurd, profane, joyful improvised podcasts, often filled with shoot-from-the-hip moments and real reactions from their fellow actors. This is not the kind of comedy you'd expect to come out of any other improv company.

Perhaps due to its games-centric nature and the fact that it has franchised all over the planet, ComedySportz's progenitor, Theatresports, isn't always discussed among your Second Cities and iOs. ComedySportz itself, being family-friendly and high-energy and stressing the entertainment value above all, is mentioned even less. "It had a huge following. It really did, but they weren't tastemakers, and it was never on the edge of anything. But it was doing the mainstream thing really well," Gourley points out.

Perhaps there's something about their shows that feels like a series of shortcuts, and maybe that perception is correct. In improv theater, though, the shortcuts, short-form improv and long-form are all a means to a very similar result. In the end, most performers who genuinely love improv and find an aptitude for it find their way around to the same sets of rules as everyone else; when the performance styles and approaches differ, it can be a thing of beauty, if everyone is elevating everyone else on stage. The rules of improv are codified in different ways at different places, but water finds its own level when everyone just wants play.

24

Leave Them Wanting Some: One-Offs and Pilots

When you're talking about the impact of '90s sketch TV on comedy and popular culture in general, you're typically talking about shows people have seen, because that's typically how TV has an effect on things. Throughout my research on the subject, a number of pilots and "specials" (usually just pilots that actually aired due to contract requirements or a desire to get something from the investment) came up that were worth discussing, especially since you can now, at the time of writing, find many of them online. Even among these, you'll find current box office and TV stars and some of the biggest writers in the business; for many of them, these were the first stepping stones to what you know them from best.

The Comedy Castaways: The Onion Makes a Sketch Pilot

The Onion was the first satirical paper in the US to have any real reach beyond college campuses. It started in 1988, and by the early '90s, then-owner and editor Scott Dikkers was looking to expand, even if he wasn't sure what *The Onion*'s brand was just yet. "We had built up this great staff with funny people, and I was incredibly ambitious, and I wanted to do more." This led to a sketch comedy album entitled *Not for Broadcast*. "It was like a National Lampoon comedy CD. We didn't really quite understand that *The Onion* was different, that it was a news parody." The natural progression, it seemed, was to work on a sketch pilot for TV, so in 1994, they started putting one together.

"*The Comedy Castaways* was a very similar idea [to the CD]. Let's do a sketch show. It's like just all this ambition, all this drive to try to get *The Onion* out there more. We didn't even think to do a fake news show." Each episode would have a different animated opening, where the cast—consisting of Andrea Gall, Todd Hanson, Rich Hutchman, Matt Spiegel, Brian Stack, and Nancy Carell (a year before her turn on *SNL*)—were chroma keyed over it. In the first episode, they are lost on the ocean, so Poseidon demands sketches from them. In the second episode of this two-episode pilot, the outlaw Black Bart tells them to make sketches at gunpoint. The staff of *The Onion* felt prepared to write their own sketches, though they did also get pieces from future *Simpsons* writer Dan Vebber and Adam McKay (also a year before he started at *SNL*); Dikkers says they changed the ending to McKay's submission.

The sketch in question features Nancy Carell as someone speaking to the company therapist (Gall) about the scores on her creativity test. They try some word association. When the therapist says "bike," she thinks about it and says "bike." When pressed, she pluralizes the therapist's words, then starts looking around the room for answers to a Rorschach test. "That's a sketch I did at Second City," McKay says. "The crazy thing is we later did it on *Saturday Night Live* with Tom Hanks. He was fantastic in it. It's one of my favorite sketches." If the sketch feels familiar, McKay says it is a "first cousin" of Steve Carell's character Brick Tamland in *Anchorman* ("I love lamp") and the similarly-themed "Gump" from *Piñata Full of Bees*. "The whole character type comes from the moment in life we all realize there are some people in charge who really and truly don't have a clue . . . The sketch I would write now would be the same character whispering 'help me . . .' to the company therapist."

With a budget of $10,000 (around $20,000 in 2023 money), Dikkers chose to make two pilot episodes, hiring a local news camera operator to shoot the whole thing in under two weeks. Staffers at *The Onion* also participated in the production, with writers Joe Garden and Kelly Ambrose on props, and future co-creator of *The Colbert Report*, Ben Karlin, assistant producing. They cast the show in Chicago, seeing people like John and Kevin Farley (brothers to Chris) and a group of actors from Second City's e.t.c. company. "I was mostly casting for chemistry between the people. I wanted different types with different vibes, so it'd be a good, well-rounded cast that you could plug into almost any sketch."

The quick shoot somehow turned out footage that doesn't look rushed, or nearly as cheap as the budget suggests. Nearly every sketch works, and there are solid laughs throughout. There's a man on his deathbed who wishes he'd spent less time with his family—not just more time at work. A Brian Stack character is convinced a carton of eggs is his secret fighting force, who eventually turn on him as he smacks himself with raw eggs. A runner of idiot movie producers trying to come up with blockbuster ideas like buying the film rights to the Q&A section of *The Carol Burnett Show* wraps around all of episode two. In one sketch, another Brian Stack character introduces his business to the millennia-old concept of the written word: "The entire epic poem and storytelling divisions could be retrained in computer science," and taking control of the meeting with a flashlight: "Thaniker controls the fiery light of the sun!" It almost makes no sense that this show wasn't picked up by someone. Almost.

"We had no idea that you had to be in Hollywood, and you had to have development executives or, you know, a production company, a distribution company, we [didn't] have any of this stuff," Dikkers says. "So we just aired it on local television, and bought some local ads that make it, you know, worth its while or whatever." Until Dikkers and I spoke, it was sitting on a tape in his archive, maybe last handled when the local ABC affiliate in Madison aired it. "They didn't know how to deal with the surround sound on the tape . . . You could barely hear the show when it aired. So it was really embarrassing. People who watched it were like, 'Oh, is this some sort of prank? *The Onion* put out a show that you can't hear.' And that was it. The show ran and we didn't we didn't do anything else with it."

Life as We Know It: The New SCTV

In 1990, The Second City decided, once again, to try and make a TV show happen. Andrew Alexander, who had originally purchased the TV rights to The Second City for $1, would be producing this new concept, too. The plan was to air on the HA! Network, which eventually merged with The Comedy Channel to form Comedy Central. Jay Levey, music video director (and manager to "Weird Al" Yankovic), was involved early on. "I happened to be chatting one day with my friend David Jablin and he was talking about a TV sketch show project that he had developed and had been green lit . . . I told him it sounded like a great project and offhandedly suggested he should let me know if he needed a director. He said he actually did, and I was offered the gig."

Meanwhile, Ken Hudson Campbell, fresh off of *Home Alone* and only a year and a half into his tenure at The Second City in Chicago, was also getting an offer. "They said, 'You're being hired to be in the next *SCTV*.' And so I was like, 'Wow, what are you talking about?' They're like, 'You're going to Hollywood—you and Carell. You're gonna star in this half-hour show.'" He was given a contract for thirty-five episodes, in case the show took off. "You have to write them and perform in them for $1,700 each job." The show was going to be loaded with top-drawer Second City performers, like Campbell, Steve Carell, Sherry Bilsing, Brad Sherwood, Ryan Stiles and Diane Stilwell.

It almost included one other Second City legend: Colin Mochrie. "I believe Steve Carell got put into the show last minute because they couldn't get a work visa for Colin," recalls Brad Sherwood, who would go on to co-star in *Whose Line is it Anyway?* with Mochrie, and onstage in their two-man show. "So my first time working with Colin would have been on that show." For most of the cast, Hollywood was a brand-new experience. Campbell and Carell roomed together in Santa Monica, and for what they assumed was just a pilot, they only had to rehearse, not write, since the pilot script had already been written. Three pieces are credited to Letterman writers Michael Barrie and Jim Mulholland, with two other sketches based on existing Second City material.

The show opens on one of the old Second City pieces, "National Debate," where Campbell and Stiles play politicians competing for who can confess the most heinous truths on camera. Carell and Sherwood star as two ad men in "The Ad-Guys" pitching new concept after new concept as their boss (Campbell) continues to reject their pitches. When they accidentally kill him, they pitch the cover up to one another, only to have him wake up right before they accidentally drop him out the window. The cartoony sound effects do a lot to diminish the overall effect, but the performances are polished. There's a black and white gangster movie parody, an extended sketch in which Sherwood's mime stalks Stiles, and a sketch about a guy who time travels to prevent himself from getting married, which has a weirdly sweet, romantic ending. Everything is pre-taped, with no audience or laugh track. Overall, the show looks better than the material demands—this could be the one time in a '90s sketch pilot where a little more edge would've been alright.

The show did end up airing on Comedy Central, just after the new channel had been created, Levey says. "We were all very proud of the show, but apparently some kind of internal politics between the network and Second City prevented the show from being picked up." *Brad* Sherwood saw more in the show's future, had it not come at such a weird time for the new network. "You know, when there's a merge and a reshuffling regime change, all the pilots and stuff in the pipeline that were the little darlings or babies being incubated by whoever was in charge at that network, those look like used car parts now to the new network that's rebranding itself."

Live on Tape: The New SNL

Gotham City Improv, in New York City, was originally opened in 1986 as Groundlings East. By the early '90s, it was the traditional place in New York to go to for comedy training, while nearby spots like Luna Lounge thrived presenting New York's version of alt comedy. Mary Birdsong, who would go on to co-star in *Reno 911!*, already had some improv experience when she discovered Gotham, so she had to perform improv with a friend in a small back room to get bumped up to the second level. "I thought musical *theater* was the thing—this is *really* my thing. I just was in love with everybody in the class. I couldn't wait to get to class. It was that thing of like, 'Oh, this isn't just a class, this is going to be my social world. This is going to be my dating pool. This is going to be my career resources, my support system.'" Like other schools around the country, Gotham was also an occasional source of work, getting its students acting jobs in industrial videos.

Around this time, a sketch group called Live on Tape was performing shows in New York featuring pre-taped sketches in between their live stuff. The shows were produced by Mike Stafford, who often checked out Gotham City Improv for new performers for his group. "It just reached a stage where I love Gotham City, but I was broke. And we were having too many conversations about 'there are more people [onstage] than there are in the audience,'" Birdsong says. It was at this point when she finally considered joining Live on Tape, because it couldn't be worse than performing for no one.

It was quite the opposite, in fact. Stafford would call everyone he could think of to get an audience together, including press. "He would call up Cindy Adams from *The Post* and be like, 'You gotta get down here, this place is hot. And these kids are on fire.'" The audiences continued to build and attract industry attention, like agent Peter Principato, who Birdsong describes as "The Louis B. Mayer of comedy." He wouldn't sign the group, though, until they polished their writing and found the right performance venue. "It just seemed like anything was possible, and all of a sudden we were doing this really good run at West Bank Cafe in New York City, in their basement space and packing the place. It just felt electric." The president of NBC, Warren Littlefield, came to check the show out. Soon after, he signed the group to a development deal. The cast for the pilot would consist of Birdsong, Barbara Herel, Tony Mennuto, Amy Wilson, Tom Bolster, Alec Holland, and Jimmy Palumbo. They would be shooting in Studio 8H, at Rockefeller Center, where you'd normally find *Saturday Night Live*. This was also right around the time of yet another incidence of *SNL* teetering on the edge of cancellation.

Birdsong remembers getting wind that *Live on Tape* might be being treated as a backup for *SNL*. "From what I understand—and this is just me hearing from different people involved—I guess at the time, Lorne Michaels' contract was about to expire. I think they were negotiating and wanted to have some sort of plan in place in case that didn't work out." The group filmed five hours of sketches—enough to pull a pilot and more from—in the event of NBC needing to fill a gap in their schedule.

Watching what is available from *Live on Tape*, it's clear that, at the very least, NBC would have had a huge slate of characters to choose from. In the tradition of The Groundlings, these were clear-cut, easy-to-understand sketches, and some of them, not unlike *SNL*, run over five minutes. There are three Jersey ladies hanging out in a line for a confessional with a sexy priest, trying to figure out why he's giving them different penances. Two '90s hipsters are shitty to a foreign waiter and brag about the wonderful humanitarians they are, passive-aggressively assuming superiority over the room. Then there's Birdsong doing what she does best, singing and being old-timey; she plays Scatwoman, the alter-ego of a songbird named Janet Lamé, who uses jazz scatting as her weapon to disarm her enemies.

The group got to choose their own producer, so they went with *Kids in the Hall's* Jim Biederman. Their director would be the ever-flexible

John Fortenberry. "I have great memories of that. I loved those guys. I thought they were all incredibly talented, and I liked their material. It reminded me of early *Kids in the Hall* stuff." Fortenberry says that while the budget was low, he was hoping for NBC to get the group a little exposure. While bits of *Live on Tape* are rough around the edges, there's not a single performer who isn't good on camera, and big personalities like Mary Birdsong would have shined with a national audience.

Deep Dish TV

Comedy sketches being bridged by the concept of changing channels goes back at least to The Firesign Theatre's 1970 album *Don't Crush That Dwarf, Hand Me the Pliers*. With the advent of cable and satellite TV, and the promise of hundreds of channels with nothing on, it was only a matter of time before someone used this basic premise again. *Deep Dish TV* aired in 1991 on Showtime, the brainchild of actor Paul Chepikian, who wrangled his fellow actors at The Harvey Lembeck Comedy Workshop to film a show that could feature all of them. The story of *Deep Dish TV* is that of a man trying to overcome tragedy and depression by doing what he loved most with his friends—comedy—and being rewarded with a Cable Ace nomination.

Deep Dish TV was a hopeful pilot, but entirely self-funded, so Chepikian knew from the beginning that this might be all he would get. Typically, especially then, someone at a network would see you, you'd get to pitch your show idea, and they'd decide your fate in the room, or a bit later. Maybe they'd have seen a tape of your work, first, but Chepikian went fully DIY a full decade before cheap cameras and fast internet would have made the process a hundred times easier.

While at the Lembeck Workshop, Chepikian lost both his father-in-law and his wife to suicide within the span of a year. He took some time away from classes to figure life out. After about a year away, his friend Tony Nassour advised him to get on with his life while also doing something he cared about. "Let's not wait for them to hire us. Let's create something." Chepikian had recently sold his house, so he took some of that money and decided to fund the new project, along with Nassour. Kind of. "I put up I think maybe fifteen or twenty grand," Chepikian says. Nassour then asked if he could borrow the money from Chepikian for his portion of the budget. "And then I loaned Tony $20,000 to put up . . . He was a good friend."

The sketches are very high energy, and the money was clearly put mostly into sets and lighting (the cast and others worked for deferred pay). In between sketches like one in which a man has to defuse a bomb on a gameshow to win some furniture, and an ad for "The Nun Channel," the voices of Lou Jacobi and Betsy Palmer play over footage of beslippered senior citizen feet in front of a TV. They both comment on what's on the television, most of which they hate, so that they can flip to the next channel and give us a new sketch. There's a commercial for "poultry bowling," and a weather report by a hacky stand-up, played by Chepikian's friend, Paul Feig.

The bridging elements were Nassour's concept, and the sketches themselves run the gamut from gameshow parody, to reality, to instructional, religion and sports; a lot of the bits are revisited throughout, as the couple check some of these "shows" out to see if they've gotten any better. We see a commercial for a 900 line you can call where, instead of phone sex, you're read a passage from a book, though it seems the narrators might read it to you sexily. There's an action show called "Frank Strap," written by Chepikian, an intentionally one-joke bit of a detective who is always chasing someone every time they cut back, getting injured at the end of each bit. It's a mix of vaudeville and satire of mixed effectiveness, all of course cloaked in pastiche.

One piece they produced was based on the home repair show *This Old House*, entitled "This Old Box," hosted by an unhoused person. This sketch might seem familiar if you watched *In Living Color*'s first season. "I basically said, 'Look, it's a funny sketch, but we're making fun of homeless people. I don't want to do that,'" Chepikian recalls. He thought about the sketch to see if the concept had any way of working outside of how it was already framed. "'Why don't we say that it's funded by the Presidential Council on Fair Housing?' Because now we're making fun of the government . . . because the government now thinks, 'Well, these people living in boxes, they can fix them up. It's not so bad.'"

They took the finished product and pitched it to HBO (where Chepikian says Nassour called Chris Albrecht "babe"), as well as to network TV—specifically, Fox. "They said, 'We're working on something very similar.' 'Oh, really?' 'Yeah. It's called *In Living Color*.' So they weren't interested in our little show."

After *In Living Color* started to air a few months later, Chepikian says he got a call telling him that *In Living Color* was doing their own version of "This Old Box," starring Damon Wayans as his Anton Jackson character. "I found out that Tony, my so-called friend, had sent them a copy of our show because he wanted to direct *In Living Color* . . . I was very proud that they felt comfortable enough to steal."

Chepikian had pitched another show to Showtime a few years before (the idea for which he believes they took and repurposed), but once *Deep Dish TV* was completed, the person they originally pitched to had been bumped up to head of the network. Chepikian, a former graphic designer, sent a custom box with Dom Pérignon, a three-minute tape of congratulations written and produced by his group, and the *Deep Dish TV* tape. He invited the executive to lunch and he bought the show on the spot. "Tony and I are so excited. Under the table, we're playing footsie, you know, it's like, 'Holy shit, we just sold our show!'" Chepikian finally got to cut checks to his friends for making *Deep Dish TV*, which would end up airing several times over the next year.

The Cable ACE Awards were the only award in town for cable shows, but the *Deep Dish* crew were shocked when the nominations were announced. Their entire budget was smaller than the costume budget for some shows, Chepikian says. Whereas for a cop scene in *Deep Dish TV*, they had to employ clever editing to spread two bullet-proof vests among several actors playing cops. They were up against a Rita Rudner comedy special, *Not Necessarily the News* and an Ernie Kovacs special. Even though *Deep Dish* didn't win, they had sold a show for television that the network made no changes to, that they had made on their own dime, in their own way.

Head Cheese

"MTV was such an important pop culture brand. Arguably, maybe the most important there for a minute or two," says Doug Herzog, who was there as MTV experimented with movies and TV shows. As with any production company, MTV Productions could make movies that got released by any distribution companies; the same would have gone for TV shows, but MTV avoided that. "We don't really want to make TV shows for anybody else, because then if they're watching something else, they're not watching us." One rare exception was when ABC gave MTV a deal to produce a sketch show for them. "I just remember it being incredibly, like, way out there. There was no way network television was gonna pick this up."

The creative team behind Chicago's (and later New York's and LA's) *Real Live Brady Bunch* were not a sketch group yet, but they had worked together for long enough that there became a certain shared sensibility. Joey Soloway would head the show up, and Bruce Leddy, an MTV veteran who cut his teeth producing *The ½ Hour Comedy Hour* (to which he later added sketches) and promotional half hour specials for sketch movies like *Wayne's World* and *The Coneheads*, was brought in to direct. "ABC thought they could get some of their heat by making a show with them. And then discovered that they were they were too cool and too edgy for ABC."

The cast of *Head Cheese* was Ben Zook, Andy Richter, Madeline Long, Sarah Thyre, Eric Waddell, Becky Thyre, and Tom Booker, with music by Faith Soloway. Zook, who uploaded the show to You-Tube, writes that the network executives called the show "too fat and too gay." For the early '90s, it is indeed incredibly, refreshingly gay. There are sketches like "Hard Action News," from a fictional gay cable network, and a commercial for HomoRooter, a company that helps you hide your sexuality from your visiting, judgy relatives; for men, they give you sports clothing, posters that both show and say "boobs," and replace your Tyne Daly poster with a Frisbee.

Leddy also captured a lot of behind-the-scenes footage, including writers' meetings, which was later cut into the show. "We couldn't hire a full crew or anything, so I was literally just holding a camera most of the time while shooting behind-the-scenes stuff so that you could kind of see the evolution of an idea."

To avoid overlong sketches, the group took some of their extended bits and simply placed them throughout the show to give you some breathing room, so you could enjoy Andy Richter as Cindy Crawford's sister, Mindy, get a bit of gay news, and then find yourself on someone's scalp with some nematodes. "I think it was a really huge missed opportunity for MTV and ABC that they didn't get ahead of that," Leddy says. "I'm sure once they saw the accolades that came for the Soloways later . . . it's the same with *The Ben Stiller Show*. I mean, how could anyone have passed on *The Ben Stiller Show* with the most insane cast? But executives—you never know what they're gonna do."

25

Veal Chops in Dill Sauce: The Bert Fershners

A TV pilot's state of being is very much up to the beholder. To some, it's pure potential. To others, it's the beginning of everything good to come. To executives, it's a thing they put money into which, regardless of the quality of the piece, they can't take back. The Bert Fershners were a sketch comedy group that got their shot, didn't get picked up, and yet still came back to the same network and got their own half-hour special. Not long after, the group called it quits. Whether you know who they are or not is irrelevant; they are the story of every artist who almost makes it. It's basically the story of *That Thing You Do!*, only the music is sometimes about a truck filled with jelly.

Who is Bert Fershner?

Mike Rock: There is a car in the '40s or '50s known as the "Tucker," which was this car that never became, it never—it got squashed. There's a movie about it actually, by Francis Ford Coppola, called *Tucker: The Man and His Dream,* starring the Bridges brothers. Bert Fershner worked for Tucker, and he created the servo device that causes the headlamp in the center of the grill to actually follow the car's direction and didn't get credit for it. Because Tucker, for all his, you know, heartfelt glory or his reputation, whatever, he, like Thomas Edison, took credit for some of his underlings' ideas. And so Bert Fershner kind of goes down in history as just this guy who had worked in the automotive industry, and then later became a grocery bagger in Shreveport. Which is fine, I mean, nothing against grocery baggers, but it just wasn't the same kind of glory as inventing a really cool device for a car.

Chris Tallman: Well, my understanding of Bert Fershner is that he was an Austrian composer. I think it's like sixteen—I don't, I'm not good with these, you know, how like they say "sixteenth century," but it's actually like 1785. So it's somewhere in there. I think it was it's like Bertrand Feishner, or something like that, but like through the Americanization of it all and seeing it like in a textbook, I think it's like, "Oh, yeah, Bert Fershner." I think that's what it was.

Joey Garfield: He invented dice. And he was a barnstorming airplane stunt pilot and would promote whatever you needed to promote, or promote his own little show that he did, mostly in the Midwest. And since we were all Midwesterners we took on that name. That's *the* Bert Fershner. As far as Bert Fershner lore, I mean, I've heard crazier things . . . He owned a fleet of trucks, Bert Fershner Trucking. He's Chris Tallman's great uncle. Something like that. So it changes, but I will say this now, on paper, Bert Fershner is real.

Mark Hervey: Bert Fershner, I think he was a test pilot that crashed his plane in the Tijeras Canyon in New Mexico.

Dan Berrett: The guy who invented dice. Was that the one that you heard? The guy who invented the loop de loop? This was much easier before the internet.

The seven nice boys that make up The Bert Fershners are Dan Berrett, Dan Fleming, Joey Garfield, Mark Hervey, Josh Lewis, Mike Rock, and Chris Tallman. Just as The Kids in the Hall set up shop after Theatresports, so did The Bert Fershners put on their own sketch shows after ComedySportz in New York, in a small room in the back of the Telephone Bar & Grill.

"A group of us moved from Madison to New York City and started doing [ComedySportz] in New York," recalls Mike Rock. "We were doing this improv show that we had fun with, but we didn't see a future for it, beyond just the back room of a restaurant. So after our improv shows, we would perform a few minutes of our sketches. Captive audience, they've just enjoyed our improv show, so why don't we do some of our sketches and see how they like them." They called these shows *The Postgame Show.*

Mark Hervey worked at the Telephone Bar, and recalls *The Postgame Show* going on there for about a year. "Anybody that was involved in ComedySportz was welcome to do it, but then we realized some of us really wanted to sort of make this a thing." They asked for a show of hands, and eight of them were in for the long haul. "There was one more . . . but he had had an incident where he was waiting tables at a Pizzeria Uno on Third Avenue, and it was held up and he was tied up. Had a gun held to the back of his head." The eighth hopeful Fershner is alive and well, and is now a successful playwright.

The Postgame Show eventually made its way to the Red Room at KGB Bar, and then The Kraine Theater, by which point they'd chosen a name. "Caution: Filling Hot" and "French-Bread-on-the-Forehead Men" were two options, but they settled on The Bert Fershners, for a reason they will take to their graves. "When we became a sketch comedy group, we all had kind of like a come to Buddha moment with each other, where we said, 'No one's in charge,'" recalls Rock. "We're going to be a socialist democracy, where each person is going to bring to the table their skills, and we're going to make the whole greater than the sum of its parts." Rock, Josh Lewis and Mark Hervey took part in promotions and getting agents and producers to come see them perform. Joey Garfield was the one to bring a lot of the show to life visually, with sets and props.

They were methodical about choosing their material—each sketch would be voted on by the group. If a sketch got seven votes, it was immediately in. Five or six votes was workable, but four or less didn't stand a chance. They combined an hour of their best material into a single show and decided to hunt for a theater.

"The very fast-paced nature of what we did in ComedySportz probably is part of what made a lot of us want to sort of write our own material," says Dan Berrett. "I think what it taught us was be quick, get in, get out, if it's not working, just move on." The sketches were separated into groups: longer sketches (some of which were musical numbers), medium-length sketches, and what they called "nuggets," typically thirty seconds or so—similar to what might typically be called a "blackout sketch." They paced the shows out so that these sketch lengths would properly play off of each other, all skills they'd learned while doing competitive improv in jerseys.

In May of 1995, The Bert Fershners put on a show at the Kraine and got a positive review in the New York Daily News. Hervey recalls this being the first step toward something bigger. "*Saturday Night Live* was just tanking, and all the networks were like sharks circling, going, 'Oh, what's the next comedy show?'" The positive press made them schedule their next show right away, and they were soon booked at Caroline's Comedy Club, which meant even more eyes on them. Right after the booking, one of the Fershners had a medical issue and was unable to speak, so they had to write two different versions of the show, in case they were short a man. "Mike came down with Guillain-Barré syndrome, which affected his ability to speak . . . We were writing two shows simultaneously, one with Mike and one without." Rock didn't make the show at Caroline's. There was a genuine fear that the Fershners might end up a six-man, still very White, group. One night, as Hervey, Dan Fleming and Josh Lewis were at a Ray Charles concert, Lewis' phone rang. "Hey guys," Rock said.

That night, at the Ray Charles show, the guys busted out their notebooks and wrote up a sketch about a sketch, which would end up in their pilot. It opens with six of The Fershners frozen in motion, then goes to black. Back at a control room, a group of engineers are in panic mode because that last sketch got no laughs. "Sir, we have six men trapped in a blackout. We have to find a way to get them outta there," one man says.

"Why don't they just go on to a new scene?" a military-looking General asks. As it turns out, they can't. The laugh that never came was supposed to propel them to the end of the show. They spend the next six minutes figuring out how to land the show. They can start by sending The Fershners back to the beginning of the episode, because "There's enough residual audience reaction there to keep them warm for a while and buy us some time." One of them leaves to run a simulation to find their options, but he's stopped before he gets out the door.

"Here, take this rubber chicken."
"Do they have a rubber chicken out there?"
"No."

"If *they* don't have a rubber chicken, *I* don't have a rubber chicken." The men soon discover that if they pluck some elements from other sketches throughout the show, the show will work. They grab a shirt from scene seven, a cane from scene six, and a hat from scene eight, and they take an engineer's glasses from the sketch we are watching. Fade back up, and one of them is Waldo from *Where's Waldo,* paying off only because of the sheer anticipation.

The Fershners were invited to the 2nd US Comedy Arts Festival at Aspen in 1996, and were recorded for the TV special *Kicking Aspen,* which was hosted by Drew Carey and featured Janeane Garofalo, David Cross, and Marc Maron, among others. The Fershners' sketches ran throughout the special, ending with their song "Tube Tops," a musical celebration of men in said garment. "And it killed," Berrett recalls. "So that was our first exposure to TV . . . and then we started talking to Comedy Central about a development deal." Not only would they be writing their pilot, but they'd be producing material that would serve as "bumpers" between shows and commercials, to get the Fershners' name out there.

"I remember The State, when they heard we were developing the show with [The Fershners], got very competitive and, you know, would shit talk them all the time," says Doug Herzog, then President of Comedy Central. At the time, Comedy Central was developing at least two sketch shows, with offices near one another: *The Bert Fershners*, and *Viva Variety*. Some of The Fershners felt perhaps they weren't given the flexibility other shows were getting. "Doug [Herzog] just could not, in five weeks' time, ever find a free Wednesday night to come down for an hour to see the sketches," recalls Hervey. "So he requested, in his almightiness, that we come and perform the pilot in his fucking office." Being a socialist democracy, though, Hervey was outvoted.

"It was so humiliating. Like, we did it. If I can do improv on a flatbed trailer at some Podunk county fair in Wisconsin in front of like little kids whose parents just set them down in the front of the trailer and they're all heckling me . . . I've been in crappy situations, I still know how to perform. And I did—with a smile on my face! But man, I have to say that was probably the most humiliating thing that I've ever experienced as a performer."

Garfield admits they were clueless as to how to make a TV show. "You have to look at camera three and then you gotta go to camera two, like that whole choreography, when you're just used to just interacting, to do it for camera was very disorienting. To me it untethered the comedy." They had a few options for their director, including *Sesame Street* director John Ferraro, and a friend of Comedy Central executive Eileen Katz. "That was our first mistake, not hiring her, because she was Eileen Katz's friend and she had some cool ideas." They filmed in the same building where *Sesame Street* was filmed, so Ferraro gave them the Sesame Street tour, perhaps to let these kind, inoffensive boys feel at home with their fellow Muppets.

Comedy Central—when they came down to see the sketches— would pick the ones they thought worked best for the pilot. Garfield recalls executive Kent Alterman making some of the bigger decisions for how to move forward, perhaps because The Fershners were still not TV-ready. Still, they didn't quite understand why some decisions were made. "He [had] the bigger vision and bigger idea, and a *TV idea* of how to do our stuff . . . Kent Alterman was a big advocate of ours; I mean he was more a big advocate of changing Comedy Central into what it is now. I think he should get a shit ton of credit for that."

"Live is where we really were the best," Hervey says. "Personally, I've never dug doing television . . . It's taping and waiting. Just put me in front of people." The Fershners wrote their own songs, made their costumes, did all their own booking—TV was suddenly a very different beast. The full pilot is hard to find, but there are a number of sketches out there, including "Magic Trick Joey" and "Racquetball Rabbi." There's a near-consensus among the Fershners that the pilot didn't make it because *Viva Variety* had a leg up because of their connection to Herzog, though Tallman recalls a meeting where Eileen Katz proposed bringing in celebrity hosts to their show, since The Fershners were a relatively unknown quantity. The Fershners didn't give in to that idea 100 percent.

"It didn't go forward because *Viva Variety* went forward," Rock says. "One of [the Comedy Central execs] said to us immediately, 'Well, we're going to do something else, so don't worry, we'll be in touch shortly.' And six months later, they called and said, 'Let's make another pilot.'" The Fershners' representation agreed to shoot a second pilot on the condition that this one would actually air as a special, whether it was picked up or not. The show is a taped live show; the stage is clearly a stage, the audience is clearly in the room . . . it is intended, at least, to reflect a real Fershners show. It opens with The Fershners as a bunch of adorable young fellows in nightgowns, who sing the words "Veal chops in dill sauce" to the tune of "My Favorite Things" from *The Sound of Music*, to cheer themselves up and get over their stage fright. It is the least-offensive sketch ever committed to video that is actually funny.

"When the second pilot didn't go forward, we were crushed like a bug," recalls Rock. Shortly thereafter, Tallman moved to LA for his successful TV acting career, and the rest of the group picked up and headed to Edinburgh for The Fringe Festival. "When he went to Los Angeles, we had that real introspective moment of saying, like, 'Okay, do the Bert Fershners still exist?'" The shows and plane tickets for Edinburgh were booked, and for that month, The Bert Fershners—all six of them now—played The Fringe. They were also followed by the BBC for the TV documentary *Edinburgh or Bust*, featured alongside numerous UK acts, including The Mighty Boosh, who premiered their first stage show that same year. The Fershners end the second episode of the documentary with their closing song, in which they're dressed like a piece of broccoli, some fish and some water, some guys in a boat, and the sun in front of some clouds. Everything is cut out of foam board and hand-painted. They're back at the beginning, at least for a bit.

They close with the lyrics, "But the fishes and me and the big broccoli must say goodbye."

The Fershners pitched a few more pilots, including a sort-of kids show and an animated Scooby Doo-ish one, but nothing came to fruition, and they began to drift apart, at least professionally. "Josh wanted to make a movie, and Joey wanted to direct things, and Dan Barrett was already working as a journalist. Chris was in LA, Dan Fleming was starting to do stand-up," Rock says. "We just didn't have gas in the tank to push anymore. I wish we had done that thing that best friends do in rom-coms where they say, 'If you're not married, and I'm not married, when we're thirty-five, let's meet at this restaurant at midnight, and then we'll . . .' you know what I mean? I wish we had done that. In retrospect, I wish we had said, 'Okay, you guys, in a year or in two years, let's meet at Veselka in the East Village and see if we want to do more together,' you know?"

— 26 —
Staging a Comeback: Viva Variety

Season four, episode three of *The State* contained a sketch entitled "The Mr. and Former Mrs. Laupin Variety Program," presented to us from The State's idea of Belgium, and featuring most of the cast playing European variety and sketch show performers. "The way it started was because Tom and I could not do different European accents," recalls Kerri Kenney-Silver. "So we had just this one, and we would do these people together." Naturally, this sketch was never intended to go any further; it was too big, too amped in terms of energy to repeat, but it's a great, anxiety-inducing one-off. Along with the Whitman's Sampler of European accents, Kevin Allison's announcer character is hung upside-down from the ceiling for the entire sketch, Joe Lo Truglio is a walking cuckoo clock, and Ken Marino is a vegetable-destroying ape man, hiding from Ben Garant as a goose-stepping Nazi-like police figure. All the while, the Former Mrs. Laupin (almost a European take on Kenney-Silver's fantastic Nancy Spungen) is making out with her new boyfriend, played by Michael Showalter, much to Mr. Laupin's chagrin.

As *The State* came to an end, everyone at the show was figuring out their next steps. "Okay, we don't really have a home. What's the plan going to be? Tom and Ben and Michael Black went and pitched it to Comedy Central," recalls Kenney-Silver. Kent Alterman, then fresh to Comedy Central, says Jim Sharp's contribution was a major factor in *Viva Variety*'s success. "When I came into Comedy Central, he was a development executive . . . Jim basically brought me in and said, 'Hey, if you want to be the head of development, come in,

because I think I'm gonna leave,' and that was a funny transition."
Sharp would be the boots on the ground producer and showrunner,
once again helping the folks from The State shape their ideas for TV.

Doug Herzog and Eileen Katz had both hopped over to Comedy Central from MTV, countless successes and interesting experiments under their belts. Herzog became president, and Eileen Katz
headed up the creative side of the still-young cable network. Sharp
remembers being reticent to give development a shot. "They called
me and said, 'Hey, come and be our development guy, it's gonna be
really cool,' and I said, 'Ehh, it's not what I do, you know, I'm not an
executive.'" They talked him into it, reminding him he'd still get to
put shows together. "It was a disaster. It lasted nine months. But while
I was there, I remembered this sketch on *The State* . . . and I thought
it was a TV show. So I talked to Tom, Ben, and Kerri, and they said,
'Yeah,' so we did a pilot and we picked it up."

"I got it immediately," recalls Herzog. "I grew up on variety
shows, and I always loved the idea and tried unsuccessfully to do
variety shows for many years at a lot of these cable networks I worked
at." Herzog, like most everyone else involved, knew and trusted the
folks from *The State* and was excited at the prospect of booking rock
bands in addition to the sketches/extended character bits and
third-party performers they'd be booking. "One of my things about
sketch . . . the show has to have a reason to be here . . . *Viva Variety*
had a real premise, and that gives it a reason to live. There's a lot of
comedy that can come from that." Kenney-Silver gets to the heart
of why the show could live on today (something she, Lennon and
Herzog have discussed): "It's 'free' to do. Because the cheaper the
sets look, the better."

In the spring of 1997, *Viva Variety* started shooting at Metropolis
Studios in New York City, each episode featuring a real variety act
like a table spinner or a contortionist, a musical act, fake commercials,

as well as conversation and interstitial bits between the main characters. These consisted of Mr. Meredith Laupin, Agatha (the former Mrs. Laupin), and Black's pompadoured Johnny Blue Jeans, the one amongst the group trying his hardest to be American at his core, meaning he kinda, sorta succeeds. While *Viva Variety*'s sketches were usually in studio bits, they would occasionally have pre-recorded pieces, like when The Former Mrs. Laupin plays a clip from her other show, "Xentra: The Warrior Goddess."

"You had a pilot for one of the major networks?" asks Mr. Laupin.

"No, no, not exactly, it was CBS," The Former Mrs. Laupin explains. The clip from her show then features the line "Tell it to my magic sword, ya' a-hole." Other bits include taking Johnny Blue Jeans out to perform in a mall to almost no one, exploring the history of the man who they say invented the Speedo, and in-show ads like a combination baby doll and instrument called "Baby is the Bagpipes."

There aren't too many analogs to *Viva Variety*, where a reality-based premise like a variety show is imbued fully with satire and presented as though real. The closest might be the brilliant late-seventies talk show satire *Fernwood Tonight*, starring Martin Mull and Fred Willard (and later, *Comedy Bang! Bang!*). Where *Viva* differs from most shows in this micro-genre, though, is by bringing in real variety acts, real music acts like Dionne Warwick, Rick Ocasek, and Duran Duran, and movie and TV stars. "We're all musical theater people at heart," says Kenney-Silver. "We would have Shelley Long, and we had Run-D.M.C., Whoopi Goldberg, Ben Stiller, Kathy Griffin, and people would come in for dance and song rehearsal. And these were complicated, some of these big dance numbers." Cable still couldn't easily nab big stars for certain shows, but Sharp says the atmosphere of the show made it easier. "We just kind of got a reputation that this is a lot of fun."

It was a big theater production every episode, and very much about suspension of disbelief, at least slightly, as Kent Alterman remembers. "Not only are they pretending to be these bizarre European entertainers in the classic throwback sense, but also [pretending] to be like forty years older than they were . . . what was really cool about that show is that it allowed them to exercise so many different kinds of muscles." For Kenney-Silver, it was all about the acting muscles. Being busy recording and touring with her band, Cake Like, while also making the show, meant that she was only acting on *Viva*, while the other three also wrote (Garant was not a regular, but did appear as various characters throughout the series).

The show's satirical atmosphere did occasionally cross into stark reality, especially when the opportunity came to bring in acts who were genuinely placing themselves in harm's way. At least once, Black was put there, too. "There was one episode where we had a knife thrower," Alterman says. "Tom and Kerri and Michael and them decided it would be such a funny bit if Mr. Laupin just cavalierly volunteers Johnny Blue Jeans to stand against the wall with all the balloons around him." The knife thrower explained that that was well within his skillset, and it would in fact not be dangerous, even if it looked like it was. "The main lawyer at Comedy Central was like, 'No way are we doing that!' So I remember getting into an argument with her and saying, 'You know, Michael is willing to do it, he'll sign a release.'" Still, they didn't budge.

"As a joke I remember saying to her, 'Sherry, imagine—I'm not saying I'm hoping for this—what if the worst thing that would happen was like he gets a knife into his arm or something. Can you imagine the publicity we're gonna get? The show will take off.' And she's like, 'I cannot believe you're suggesting that!'" Somehow, even after that, Alterman talked legal into letting it happen. "It was great because it just heightened the stakes, not just in terms of there's some danger there . . . but comedically it was just so well executed, because it wasn't Johnny Blue Jeans going, 'Hey, I'll do it;' it was Mr. Laupin, who just was abusive." Watching the scene now, it's remarkable

Black can keep any kind of character up, though it's quite clear he stuck to the script. "That knife thrower, I guarantee you, never did improv. It was a collision of different cultures, from different worlds, but they made it work in a way that it just felt really cohesive."

The show lucked out with great guest stars, too. In the knife-throwing episode, the guest is Ben Stiller. Moments away from being a movie star, despite an already considerable movie career, Stiller is brought in for the *Viva Variety* tribute to the show *Happy Days*, only all of the stars of the '70s sitcom have dropped out. Stiller, they hope, will be their Fonz. Begrudgingly, Stiller agrees to roll in on a motorcycle. Alterman recalls him trying to nail even this small bit. "I remember Ben saying, 'What do you think?' And they're like, 'Yeah, we got it. It's great. Let's move on.' He's like, 'I don't know. I feel like I could do one more. What if I did one more and I tried doing this?' and they're like, 'Sure.' He probably did that six or eight more times . . . I just got a little glimpse into the window of a super perfectionist craftsman who is not going to stop until he has it perfect."

For the third and final season, *Viva Variety* shot entirely in Las Vegas, after shooting in New York for two seasons. Alterman recalls wanting to see who they could get on the show if they were now in the middle of it all. "We thought this could be interesting. We're getting all these acts from Vegas, but why don't we go to the belly of the beast and really steep the show in the weirdness of Las Vegas. I would say the thing we probably didn't contemplate the most was, what is it like to live in the Las Vegas Hilton Hotel." The first episode of this new season is as big as promised, with a fantastic opening number featuring a new cast of the Swimsuit Squad (the show's dancers) and Johnny Blue Jeans bringing out his surfboard to go "hang ten" in this desert town.

"We did several episodes in Vegas with the Rockettes and four-tiered stages that would spin," says Kenney-Silver. "My hair was like a live bird cage. I mean, it was a dream come true for an actor who likes to sing and dance, but who's not very good at it . . . I would do that show again in a heartbeat." *Viva Variety*'s final episode aired on December 1, 1999, and not long after, papers were reporting that Fox had picked up a pilot about "life in the suburbs from the comedians who did Comedy Central's *Viva Variety*." By now, Herzog was President of Fox, so they had brought their next idea to him.

"That was the origin of *Reno* [*911!*]. Because I hired Ben and Kerri and Tom to create something and they did. And then I left Fox, and it died on the vine as a pilot. But Fox had fallen in love with them. That's what ultimately led to *Reno* getting developed through Fox." Herzog, like Lennon and Kenney-Silver, still has fond memories of *Viva Variety* as this show that realized a few people's entertainment dreams in one fell swoop.

"We were just actually talking to Doug Herzog recently," Kenney-Silver says. He's like, 'We have to get this back on. You guys have to do this again.' Because now we are the age of the characters that we were playing back then. I look back at clips of it, and I was like, twenty years old, playing a fifty-two-year-old woman faking this old smoker's accent and now I'm just that old crinkly lady. It would be perfect with like, waddly underarms in those dresses."

Herzog says, "I just loved the whole idea. I would do that show again, today. It's one of my favorite shows I ever did."

Not Another Pineapple: Improv Comes to TV

Sometime after the Upright Citizens Brigade opened their first theater in New York City, the group visited iO West in Los Angeles for the Chicago Improv Festival. Jim Wise was part of the group representing The Groundlings in this showcase of nationwide improv comedy. "We're all like short-form at The Groundlings. The people from UCB were before us; Besser says at the end of their show, he's like, 'If you're ever in New York, please come by our theater! We want to thank you all so much! You've been so supportive over all these years, and *long-form lives!*'" The crowd went nuts and the announcer at iO West then introduced The Groundlings. "He might as well have said 'and now the short-form comedy of The Groundlings.'" They then performed a parody of "Come Out and Play," by The Offspring. "It just didn't work."

Short-form improv certainly attracts audiences, but thanks to iO and UCB championing and evolving The Harold, long-form was becoming a viable entertainment alternative. If you don't want to see games and blackouts and—in some cases, anyway—joke-centric improv, The Harold is going to give you something a little more dense and layered. You're not likely to see a Harold on TV any time soon, though.

It is strangely impossible to write a history of sketch on TV in the '90s without addressing the elephant in the room. Improv was becoming too big to ignore, and for the first time ever, there were several attempts to bring short-form improv to TV. The entire landscape of television comedy in the '90s was already steeped in improv, so maybe it seemed logical. Most of the big-name performers and writers in TV comedy were either stand-ups, or trained improvisers, anyway, and improv does mean good business, when it's live and in person. On camera—outside of *Whose Line*—it rarely works.

Whenever an improviser asks an audience member for a suggestion for a thing to center the scene around, the most common suggestion, by far, is "pineapple." It could be because the word feels funny; it's multisyllabic, it has a couple of plosives in it. Whatever the reason, it is the last thing an improviser wants to hear, while at the same time the one thing they're all prepared for.

Kwik Witz

Kwik Witz, also known as *Quick Witz*, hit the airwaves in 1995, three years before *Whose Line*. Created by Steve Belkin and hosted by three hosts over the years—Jillian Hamilton, Andi Matheny, and Robin Nance—this heavily-improvised show featured four actors in each episode, in two teams. Each had team names like "The Comedy Pimps" or "Shaky at Best," and would compete for audience votes. The show's cold open would feature a single prop (like a mop or a loofah), and each performer had to do a physical gag with that prop and pass it to someone else.

While *Whose Line* would later subsist on quick bursts, *Kwik Witz* would start with some simple games but go into slightly longer scenes. They also did their own version of the *Whose Line* classic bit "Film Dub," where the actors come up with new dialogue for a clip from a crappy film. *Kwik Witz* also featured pre-taped, clearly scripted pieces between the improv with each of the teams, many of which were loaded with to-be-famous folks like Steve Carell, Jack McBrayer, Wayne Brady, Alex Borstein, Kevin Dorff, Jeff B. Davis, and improv legend T.J. Jagodowski.

"I put in my hours with Theatresports; I put in my hours with [my improv team] Houseful of Honkeys. We became really well known out here in that alt comedy niche," Wayne Brady says. "*Kwik Witz* was my foray into writing sketch. That's when I went, 'Oh, if I start off with this idea, I can blow it up into this scenario, and I can apply my skills and it can be funny.' No one had ever asked that of me before. So I'll always be thankful to Steve Belkin for that crazy little show that would come on after *SNL* at 1:30." Brady also discovered here that he was particularly good at musical pieces. "That really prepared me for the *Whose Line* audition later." Another performer got in through his high school pal, Jeff B. Davis.

"There were two guys that I remember from ComedySportz, Jeff Davis and Frank Maciel, that had started doing the show, I think fairly regularly, along with Wayne Brady and a few other people . . . [Jeff] brought me on because it would be two teams of two," recalls Matt Gourley. "He and Frank would have performed together but then they were doing so many shows that they started spicing it up a little and I did, I think, two episodes." The show was produced and distributed out of Chicago, but shot in LA, hence all of the LA actors. "I don't remember doing a good job. I can tell you that."

"I also remember it not really being all that improvised. It was fairly written and rehearsed and structured," Gourley says. The show had a big crane camera, the kind of bulky equipment you need to plan around, especially if it will be heading toward your actors' heads with any speed; they needed to hit their marks, so a little rehearsal would be necessary. "Like if you were doing a punch line, rapid-fire thing, you'd know what it is. It was this unspoken thing, if I remember correctly, where they'd say, 'It might be this, or it might be one of these two things,' so that the 'wink' was that they wanted you to prepare." Improv being new to TV, it shouldn't be surprising that the producers might not have full confidence in a format that was practically untested on camera.

The show ended in 1999, but one of the producers, Steve Belkin, had one more gig for the actors he'd plucked from ComedySportz, including Gourley and future *Superego* co-creator Jeremy Carter. "He had discovered a loophole in one of the major airlines' mileage programs," Gourley says. He paid each person $50 per trip to hop a short flight, then sign their miles over to him. "He would make more money in mileage than it would cost for the plane ticket. So there were a bunch of us flying sometimes three round trips a day." There were plenty of easy flights like this—LA to San Francisco, LA to Las Vegas— Gourley and Carter took the San Francisco flights because of the cool weather. "You'd just have flight attendants looking at you like, 'Why are you getting back on? Are you like a drug mule, what's going on?'" The airline eventually caught on to what was happening and settled with Belkin, who would go on to write a book about how he got forty million miles in a similar way.

Whose Line is it Anyway?

The original version of *Whose Line is it Anyway?* premiered in the UK on December 31, 1987. This likely pilot was eventually picked up, and the regular series premiered the following September. Created by Dan Patterson and Mark Leveson, *Whose Line*'s premise is simple: Everyone on stage is awarded points based on their improvisations. The UK version lasted for nine seasons, at which point the US version kicked off, featuring Ryan Stiles, Colin Mochrie, and Wayne Brady as recurring cast members. Most recently, a third incarnation has launched, with both new and classic cast.

"I was working at Universal Studios [Florida], doing the *Beetlejuice Rock and Roll Show*," brags Wayne Brady. He and his comedy group, Houseful of Honkeys, had already auditioned for *Whose Line* once before. "We were horrible. If somebody reading this gets offended, too damn bad, because you know that you were bad. I know that I was bad. We were horrible." That was the experience that could've turned him away from improv forever, outside of doing Theatresports for the fun of it. Between shows at Universal, he got a call from his agent asking him to audition for *Whose Line* again, with another giant roomful of people. "I'm making just as much money as somebody who's on Broadway. Why do I want to go to an audition that I know that I'm going to suck at?"

"Just go, Wayne." Wayne headed out on his lunch break, planning to get back to the rest of his shows at Universal that night. "I'm driving there in full Wolf Man makeup. I pull up to the audition, taking off the makeup, because I don't take it seriously. Because I'm laughing at myself. I'm like, 'This is some bullshit. I'm just gonna walk in and Dan and Mark are gonna send me home.'" During the audition, they quickly got to his least favorite game, "World's Worst," where a card tells you to make up the world's worst something. "It's like, 'Well, this is me going home.' But I did it. 'Oh shit, I actually said something funny!'" He knew he was going to miss his show at Universal, but it was worth it: When they got to the improvised songs, he shone. He'd been doing this kind of thing in his bedroom since he was a kid. They quickly cut the list down to two people: Brady and his SAK Theatresports compatriot, Clare Sera. Brady was on the American version of *Whose Line* not long after, hanging up the Wolf Man costume.

Brad Sherwood was given the inside scoop from Second City buddy Ryan Stiles (already a veteran of the UK show) that *Whose Line* would be casting in LA. "I basically had performed with and was friends with everybody that was in that audition. It was like *A Chorus Line*. It went on for three hours." Like Brady, Sherwood was the only one to make it all the way to the end, and eventually on to the show. There were other auditions, of course, so the show was already building up their LA contingent. "We went to a morning rehearsal just to run through so that everybody sort of knew the structure of the games and scenes that they were going to do on the show. We were all hung over—it was 11 AM—we were just in a little rehearsal space, fucking around, not really thinking we had to try too hard." One of the other new cast members was sent back home to Australia because this was, apparently, not fuck-around time.

Whose Line, despite of and because of its longevity and ubiquity, is not a universally-loved phenomenon in the improv world. "A lot of people look on short-form as sort of where you start out, but then you graduate to doing something a little more 'elevated,'" says Sherwood. The show is, of course, all games. No stories, not a lot of time to build any sort of character, and definitely focused on the joke. "But, you know, there's no way to put long-form improv on television. You know, this is kind of like Warner Brothers cartoons with humans. This is what it's supposed to be. It's supposed to be goofy and silly."

Instant Comedy with The Groundlings

For one brief shining moment, American TV had three improv shows airing at the same time. One of them was on the still-young FX network, and featured The Groundlings—mostly current members, but with visitors from the past, like Lisa Kudrow and Phil LaMarr. "For a while it looked like they were gonna go with Chip Esten, who went on to be on the show *Nashville*," recalls Jim Wise. "He's great-looking, a really good actor, and a really good improviser. He's really an aggravating person. He definitely has it all." The main cast was going to be Esten (who now goes by Charles), Michael McDonald, Amy von Freymann, Brian Palermo, and Mindy Sterling. "And then Chip I think got a TV show. And they're like, 'Who's our low-rent Chip?'"

The schedule for *Instant Comedy with The Groundlings* was grueling. They'd shoot at The Groundlings Theatre, all day, trying to get enough material for five shows. They shot for thirteen weeks, gathering up sixty-five full episodes of footage, which would be cut down to a few half-hour shows. It took its toll on everyone, with some of the actors on edge even while on stage, when you're expected to be loose. One actor took a suggestion and used it to rib one of the other actors on stage. "'Cut, cut, cut! Are you gonna let him say that?' Like, it would have been a fight on TV. Everybody was a little frayed."

Combine the overworked stress with the fact that one of The Groundlings, Michael McDonald, had just started on *MADtv*. "He had had a taste of a network show," Wise recalls. "I remember him sitting next to me, and bitterly saying, 'I never want to work at this level again.'"

Instant Comedy was as close to seeing a Groundlings show live as you could get on TV. While The Groundlings does do long-form, like *The Crazy Uncle Joe Show*, you can see plenty of short-form there, too, and the TV version reflected that experience. It was a mix of games and short scenes, and the producers made sure to find room for the one thing that always brings the house down—on *Whose Line*, too—musical improv. Wise was particularly adept at mimicry, and his Led Zeppelin-style songs wowed the room on numerous episodes. While it only lasted a season, *Instant Comedy with The Groundlings* remains the only TV show to make a weekly showcase of something approaching real live improv, from one of the best-known schools in the world.

— 28 —

Hit and Run Comedy: Upright Citizens Brigade

Matt Besser moved to Chicago in 1990 to be in his own sketch show. He was doing stand-up at the time and wanted to find other like minds to form his own Kids in the Hall. "I didn't even know what improv was when I moved to Chicago. I didn't understand the concept of it. I'd seen *SCTV* and knew it had something to do with Second City in Chicago, but I didn't get any kind of improv link." When he finally saw a Second City show, he thought it was corny, and the improv at the end he thought was worse. He was then told to check out the ImprovOlympic, where he saw in the same show Tim Meadows, Dave Koechner, Chris Farley, and the to-be-legendary team, Blue Velveeta.

"I think they're cheating, I think it's bullshit. I'm like, 'You guys totally must've written that.' I went up to someone after the show. I forget who it was, I think it might've been Koechner. And I was like, 'Come on, buddy. You guys just came up with that song?'" Besser insisted the song must've been written before they came out on stage. "'And the fat guy won, right? He won the night, right?' Like, I thought there was a winner, and I had declared Chris Farley the winner." After being explained there was no "winner," he asked who the team captain was. "It was just funny how little of a concept I understood, but like a lot of other people [I was] discovering that what was *really* happening in Chicago wasn't Second City."

Ian Roberts had been acting in Milwaukee, trying to get into the bigger theater companies in town, like The Milwaukee Rep and Theater Tesseract, but couldn't crack them. He thought about his options, knew he could do improv, and decided he'd head to Second City. "I had this vague sense that Second City used improvisation. So in my mind, I thought I'd get there, and within a few months, I'd audition and I'd be in Second City, and Second City leads to *Saturday Night Live*. I thought that would be my career." He auditioned twice, and while his improv skills were clear, he didn't have the three requisite characters you needed to potentially shine on their stage. He still checked out every comedy space he could, wandered into the basement space where iO was, and sat down to watch the show.

"It starts with about eight people just sort of wandering around on stage, saying a word at a time. So like, 'butterfly,' 'flower,' 'garden,' 'Garden of Eden,' 'Adam,' 'Eve,' and I'm like, 'What the fuck is this?' And I'm really just thinking, 'How quickly can I sneak out without being insulting? Because this is strange.'" As it turns out, this was how they were opening the Harold at the time, with a word association game that slowly led into the first scene. "Then they stop wandering around saying one word at a time and doing this word association. They start doing scenes, and I'm like, 'Oh, okay, this is what I like to do.' They're just starting from nothing and coming up with a scene." He stuck around long enough to watch another show, this time featuring David Koechner and Kevin Dorff. "Instantly, boom, this is what I've been looking for. I gotta get in this place."

Roberts started classes at iO and got on the house team quickly, alongside Besser, who eventually jumped ship and went to another team, The Family (known as "The Victim's Family" until the tragic death of member Rick Roman). Rich Fulcher was also involved in The Family, if only briefly, as he says happened often with members of iO. "Charna did this all the time. She would put you on with The Family, and you were thinking that you were on The Family, and you weren't. And The Family would get so pissed off." When the Upright Citizens Brigade starting truly becoming a thing, there were a lot of members and potential members, but at least they could control who came and who went. The original three members of the Upright Citizens Brigade were Besser, Adam McKay, and Ian Roberts.

"The very first sketch show where we used the name Upright Citizens Brigade, the name of the show was 'Virtual Reality,'" Besser says. "This is in 1990, '91, when most people don't even know what that word is. I was reading William Gibson, and really into *Neuromancer* and all that kind of shit." In character as the all-seeing Upright Citizens Brigade, they would bring audience members up onstage, and create scenes inspired by them. "We liked the concept of that group so much, we kept that as a thread through our other shows." Besser, McKay, and Roman were all fascinated by secret societies, conspiracies and numerology, seeing the obvious comic potential. Roman even hoped to start a religion called "The Temple of Industrial Leisure," a concept he developed (and wrote pamphlets for) with McKay. Beyond the onstage live presentation, they wanted to use videotaped elements and to bring the audience outside the theater as part of their shows.

"We're all specifically fans of *Kids in the Hall*, and we saw the route they'd gone, and it seemed like, if they could do it, why can't we do something like that?" Besser says. Other actors would show up and be part of UCB early on, too, including Amy Poehler, Matt Walsh, Neil Flynn, Susan Messing, Rick Roman, Laura Krafft, Rich Fulcher, and Horatio Sanz. "Comedy Central was also becoming more of a thing about that time, and it seemed like a logical place for sketch shows to end up."

While the group was certainly made up of iO alums, iO was not their space. "We never did one UCB show at the ImprovOlympic until right before we left for New York," Besser says. They were a unit, but a comedy group in Chicago has its choice of theaters. Not that any one theater would necessarily remain their only venue, even for an individual show. "We used to fuck with the audience," remembers Roberts. "There was one show that ended with us taking them out to Adam McKay's apartment, which was two or three blocks away from the theater, looking through the window of the apartment and having them witness a murder. Then a car pulls up, and we get Pillsbury dough, like to make croissants or whatever, and throw it at the audience, and get in the car and never end the show. We just drive away and the people go back to the theater, or don't."

"There was one where they staged an accidental hit and run," remembers Fulcher. The idea started with a Thanksgiving dinner between four people, each on their own corner of an intersection at North Avenue in Chicago. They'd pass food across this four-lane road and play the scene as though nothing was out of the ordinary. "At one point, we have a family argument," Roberts says. "Horatio Sanz would angrily cross the street, and then Adam McKay would hit him with my little Ford Festiva . . . Then everyone would run over and he would jump up, somebody would hit a boombox and start playing some clips of music, and Horatio would pull flowers out from under his shirt, and then we'd all dance back in the theater." Back in the theater, one of the video pieces they would play during the show was a virtual road trip, which is interrupted by the very accident the audience has just seen, from inside the car. Not easy in an era of VHS editing.

As TV sketch of the early '90s was trying to be edgy without being successfully subversive, the Upright Citizens Brigade was leaning toward the strictly subversive, through stealthy commitment to bits. Like when Adam McKay announced via fliers around Chicago that he was going to commit suicide. "This whole thing came downstream of Adam McKay getting headshots done [where] he thought he looked like a jackass," Roberts says.

"So we make up these flyers with that big smiley face, and it's like a suicide note. It's a guy saying, 'Hey, this is Adam McKay. I'm gonna kill myself. This is no fucking joke. I'm done.' And we plaster these up all over Chicago." They found a tall building near where they were putting their next show on and spoke to the owner of the building. "'Can we do something where we throw a dummy off your roof?' He's like 'Yeah, okay.'" McKay played it real and threw the dummy off, to the absolute pleasure of one audience member: Del Close, the group's mentor.

New York

Jake Fogelnest condenses it all nicely. "The UCB showed up to New York City and said, 'Hi, we're the Upright Citizens Brigade. We're going to start doing shows. We're going to do this long-form improv. We're going to get our own television show. We're going to open a theater and a school.' And New York just went, 'Yeah, that sounds great.' And that's what they did."

During the years that UCB was starting up, Besser was still doing stand-up, and now had a manager, who had booked him to write on a pilot for MTV VJ Kennedy, while also performing the warm-up comedy for the show. "I'd pretend to be her guest and just improvise and do characters, and do too much, really. But the MTV people saw me." This became Besser's first opportunity to pitch something, but he had nothing in his back pocket, at least not for himself alone. "Well, I don't have an idea for me. I got this thing called Upright Citizens Brigade. And I'd show them these shitty VHS tapes of us on stage and the shit we did out in the streets. I can only imagine what was going through their head[s] when I would show them these things." It wasn't something they could commit to in the room, so they told Besser that he should bring the group to New York and do some showcases.

With no internet, having someone in the room to see you was a necessity, but asking a whole group to uproot from 800 miles away was a huge request. At one point, they got MTV to come see their live show, "Thunderball," in Chicago, which only furthered their interest, if not their commitment. "So when we came out there it was with a very specific goal to put on showcases, and sell it as a pilot. I think we said we'll give ourselves a year. I don't know what happens after a year, then we self-destruct." The final piece of the puzzle was cementing the lineup. "Amy and Walsh didn't officially join the group until right before we left for New York."

With consistently sold out shows in Chicago and all of this motivation from a huge cable network, the group officially committed to the New York move in 1996. When they arrived, they felt pretty good about their chances. They saw some of the other sketch offerings at the time and weren't concerned. "Comedy Central, MTV, everyone else, they may not like us, but it's not because they like someone else." They would put on their showcases, as well as improv shows, at various places around town, starting at KGB Bar. Their form of improv pretty closely mirrored their now long-running show ASSSSCAT, the long-form improv show that sprouts from a monologue.

Their main live show was still very much what the TV show would end up becoming. The framework of four members of an underground cabal who "look for chaos and create chaos where there is none"— Antoine (Roberts), Colby (Poehler), Trotter (Walsh), and Adair (Besser)—allowed for sketches to be disparate in tone, while also slowly bringing them together, thematically, like a Harold.

Like anyone else, though, they needed jobs, which is where *Late Night with Conan O'Brien* came in, from their existing Chicago connections. They also all received their first TV writing and acting credits for a show that never aired, and which sort of starred Jimmy Stewart. *It's a Wonderful Life* had fallen out of copyright at the time, but due to a loophole, the soundtrack and story were still owned by an extant company. Kent Alterman wanted to chop the copyright-free visuals up and give them new sound effects and dialogue. "I brought the UCB members in to help write, but also to voice all of the parts. We really wanted to be sophisticated about trying to match lip sync. The four members of the UCB were just geniuses at improvising, writing lines, but also recording it." It would have aired on Comedy Central, but Viacom, their parent company, also owned the company who had an exclusive and lucrative deal with NBC to air *It's a Wonderful Life* they didn't want to screw up.

In February of 1998, UCB won the best sketch group jury prize in the US Comedy Arts Festival at Aspen. Being there meant the possibility of a TV deal—doing this well probably sealed the deal. "I will brag and say that it was our Super Bowl, and we killed it," Besser says. "I don't even know if Comedy Central would have bought us if we hadn't have done great because it was such a concept, this underground group. Like I think they more wanted us just to be a sketch show."

The Upright Citizens Brigade on TV

Before he ever got them to destroy *It's a Wonderful Life*, Kent Alterman was in an audience in a New York show. "They randomly picked me. I still remember Matt Besser going, 'Sir. What's your name?' I go, 'Kent.' 'What do you do for a living?' I just made something up because I don't want to tell him I work for Comedy Central. I think I said, 'I do landscaping.' And he goes, 'Ah, landscaping, you're trying to alter the environment.'" They put a helmet on Alterman's head and interrogated him in a chair on stage. He loved the conspiratorial element of the show, and the idea of their inner sanctum, as well as the show itself. "My feeling was, unless you're *SNL*, it's really hard to have a sketch show where you just live or die by how funny each sketch is. So we need some controlling idea that gives it almost like a narrative engine or something that distinguishes it." He also liked that they had a core group with a strong shared sensibility. He attended every Sunday night ASSSSCAT performance he could.

"They used that ASSSSCAT show to generate almost all the material," remembers Alterman. "They would have these improvisational scenes and then they would come back in the writers' room and figure out, 'Which ones can we use that will thematically weave together to be an episode of the UCB sketch show?'" Some of the ideas went through the normal sketch writers' room experience, coming from an outside idea and developing it in the room. Besser estimates that most five-minute improvs would yield four or five lines that could have some life in a fully-formed sketch. "It's been proven to be funny already. So I'm taking that line, I'm gonna put that line in the script, but then the rest of the script is more extrapolating and making it tighter than it was in the improv."

Where each show would go depended on the improv and the tightness of the writing, but a few things were in place. The UCB characters would frame the show, and the show's narrator would be Del Close. They also wanted the pieces with the uniformed UCB to have a definite sci-fi look. Animation director Jon Schnepp was hired to direct the framing segments for the pilot, because they thought his visual style jibed with the material they'd written for the interstitials. Other than some of them appearing on *Late Night with Conan O'Brien*, though, the group was still relatively new to working in front of cameras.

"We wanted chaotic images in the opening," Roberts says. "One image that we thought would be great was a guy sitting in his living room like a zombie watching TV while his house was on fire." They knew full-well they couldn't put an actor on a flaming set; they weren't out to kill anyone. They decided to shoot outdoors and just have a flat (a stage wall) behind the actor (a student) and they'd instead light that flat on fire. They headed out to New Jersey, with no permit, painted a flat with some rubber cement, put their actor in front of it, and set the flat on fire. "Matt Walsh is at the side, watching it just letting him know, 'The flames aren't close to you. You're okay, you're okay.' And this guy's going, 'It's really hot!' [Walsh says], 'You're good, you're good.' And at one point, he notices that the skin on his neck is bubbling."

They told the actor to leave the shot, and then realized they had nothing with them to put out the flames. "So people start getting handfuls of dirt and water bottles and sprinkling water on it and throwing dirt on this fire." They got a friend with access to a private jet to slap a magnetized UCB sticker on a plane so they could get footage of a UCB plane landing, borrowed the motorboat of one of their agents at the time, and then wanted to have Besser get into a helicopter while holding a fetal pig. Their solution was to book a helicopter tour and go for it. "So [Matt] shows up with this fetal pig in a bag or a box, dressed up in his costume, and then pulls it out the last minute. The guy gets the camera up, and he runs on and then I think just said, 'Yeah, we don't want to take the tour.' Either that or the [pilot] said, 'Get out of here, you're not getting on this helicopter with your freakin' pig.'"

Originally, the TV show was going to have a live audience; in an unusual twist, this was at the request of the show's stars. "We really strongly felt we wanted to perform in front of a live audience. And we did, and we hated it," Roberts says. They weren't used to single-camera shooting, and when they had to shoot in a real school bus for the pilot, all of the waiting really made them hate the process, at least in the beginning. Still, much as they craved that audience reaction, they moved away from having live reactions, and refused to have a laugh track. Alterman also recalls having to make sure that all this subversiveness still fit into a mold, even if it was a mold the UCB had to create themselves.

"There was always a little bit of tension, and obstacles that we had to overcome to maintain the integrity of what we set up. It was challenging. I remember from season one to season two, we tried to tweak it so we had a little more freedom . . . what's the best way to do this, that gives us the strongest controlling idea and premise, but not at the expense of being funny and contriving things to fit." Where *Mr. Show's* main stress point was the links, *The Upright Citizens Brigade* leaned right into zooming in and out of screens. It was the thematic layering and crossover that meant the most to their vision.

Jake Fogelnest went from being a real-life Wayne Campbell with *Squirt TV* to learning, performing, teaching, and at one point being the artistic director of the UCB Theatre in New York. Once the theater opened in 1999, the show now had a pool of skilled performers to pull from, often for extra/background work. A little TV work was intended recompense for performing at all hours for nothing. "There was a hundred of us, we're all doing this, and we're all doing it for no money. We're staying up until two, three o'clock in the morning, putting on sketch shows and improv shows. And at the same time, the UCB, they're barely getting paid, but they're doing a Comedy Central show. So they would always try to use us." It wasn't unlike the kind of work the original UCB were getting on *Late Night with Conan O'Brien* when they needed to avoid day jobs, or the jobs Charna Halpern at iO would find for people. You can find Jake, Paul Scheer and dozens more UCB folks in the background of UCB episodes.

There are numerous standout sketches among their three seasons. One of the most famous is probably "Ass Pennies," about a self-assured businessman whose confidence comes from knowing that the tens of thousands of pennies he's put in his ass over the years have probably been handled by people he does business with. The sketch in which a Besser character does everything through a hole in a sheet in order to justify terrible habits with religious dogma stands out as something you can easily picture him— and him alone—performing onstage. There's a sketch in which a con man installs every manner of bell, alarm and notification in a home, each containing a recording of long-dead disc jockey Wolfman Jack, which leads almost nowhere and yet is a delight to behold.

Watching an entire episode all the way through can be anxiety inducing because of how raw some of the sketches are played. Even if there's a goofy wig, crazy makeup or an insane premise, there's a legitimately unsettling layer of reality on the face of each UCB member. Roberts felt that a laugh track would kill how subversive the show is, and he's right. The commitment is what makes you question your reality just enough while watching it, especially as they occasionally pull off continuations of their sketches in hidden camera segments, amongst the populace.

The UCB Theatre

During the second season of the show, UCB nailed down a permanent location for their own theater and school. Since then, the likes of Kate McKinnon, Donald Glover, Aubrey Plaza, Ben Schwartz, Lennon Parham, Bobby Moynihan, and D'Arcy Carden have studied and performed there, honing their craft. Even by 1999, while New York City had other options, those places weren't exactly competitive with UCB. Will Hines trained and eventually taught there before moving to LA to work in TV. "The preexisting comedy communities were like Gotham City Improv and Chicago City Limits, and they did not encourage a community. They sold classes and they sold tickets to their shows, and if you were a student, you got discounted or free tickets to shows, but there was no hanging out after a Chicago City Limits class." UCB put on shows every night of the week where tickets cost $5 or were otherwise free. "No other theater had free and cheap shows that you could form a social life around."

"The UCB was a school that had a recital stage, which was the theater, that, just because the students were so good, that recital stage was as good as a comedy theater." The performances, as they do at any other improv theater, serve a double purpose. "The shows were advertisements for the classes, and the classes is what kept the place afloat . . . that's a real delicate balancing act that they get enough people from their classes onto their stage, that the student body is satisfied that justice has been served. And they're not just being ripped off of their money." Like iO before it, UCB is a place that finds work for people and, of course, it wasn't long before industry started scouting shows for new faces.

During their *Late Night with Conan O'Brien* years, Ian Roberts performed in a sketch with Nipsey Russell. "He said something that's stuck with me to this day. He said, 'In Hollywood, they've got 1,000 copy machines and one typewriter.' That was his way to say there's very little innovation, and a lot of copying what succeeds. That's why I've always thanked Kent Alterman, because I don't think getting behind our show was obvious that this was some home run success. He just legitimately liked it himself and had the strength of his convictions."

With an emphasis on long-form improv, as well as its own aesthetic that comes from decades of evolution from that four-headed beast, UCB could have been in danger of producing copy machines themselves. If there is a "UCB style" of improv, it is one that rewards individual thinking combined with team play, with a particular focus on the creation of the worlds that characters inhabit, just as those characters are being created themselves. Getting into the weeds just to pull yourself out of them is what the UCB Harold is all about.

The core members of The Upright Citizens Brigade never made a movie based off of their show, though they did produce two feature films, entitled *Wild Girls Gone* and *Martin and Orloff*. Each of the four has gone on to perhaps varying levels of fame but undeniable impact in the world of comedy, with Poehler going to *SNL* and *Parks and Recreation*, Roberts show-running *Key & Peele*, and Besser and Walsh appearing on every show under the sun. The hundreds of actors and writers who have gone through their schools in LA and New York are on a figuratively uncountable number of shows and movies. All of this, just because Matt Besser once thought you could win at improv.

. . . And the Rest:
Every Other Sketch Show (Nearly)
of the '90s

I sent out around 500 requests to speak with people for this book. These requests ran the gamut— everything from sketch shows that saw a season, to shows that shot a pilot, down to shows that only got as far as a script. I was intending to be comprehensive, which I'm now realizing borders on impossible, unless you want a 1,000-page book. The number of people out there who have completed sketch pilots is pretty much unknowable, as well, but even for shows that did make it, there's not a ton of information out there, except in the heads of the people I tried—and would still love—to interview. Stephen Colbert, if you're reading this, please let Amy Sedaris know it would be an honor to speak with her for the next edition.

Here are a few brief histories on certain shows, or anecdotes that I found particularly illuminating about some of the shows I got to dig into. Many of these deserve their own chapters or books (including shows I absolutely love), but due to space constraints, I had to make some tough decisions. Here are eighteen additional '90s sketch and sketch-adjacent shows, in brief.

All That

While I'm a few years too old to have watched this show when it first aired, I am well-aware of its fan base, and that of its spinoff movie, *Good Burger*. Like a few of these shows, it could easily fill a book, especially given that it launched the career of *SNL*'s longest-serving cast member, Kenan Thompson. Danny Tamberelli, best known as Little Pete on Nickelodeon's *The Adventures of Pete & Pete*, found himself on *All That* when he was fifteen. Two years later, he partnered up with Mark Saul—they were seventeen and fourteen, respectively—to write a sketch and see if the producers would put it on the air.

"We wrote it, we gave it to one of the writers, and they thought it was pretty good. And they're like, 'Okay, we're going to show you how to kind of flesh out the sketch more.'" After his three hours of required tutoring each day, and extensive rehearsal, they would head into the writers' room to pitch, and from 1999 to 2000, Tamberelli was consistently in the writers' room. Throughout *All That*'s run, the room was open to the kids. "I feel like the fabric of the show, while totally produced and put together and created by the crew, has everyone's little idiosyncrasies throughout."

Exit 57

It was almost called "Strangers with Candy," "White Leg," "The Day Room," or "Strange Rituals." It's a sketch show with big theater kid vibes. The world's biggest fan of this show is Matthew McConaughey. In fact, he re-enacted the *Exit 57* sketch "Forecast" with Stephen Colbert on *The Late Show* in 2018, quite possibly from memory. The show starred and was written by Colbert, Amy Sedaris, Paul Dinello, Jodi Lennon, and Mitch Rouse and was the continuation of a comedy partnership that started in Chicago. Rich Fulcher recalls the group's sendoff party as the first time he'd seen a Chicago group not just shoot for *SNL*, instead making their own stuff. "They went off to New York, and we were thinking, 'Oh, my god, doing *this*, you can actually like, do other things.'"

The show was directed by Mick Napier, founder of Annoyance in Chicago. "I went to New York City to play pool in the 1994 Gay Olympics, the Gay Games." He spent his non-competitive time visiting his friends, and watching them develop the show, since they'd just come to New York from Chicago. "Just through that, they asked me if I wanted to work on it and I'm like, 'Fuck, okay.'" He stuck around in New York and directed the show, while also directing an off-Broadway show by David Sedaris and editing a film. He helped punch the sketches up, while writing four of his own, and still isn't entirely sold on the "director" title. The first season was a lot of consulting, with Napier in a sort of artistic director function, and the second season there was a union issue with their real director, so the title went to Napier. "I directed people, but I didn't technically direct the television show. So it was just kind of mixed up that way. I would consider myself more like a creative director or a liaison between the producers and the actors. Or maybe in some ways, the head writer."

The Uptown Comedy Club

Kevin Brown would end up better known as "Dotcom" on *30 Rock*, but in the late '80s, he was booking comedy shows with hip-hop music, and from 1992 to 1994, his showcases were on TV. Comedians like Tracy Morgan, Debra Wilson, and Chris Tucker would find their way to *The Uptown Comedy Club* before we'd see them make their big breaks. Sketches, like the stand-up and music, were performed on a cramped stage in front of an enthusiastic audience and were staged as barebones as possible. It wasn't about the costumes or the lack of props; it was all big characters.

"On any given show, you would look in the audience and there's young Big Daddy Kane, young Tupac," recalls Brown. The show ran in syndication, and kept drawing new and established names; for season two, their head writer was Paul Mooney. Even before they went to TV, though, they were getting the attention of all kinds of producers. "This rap mogul dude wanted to get into comedy, so somebody brought him to my club and introduced me to him and he shook my hand and he said, 'I have this idea for a TV show. All you got to do is sit back and collect your checks. We're gonna produce this show together.'" The producer and their people brought a camera with them and shot footage all over the club. "So when you watch *Def Comedy Jam*, that was my club. The same way my DJ [Kid Capri] was in the back, elevated. The same way they were sitting auditorium style. What he did was he created the television version of the Uptown Comedy Club. So a lot of people don't know. Even when you watch *Def Comedy Jam*, you're watching *The Uptown Comedy Club*. You're watching what we created there on 125th Street."

Brown also recalls *In Living Color* running auditions at his club. "Bring a character, bring a sketch, bring a whatever. There was a lot of controversy backstage in the comedy world because sketches that people auditioned with turned out to be a sketch that they used on the show that they didn't compensate that young artist for." He's also aware of the parallels between his pioneering combination of hip-hop music and comedy and *In Living Color*'s set up. "They absolutely saw that was the way to do it. But I mean, there's nothing wrong with that, right? You see creativity and you build on it. That's the name of the game, right?"

She TV

At one point called "The Better Sex Show," but renamed because testing discovered people assumed it was about being more proficient in the sack, *She TV* was a 1994 summer replacement series starring (mostly) women. Why women couldn't have done drag is unclear. *She TV* was created by Tamara Rawitt, producer of *In Living Color*. It was an hour-long sketch show which combined live and pre-taped sketches, seemingly mostly to allow actor crossover between subsequent sketches. The show starred Jennifer Coolidge, *3rd Rock from the Sun*'s Simbi Kali, Becky Thyre, Linda Wallem, and Linda Kash, with Nick Bakay and Elon Gold as the two men.

The show's first episode opens with two exotic dancers (Kash and Wallem), singing a classical song backstage, quickly becoming a beautiful harmony. They find out that one of them had to perform it at her Juilliard audition, the other for a car commercial. A simple statement about not underestimating what you see when all you see is what you see. Wallem also plays then Attorney General Janet Reno, explaining the ethos of *She TV*: that it will "examine the issues that women face each day." She then goes on to say the show is "sort of like *Up with People*, only not so much like a cult."

She TV also features "SHENN," a news parody segment, and a segment in which Mrs. Beavis (Kash) and Mrs. Butthead (Coolidge) play the moms of cartoon characters Beavis and Butthead. The show does as it promises, so that even when it leans into a stereotype it still manages to examine it from a female perspective. The men are utility players, occasionally there to represent the idea of maleness, like an *NYPD Blue* parody in which Bakay plays David Caruso's character, who pretends to listen to and care about the women in the precinct, until one of them (Coolidge) stands up for herself, at which point he blames her perceived attitude on her period.

Rawitt had hopes for doing with *She TV* for the female perspective what she had helped do for the black perspective, through *In Living Color*. "The reason *In Living Color* was the success it was is because the network just left us alone to do what we knew how to do. That's why it was successful." With *She TV*, the typical network notes and interference didn't help. She also believes that *She TV* didn't have one designated point of view. "There were too many cooks in the kitchen. The show didn't have a singular voice, and that's why it tanked." Though Rawitt does stress that she's proudest of having found Jennifer Coolidge for the cast.

While the sketches aren't always the most tightly written (a '50s filmstrip parody about a young girl discovering she's attracted to girls drifts between "being gay is okay" and "ha, ha, look at the butch gym teacher"), the show was unique for its casting of mostly women, even if it was a heavily male writers' room. Coolidge would later go on to star in the short-lived 1996 Fox sketch series *Saturday Night Special*, in which we were asked to watch Roseanne watch other people in a sketch before suddenly remembering she has lines.

Roundhouse

Roundhouse was a themed sketch show for kids, shot all at once like it was in a theater, with moving sets and constant action, and it was the brainchild of some experienced theater producers, including Buddy Sheffield, head writer for *In Living Color*. Sheffield took time during that hit series to produce the TV version of something he and his ex-wife Rita Sheffield Hester had been working together on for years, called *Cheap Theatrics*. "Young adults acting for kids, performing all over America, in little vignettes and sketches," recalls Sheffield Hester. The show had started in the '70s, and evolved over the years as they toured the US, playing places like the John F. Kennedy Center and the Detroit Institute of Arts. "The plays were written by Buddy Sheffield and his brother, David Sheffield. David broke off first by getting hired for *Saturday Night Live*."

"We wanted to reflect pop culture and what their lives were like. So it was very topical," Sheffield Hester says. *Roundhouse* was a '90s take on *Cheap Theatrics*, with a set reminiscent of *In Living Color*. They hired triple-threat kids and young adults ranging from their teens to late twenties, to put on half-hour shows that were, if not one take, shot as though they were, with sets moving in and out in real time to accommodate new sketches. The themes were meant to be relevant and helpful to kids, like "Justice," "Nobody's Perfect," and "Feminism." They kept the comedy going in a way that managed to avoid being patronizing, even if the energy of a bunch of kids fresh from the Jim Carrey School of Comedy can be a lot (you can't blame them, he was everywhere).

The Sheffields showcased it for a while, and each company interested wanted to change something about it—make it a sitcom, make it improv—but Buddy's influence helped them keep their vision. They invited Nickelodeon to come see it, but they were no-shows. "Our agent one day was just in his office, and Herb Scannell from Nickelodeon walked in and said, 'Hey, do you do you have any clients with a kids' show?'" The pilot was shortly greenlit and the show would go on to do four seasons.

"We treated it like a live of event." Scripts were finished Monday, there was a full rehearsal with singing and dancing and blocking. "On Friday, we shot the show, live-to-tape in front of an audience. I didn't stop the show at all, except for the little brief commercials, like thirty-second spots." All this without cue cards. Typical of *Roundhouse*, their final episode was about endings, an opportunity to remind kids that nothing is permanent, in the most fun way possible.

Tracey Takes On...

In 1996, Tracey Ullman's new sketch series launched on HBO, giving the chameleon actor the budget for wigs, travel and make-up—sometimes too much, and a lot of it beyond inappropriate—to tell interweaving stories of some of her favorite characters. Don Scardino (who took over for Victor Garber in the famous *Godspell* production in Toronto) directed the pilot and nine episodes of *Tracey Takes On...*

"What Alan McKeown and Tracey wanted to do was to take these characters that worked so well in sketch comedy on Fox, and put it into a context that was more like a comedy movie." One of the keys to the show that they worked out in the development process was having characters overlap and interact. "It's more of a world of

Tracey's, that gives us a context that we can play in terms of film, which makes everything literal, as opposed to tape . . . the fact that we're in on the joke that these are all Tracey in different getups, that allowed us to play broadly enough to make the comedy work."

In order to make the crossovers function on camera, they needed—at the very least—an actor who could hide under the same makeup Ullman did, serving as a body double for when she was interacting with her own characters. Who they found was Salli Saffioti, a skilled mimic in her own right. She had booked a small part of a jury foreman on an episode of *Takes On. . .*, when Ullman approached her about her nice shirt. Safiotti had spent time working in fashion in New York.

"It was like a high end designer shirt because the designer couldn't afford to pay me, so she would give me clothes," Saffioti says. Ullman kindly said she hoped to see Saffioti back on set. Between shooting and the beginning of the next season, Saffioti had dropped her agent. "I was kind of destitute. I was like, oh, no, like, should I get out of this business? Like, is this the end of my everything?" She soon got a call that she was a "corporate request" to audition for the show. They sent a messenger to her house with a pile of VHS tapes and scripts and told her to pick five of Ullman's characters to learn. She'd been preparing for this her whole life; her dad was a bus driver in Queens, and when she'd have to sit with him on his route, she'd pick up accents and dialects along the way, *a la* a young Sid Ceasar.

Despite her skill, the producers weren't convinced. They had every conceivable part of her face scrutinized to figure out how the prosthetics might fit and didn't feel she was right. They brought Ullman down to play a high-stakes version of the mirror game, and Ullman was convinced. "They were like, 'Tracey, it's not gonna work. Look at her jaw. Look at her.' She says to her people, 'That's your problem to figure out.' And then she's like, 'We're good. I'll see you soon.'"

Director Penelope Sphe-
eris and Dana Carvey
on the set of *Wayne's World*.

The *Wayne's World* theatrical poster.

Andy Richter and Co-
nan O'Brien have
a conversation with Pimp-
bot 5000 (Brian McCann).

Conan O'Brien adjusts
his rearview mirror
in a promotional image.

*H*ouse of Buggin' cast—clockwise from top left: Tammi Cubilette, Jorge Luis Abreu, Luis Guzmán, Yelba Osorio, David Herman, and John Leguizamo.

A solo promotional shot of John Leguizamo.

*L*eguizamo and David Herman in a game show sketch.

MADtv cast photo—clockwise from top left: David Herman, Mary Scheer, Will Sasso, Phil LaMarr, Nicole Sullivan, Debra Wilson, and Aries Spears.

Debra Wilson appears as Oprah Winfrey.

Mo Collins as Doreen Larkin, Michael McDonald as Stuart Larkin, and Will Sasso.

Mr. *Show with Bob and David* promo photo—David Cross and Bob Odenkirk.

From "The Biggest Failure in Broadway History"—John Ennis, Bob Odenkirk, David Cross, and Mary Lynn Rajskub (left to right).

From "What to Think"—Jack Black (2nd from left), David Cross (3rd from left), and Bob Odenkirk (center).

Dana Carvey holds up a novelty check from Taco Bell as the first sponsor of *The Dana Carvey Show*.

Dana Carvey promotional shot.

The Bert Fershners outside of KGB in the East Village—from left to right: Josh Lewis, Dan Fleming, Joey Garfield, Chris Tallman, Mike Rock, Mark Hervey, and Dan Berrett.

Viva Variety cast photo: Michael Ian Black, Thomas Lennon, and Kerri Kenney-Silver.

Viva Variety solo shot of Kerri Kenney-Silver.

The Upright Citizens Brigade: Matt Walsh, Matt Besser, Ian Roberts, and Amy Poehler.

A̶my Poehler as Colby from *Upright Citizens Brigade*

Behind the scenes of *The Idiot Box*—clockwise from left: Lee Arenberg, Alex Winter, Krista Montagna-Gordon, and Tom Stern.

Tom Stern as Carol Channing and Alex Winter as Willard Shreck.

Deep Dish TV cast photo–clockwise from top left: Linda White, Bill Evashwick, Kerry Phillips, Tom Sheeter, Antoinette Stella, Paul Chepikian, and Tony Nassour.

*B*ehind the scenes at Nickelodeon's *Roundhouse*—from left to right: Norma Gross, Sheila R. Lawrence.

Keegan-Michael Key on a flying rig from *Key & Peele*.

Key & Peele cast and crew shot from "It's Happenin'."

The Higgins Boys and Gruber

The Comedy Channel was, for its brief lifespan, an incredibly free-form, if nearly impossible-to-find cable network that played comedy all day, often with interstitials from presenters, sometimes in character. *The Higgins Boys and Gruber* were Dave and Steve Higgins (Steve now produces *SNL*) and Dave "Gruber" Allen, all of whom had previously toured the Midwest as Don't Quit Your Day Job. They changed the group's name to The Higgins Boys and Gruber just before meeting *Mystery Science Theater 3000*'s Joel Hodgson, who wanted to shoot a pilot for them, as he was already producing *MST3K* at The Comedy Channel.

The show slowly developed from throwing to funny shorts and TV shows to eventually concentrating on the group's own sketches. They had fake sitcoms, a children's show host, and even an entire week-long telethon (that you only saw when the show was scheduled to air, of course). Hodgson recommended the show be formatted simply, as the guys just hanging out in their own living room. "We actually recreated our living room of our old house in North Hollywood," Dave Higgins recalls.

The Comedy Channel had an open concept office on their floor with performers on the outside and writers on the inside, to get shows to share material and actors, which only happened occasionally. Though you had to be prepared. "We had several times where we're we had to take over. Somebody else's script wasn't ready for their show, so we'd go in and just ad-lib."

Mystery Science Theater 3000

If we're talking about sketch-adjacent shows, you can't discount *Mystery Science Theater 3000* as one of the great low-budget sketch-fests ever committed to television. *MST3K*'s actual mission each week was to talk or "riff" over a movie, in written but spontaneous-feeling long runs of jokes. The sketches during breaks were usually themed to the movie in question, though they also would sometimes simply dip into whatever they felt like doing, like the time they made an Ingmar Bergman style parody.

Shot in black and white, the piece features the robots Tom Servo and Crow T. Robot walking down a pier, counting the slits between the wooden planks in dreary Nordic tones. When Tom can no longer count them, he has fallen off. Crow then says, "When you're out of slits, you're out of pier." I had never seen a Schlitz beer commercial, but this was so perfectly constructed it allowed me to do the mental gymnastics to reverse-engineer that there was once a commercial with the tagline, "When you're out of Schlitz, you're out of beer."

Creator Joel Hodgson was a successful stand-up and brought people into the show from all around the Hopkins, Minnesota area to perform, write and crew for *MST3K*. Eight years in, Bill Corbett would join the cast as the new voice of Crow, as well as many of the villains of the between-riff segments. Corbett explains that the sketches were pitched on their own day, separate from the riffing. "We did the traditional writers' room, index cards on the bulletin board thing for the interstitial sketches . . . We'd have a reading of the sketches that was always fun. We would usually give each other a couple of notes, and they were almost always like, 'It's got to be shorter,' because those sketches were pretty clocked. One of the best things about them actually is that they were relatively short, and they did not have time to wear out the premise."

Corbett explains that while they had a relaxed writers' room, it was a simple process, so there was never any reason for it to be too tense. "At heart, it was like a bunch of people blurting out jokes in a movie. Somebody else had the [remote] control and would stop. Every now and then we took turns, actually just trying to record it all. I think at one point, they had hired someone to do it, but it seemed harder because it's sort of embarrassing when you blurt out a half-formed dumb premise joke and some hired temp basically has to say, 'Did you say "fart," or . . . ?'"

Random Play

VH1 got in on the sketch action in 1999 when they brought in *MADtv*'s Craig Anton, *Exit 57*'s Paul Dinello, and *The State*'s David Wain, Michael Ian Black, and Michael Showalter to write the music-themed *Random Play*. "That was just goofy goofball sketches," recalls Patton Oswalt, who also wrote on the show. "We wrote one sketch and they never shot it. It was this really badly done biopic about U2, where clearly the people who had written it had done no research on the band . . . It was so esoteric and weird, and they just didn't get it, but I thought it was one of the funniest things I've ever written . . . One of the band's biggest struggles was that The Edge had alopecia. And like, 'What do we do?' and then they give him his cowboy hat, it's just stupid."

The cast was pretty loaded, too, including Nancy Carell, Jim Gaffigan, Black and Showalter, your occasional Stephen Colbert, and Jerry Minor. "Jane [Lipsitz] was a producer, and she just wanted to put together a sketch show of a lot of the people that she'd been seeing around the alternative comedy [scene]," Minor says. There were behind-the-scenes documentaries, including a sketch where Colbert plays Dénnis Froom, a pretentious music video director. At his studio, "we take things you can see, and transform them into visual images," with help from his art director, Geöan (Andy Richter). There's a commercial for the Soft Rock Café, and a sketch where you suddenly realize how much Jim Gaffigan resembles Elton John.

Random Play is one of those rare cases where an overarching show theme somehow comes together in a series of solid sketches. Minor recalls they had quite a bit of freedom, unless you stepped on a band's toes. "'Hey, we're gonna make fun of this band.' 'No, they're gonna be on next week.'"

The Carol Burnett Show (1991)

In 1990, Carol Burnett had experimented with an anthology series, *Carol & Company*. She told the press about the experience, "Some ideas were worth seven minutes, some were worth forty . . . It was simpler just to do variety." The following year, bringing two of the *Carol & Company* cast members—Richard Kind and Meagen Fay—with her, she produced a new season of *The Carol Burnett Show*. It was directed by Paul Miller and harkened back to the original *Carol Burnett Show* with simple premises—like Burnett playing a 116-year-old woman who can't blow out the candles on her birthday cake and an extended scene with a musical number in a diner on I-90 full of Sondheim fans who all know Bernadette Peters' entire Broadway career, show-to-show.

Meagen Fay was in awe of Burnett during her time on both shows. "She had a complete working knowledge of every department and treated everyone as though they were the master of their craft. I learned that that's the way you walk onto a set. With absolute respect for everyone there. Because without them, you don't end up on television."

The show only lasted seven episodes, perhaps because it was variety instead of sketch in an era where people were declaring the variety form to be outmoded. Because it was still very much the same show she had done before, though, the quality hadn't waned. Guests included Robert Townsend, Bernadette Peters, Andrea Martin, Delta Burke, and Stephen Wright.

The Dave Thomas Comedy Show

Dave Thomas sold a sketch show to CBS. "They had no idea what to do with that show," Thomas says. The series, which Thomas co-wrote with Mike Myers, Michael Short, and others, featured famous guest stars like Martin Short, Dan Aykroyd, John Candy,

Kelly Preston, Catherine O'Hara, and Chevy Chase. The sketches could be anything from a parody of the crime drama *The Equalizer* where the main character's greatest weapon is his vocabulary, to an old-style sitcom starring Thomas in pretty good Jack Palance make-up. The sketches are bridged by Thomas on a set featuring old cars and a '50s diner, and the opening of the show featured Thomas running to set, opening doors along the way to weird semi-comic situations. He was never happy with this opening, preferring the first one they'd shot.

"I had an audience, and they were characters in the show, and I had an eighty-foot blue screen behind me, which when the curtains opened, I could project anything." He has a Ford Mustang on the stage, promising to take the audience along with him, and he appears to drive off into the California desert. We cut to an actual desert location, where he is then robbed while out on the highway, sending the robbers back a mile or so to the theater, which we can see hovering in the distance, through proscenium. Eventually, he crashes into the end of the thirty-mile-deep set, and the show continues. "Well, CBS looked at that, and then they just thought, 'This is too scary for us. We don't think our audience is going to be able to follow it' . . . and the loudest sound in the room was them scratching their heads."

Space Ghost: Coast to Coast

Another show on the sketch-adjacent end of the spectrum was Cartoon Network's first original show, starring a 1960s cartoon superhero known as Space Ghost. More than influenced by David Letterman, the fake talk show consisted of chopped up old cartoons with new voice-over and background art, and interviews with celebrities ranging from Buzz Aldrin to Björk. "It was so early in the stages of Cartoon Network, they wanted to know if people knew their stuff," says writer and voice actor Andy Merrill. "They would give us a written test on cartoon knowledge, and it had everything from matching to fill in the blank to multiple choice, an essay question." He was hired soon after taking the test, thinking he was going into programming. Instead, he'd be working on what would become the Adult Swim block, under executive VP Mike Lazzo.

The original scripts were written by Merrill, Pete Smith, Chip Duffey, and Dave Willis. "[We] would write a funny script together, and then Lazzo would come in and crap on everything. Because he would read the script four times, and the joke that he thought was funny at first, wasn't funny anymore. So we would have to rewrite it. Because Lazzo was stupid." It wasn't long before actual *Letterman* writers and established sitcom writers were sending in their scripts for *Space Ghost*. "That's when we were like, 'Wow, this is kind of cool.'"

Beakman's World

In the early '90s, the FCC required that TV stations carry a certain amount of children's programming per day, so they were always on the lookout for new stuff. Specifically, they wanted educational shows. Jok Church's comic strip *You Can with Beakman and Jax* already existed, and CBS had the rights, so writer Mark Waxman was asked to do something with it. "They put it on my desk and said, 'Create, develop, make a TV series out of this, because we're gonna go sell it fast.'" They interviewed a number of potential writers, some with science minds and some with comedy minds—and at least one with both. Bill Nye was doing the rounds as a writer as they were developing Beakman. "He was down here interviewing for other shows, and we had a brief meeting, and it was very nice. We didn't really have the budget to have a huge writing staff."

Beakman's World was designed as something that looked and felt like an MTV show, but aimed for a younger audience, and director Jay Dubin had a specific look in mind. "He knows science, and he totally gets comedy," says Paul Zaloom, who plays Beakman. "Every frame looked great; he invented the whole look, the ultra-wide-angle cameras, the cameras never moving." The cameras were placed relatively close to one another to bring the audience in. "The performers move back and forth between the two cameras. It's never been done before or since. And it gave it that unique look, and the intimacy."

"We had a rule on the set that if something went wrong, you weren't allowed to stop," Zaloom recalls. The show was tightly written, but sometimes they'd add visual gags on set, and those gags didn't always go as planned, like when they'd bring in animals. "One time the alligator or crocodile, whatever the fuck it was, it's laying there for hours and hours. And one point, it just went 'chomp,' like that, towards me. It scared the shit out of me, I screamed like a little girl, ran out of the frame." That made it into the show. *Beakman's World* was staunchly scientific and equally vaudeville, giving the stations what they were mandated to have, and kids who were maybe not so good at science a new handle on it.

Square One / Mathnet

Square One Television was conceptualized as a show to teach children mathematics through the use of sketch comedy. One of the segments, "Mathnet," was a pastiche of the police drama *Dragnet*, only all the crimes were relatively minor and required math knowledge to solve, and the cops carried calculators in their shoulder holsters. The show was originally shot during a period when most TV shows were on hiatus. This allowed them to get some big guest stars who would otherwise not be working. Beverly Leech played the no-nonsense, monotone Kate Monday, partner to the looser and slightly bumbling Joe Friday (Joe Howard) and remembers James Earl Jones playing the LAPD Police Chief on *Mathnet*. "He was royalty, and he behaved like a gracious king all the time." She also appreciated the opportunity to impress him.

"We had these big speeches, you know, all filled with math and probability. [Jones asked], 'How do you get off book like that?'" Leech would usually take the script home and do the math herself as she tried to memorize it. "I'm not able to really memorize unless I understand something," Leech says. Teaching kids complex ideas through TV necessitates a slow, methodical approach to help them understand and recall the concepts. This was a perfect opportunity to load the show with the kinds of jokes that—for those of us who needed it—also patiently taught us how to write jokes. In "The Problem of the Missing Baseball," they interview someone's neighbor:

Man: I'm not very good at finding missing baseballs.
Friday: Yes, sir.
Man: I found a missing golf ball once.
Monday: Uh huh.
Man: It was in the weeds.
Monday: Yes, sir.
Man: It was, you know, round.
Friday: Most of them are.
Man: What a day that was.

Animaniacs

Stephen Spielberg wanted to get into cartoons, which originally led to *Tiny Toon Adventures*, the success of which meant he wanted to make another cartoon show, this time with headlining characters. "With *Tiny Toons*, we had network people breathing down our necks and giving us notes," recalls *Animaniacs* creator Tom Ruegger. "By now we had a hit under our belt, and Stephen said, 'Let these guys do what they do.' Stephen then went to Europe and made *Schindler's List*, while we're over here, making zany comedy. And so we had literally no one watching us." The Warner Brothers, Yakko and Wakko, and the Warner Sister, Dot, were a Marx Brothers for a new generation, each show featuring the lead characters in their main story, along with other shorts like the world-dominating mice Pinky and the Brain and the *Goodfellas* parody starring pigeons, "Goodfeathers."

Animaniacs wasn't afraid to push stuff they knew would go over a kid's head just enough so that a parent could appreciate it. In one piece where Yakko is investigating as a PI, he asks Dot to dust for fingerprints. After a couple jokes, she comes back in, carrying the musician Prince. "No, no, fingerprints!" Yakko yells. The original script left it there, but Dot saying "I don't think so" almost pushes it over the edge, though standards and practices somehow let it go. They may not have had a choice, though. "They would say, 'Hey, we don't like this bit that you're doing, we don't like you using this word,'" Ruegger recalls. The rebuttal was always easy. "'Ohh . . . Stephen *loves* that. That's his favorite thing in the show.' It was like gold. And of course, Stephen's in Bulgaria, shooting a movie. We have pictures of him looking at 'Pinky and the Brain' storyboards on the set of *Schindler's List*."

Muppets Tonight

In 1996, The Muppets were going to be revived for prime time, in much the same format as *The Muppet Show* of the '70s: a variety show starring puppets with a celebrity guest each week. The show started on ABC, but after thirteen episodes, it didn't perform well enough. It was then picked up by the namesake cable network of ABC's new corporate owners, Disney. Patric Verrone had just come from writing on *The Critic*, and wrote on *Muppets Tonight* for both seasons. "What The Disney Channel people didn't realize when they greenlit it was, this was an expensive show . . . With this kind of program, you had to build sets for every episode, you had to re-costume every episode, and you could work well into golden time."[2] Furthermore, the

---

[2] After sixteen hours of work, union employees are then paid their eight-hour day rate every hour—this is "golden time."

guests were huge, which could affect costs depending on how much potential they had to slow things down.

One stand out guest, in terms of notoriety and final product, was The Artist Formerly Known as Prince. "We were told he was going to be on the show. We were also told, 'No one talks to him. No one looks at him.'" No autograph requests, etc. All material had to be cleared in advance because they had only one day to shoot with him, as opposed to guests like Martin Short, who showed up for the whole process to write with former *SCTV* cohorts Dick Blasucci and Paul Flaherty. On top of this, Prince had recently experienced a never-publicized, traumatic personal event. "So we get word that not only is Prince his normal, difficult self, but he's also going through a genuine tragedy . . . He was a showman." He could shut it on and off with ease. "When the time came, this guy could do it. He pulled no punches." This ended up being the episode that won them an Emmy, even if they were now up against kids' shows instead of *Letterman*.

"They said, 'Spend whatever you have to make His Purpleness feel comfortable' . . . So this $2 million 'children's program' [is] up against 'Linda Ellerbee Talks About Divorce' and a couple of $10,000-per-episode Nickelodeon live action shows." They tied for the Emmy that year. With a different Linda Ellerbee special.

On the Television

After writing on *Pee-Wee's Playhouse*, George McGrath was asked to write for and star in a show called *The Do-it-Yourself Sitcom Search* for Nickelodeon, where viewers would submit their ideas and Nickelodeon would shoot their pilots at their homes and jobs (Viacom again). After this, he was offered a pilot, which became *On the Television*, essentially a parody of the movie review show *At the Movies*, hosted by Siskel and Ebert. This framing device allows the sketches to be thrown to easily, with some easy-to-shoot dialogue to fill in any gaps.

"It was a fantastic time for me because I got to give so many people their Writers Guild memberships," says McGrath. He brought in Groundlings and other folks he knew to write and act on his show, putting on sketches based on characters they had developed at the theater, and some brand-new ones for the show. "Torty" is a Lassie-like show about a boy and his tortoise who can very slowly get help if something life-threatening happens. "Tobacco" is a parody of the glut of prime-time soaps in the '80s, only this one is produced by big tobacco to get around the ban on TV advertising.

"The sad part of it was the misuse of our budget. I was the co-executive producer, but no idea about the money side of anything. I was writing it, I was starring in it, I was casting it. So when that happened, it was so scammy." They shot thirty-nine episodes of *On the Television*, but money management ended up being a problem. For cheap-to-produce shows, disappearing money was not an uncommon problem.

The Newz

If you think a daily sketch show wouldn't have legs, you'd be both right and wrong. *The Newz* ran from 1994 to 1995, and featured future *Whose Line* star Brad Sherwood. "It was singularly one of the most fun, creative sketch times of my life. I was writing stuff for that show, I had really great relationships with a bunch of writers, so I would go in all the time—I lived and breathed it." While it was called *The Newz*, there was no anchor desk or journalist characters or news satire framing the show. The only news satire was in the segment "Top Story News." It was straight sketch throughout, in bright, early-'90s colors and a lot of big sketch acting energy to support pieces like "Dead Girl" (a show about a corpse), and a commercial for 1-800-HARRASS [sic], a special phone plan for social monsters to save money when they call up people and make their lives hell.

The show did well enough in first-run syndication that the production company wanted more, but they never got them. "After we had done, like, sixty shows, Columbia TriStar and the studio loved it so much . . . they were going to pay for more episodes, give us more money per episode, but they needed an accounting." In fact, the producers owed Columbia TriStar thirty more episodes. "Two of the executive producers were embezzling money from the production. They thought this was a one-time cash grab." Around $600,000 went missing, and the actors ended up being owed at least $21,000 apiece.

EPILOGUE

"Everyone can act. Everyone can improvise. Anyone who wishes to can play in the theater and learn to become stageworthy."

—*Viola Spolin, Improvisation for the Theater*

Viola Spolin's words can easily be expanded to include comedy; they've already been used for decades to make it. Interestingly, you'll find that many professional, successful comedians feel that "you can't teach funny," but, in fact, that happens all the time. Some comedians forget that before they could ever get a laugh, they were learning why and when to laugh by watching what their parents laughed at. Extrapolate from there and some people figure out the math of comedy. Skip a few, and you've got someone who was "born funny," rather than someone who busted their ass to be hilarious, legitimately earning those laughs. "Talent" belies hard-earned skill.

The sketch comedy of the '90s was—whether by the sheer math of it, or coincidence, or subconscious effort—a perfect opportunity for future sketch comedians to learn that sketch was the thing they wanted to spend their time making. It was a saturation point that meant we had seemingly unending examples at our fingertips, as long as we were at home when it aired or knew how to program a VCR. The World Wide Web had been invented in 1989, and by 1999, high speed internet was starting to spread, so it was only a matter of time that the people raised on sketch TV would have a publishing platform for the stuff they were putting together at home.

The promise of the internet was supposed to be informational equality—a digital community—and for creative people it was a place to put your dumb sketches, usually on your own website, or emailing it around; this was just before the term "viral" had come to mean what it means now. For some comedians the internet was a relatively level playing field, for a while, where you could post funny stuff alongside everyone else on new publishing platforms and have the same (low) chance of being found as those people. Inevitably voting, ratings and comments entered the game when people running these websites discovered that "engagement" (convincing people they need to opine on everything) means people staying on your site for as long as possible. For a while there, it was pure, if not a way to make a living.

Notwithstanding the impact of *Chappelle's Show*, there was something of a sketch comedy drought in the 2000s. While for decades, sketch and variety were the cheapest forms of entertainment TV to produce, with *COPS* and *The Real World* proving to be moneymakers, reality TV shows rapidly took over as the go-to cheap productions for networks. Rob Cohen has a stock answer when he's asked by executives what the greatest sketch shows of all time are: *Monty Python* and *SCTV*. Half of them, he says, haven't heard of *SCTV*, and their awareness of Python as a group doesn't always translate to knowing any of their sketches. "There's a huge gap, because in the 2000s and beyond, sketch went away for so long, that a younger person may not even have a frame of reference of any sketch show. It's this weird thing that pops up, it goes away, it pops up, it goes away. Lately, it's been going away more than it's been popping up. So I think if somebody remembers the '70s, or the '80s, or the '90s, that was the golden era of sketch."

The reason for this drop-off, along with the increase in reality programming, may well be another perfect confluence of events. I uploaded my first comedy video to the internet in 2000 or 2001, but I didn't have a platform that made it easy to find. The Lonely Island, consisting of Akiva Schaffer, Jorma Taccone, and Andy Samberg, started at the same time with the same limitations, and just four years later they found themselves as the first internet-originating performers to work at *SNL*. Shortly thereafter, some cupcakes may have changed how we get our entertainment, as everyone started heading to the magical new video sharing platform where they could be found.

The internet had its share of videos that went viral (not in the numbers we'd associate with that term today) before December 2005, but none of them hit the way "Lazy Sunday" did. YouTube officially launched on December 15, 2005, and The Lonely Island premiered their video featuring Chris Parnell and Andy Samberg rapping about seeing *The Chronicles of Narnia* at the movies and eating cupcakes two days later on *SNL*. "Akiva, Andy, and Jorma were already making videos before they got on the show, and they knew what they were doing," recalls Chris Parnell, who also co-wrote "Lazy Sunday." "I think Jorma made the track, and we just recorded it in their office."

"We just went out one afternoon and shot it all, because they knew how to do that already. So we were able to do it pretty quickly." The video aired and was well-received by the studio audience and, soon enough, *SNL* would finally amble into the digital age. "We were kind joking about 'We're gonna be huge. It's gonna blow up.' But I don't think anybody really believed that. 'That would be fun, but I don't actually think that's gonna happen.' But then it did." Parnell and the Lonely Island guys were interviewed by the *New York Times*, and Samberg was getting recognized much more all of a sudden.

SNL did not have a presence on YouTube yet, because the site was young, but bootlegs did start appearing on the site shortly after it aired, getting about seven million views. A year later, after things snowballed, YouTube was bought by Google for $1.65 billion. Because NBC had the clips pulled from YouTube, and because people persisted on uploading old shit they loved, as well as their own crap, corporations were paying attention to the internet as a place to put your creative works and give them a worldwide audience. Eventually, of course, it all became called "content" (which might seem a small price to pay for legitimizing internet sketch comedy in the eyes of commerce, but please stop calling it that), and the possibility of getting paid for your work, or "monetizing it," suddenly became a reality for some people. Since then, there's also been a change in the type of comedy people put out.

"I also think something happened in the 2000s into the 2010s," says Adam McKay. "Where America shifted so hard towards this corporatist point of view, or countering the corporatist point of view, the extreme right." He recalls a visit to Yale a couple of decades ago, in the late '90s or early 2000s. He got invited to visit the *Yale Record*, their humor magazine. "They were really wonderful people, very smart. But I noticed: these are the winners. There was no anger in what they were doing at all. It was all references to shows they had watched as kids being recycled and twisted." He dug in to see what kind of subversive stuff they were getting up to—after all, McKay and the UCB had taken over Navy Pier when it opened and almost got arrested—and he was met with confusion.

"All the places you're making the stuff at have been corporatized more, they've been taken over by Wall Street more. All of the incentives have changed, or culture; I mean, your very identity now can be identified as a 'brand.' The way you carry yourself has an economy to it. So I do think that played a part in it. I really do."

Skye Townsend, who joined *A Black Lady Sketch Show* in season 2, has been doing comedy since this shift, but her priority is the actual comedy she produces. "When I joined the show, I was like, 'I need to make it clear that I love this,'" Townsend says. "I need you to understand that I'm not just going to come in and do a mediocre voice, and then tell you how many followers I have. I'm not entertained by anything subpar, and so I think sketch is in a weird place, because a lot of people are getting by by being mediocre if they have numbers."

As cameras have shrunk to be pocket-sized and smaller, the ability to make a professional sketch show look like a million bucks has become increasingly easier. There were some awkward middle years, where otherwise groundbreaking shows (in terms of representation and visibility) like *Big Gay Sketch Show* came about, looking a little old-school but still introducing the world to Kate McKinnon. Pre-taped sketch shows in HD as a standard could mean that the entire perception of sketch comedy will either one day change to be "sketch comedy must look sexy," or the sexy look will, instead, eventually be perceived as the boring old way to do sketch. Early on, though, this technology did find its way into the hands of the right people at the right time, and suddenly a generation of internet filmmakers were making the best sketches on TV.

"I was drawn to sketches that were more like short films and [that] sort of removed the artifice of proscenium and doing it live," says *Key & Peele* director Peter Atencio. Every sketch of every episode of *Key & Peele* looks like a movie, many of them genre parodies and pastiche, and the show's stars, fresh off the heels of *MADtv*, suddenly had a sandbox to play in that didn't condemn them to the harsh overhead lights and playing to the back of the room that came with standard-issue TV sketch. "I'd done a web series pilot for MySpace with [Keegan-Michael Key]." This led to him being interviewed as a potential director for the new series. "I was like, 'I've always wanted to do a show where it's sketch comedy, but we make it as cinematic as possible, and we tailor the look and the feel to the sketch and what the game of the scene is. I want it to feel like it's the funniest set piece of a movie, and we've just lifted it out and presented to you.'"

Both Key and Peele loved his pitch, but Comedy Central didn't like Atencio's lack of credits. The director they hired, though, wasn't feeling this concept, and soon dropped out, giving the 28-year-old Atencio an opportunity to prove himself. As he did, he made it clear that some sketches should be letterboxed and that none of them should have laughs over them. "Comedy Central was like, 'No way.

You can't do that. We'll get so many calls from people in the Midwest with their [non-widescreen] televisions.'" He negotiated for a few such sketches and got them, and then eventually, down the line, there was no limit on how many they could do.

As for laughter, even the show's stars were used to hearing that on sketch shows. "I was adamant from the beginning, no laughs on sketches. It totally breaks the immersion. That was pretty unheard of on television at the time; I was coming out of the world of You-Tube and what was happening on sketch comedy [there]. There were so many people doing groundbreaking things on YouTube at that time, so to me, why would we have people laughing over the sketch? That just felt offensive to me."

They cut two versions of the pilot: with laughs and without. "When they saw it without, I remember Jordan was really the first one who was like, 'Oh, this is—no, yeah, we can't have laughs over these sketches. It would be totally wrong.'" They cut with and without versions of every episode that first season, and forward-thinking heads prevailed two weeks before the premiere. Comedy Central tried for laughter again for season two, but no dice. By season three, there were no more requests for it.

Later in 2012, *Comedy Bang! Bang!* took the cinematic approach and applied it to an entire satirical talk show, and the following year *Inside Amy Schumer* premiered, using it much to the same effect as *Key & Peele*. *A Black Lady Sketch Show* uses the cinema look to its full potential, while also realizing the dream of a female-led sketch series, inviting everyone in because of its specificity; it isn't written for me, but it allows me in, nonetheless. It also might be the most rigorous pre-production process in sketch. "We audition for every single part in the entire script," Skye Townsend explains. "We have a week to prepare 150 characters. From that, we audition against each other in the room." It's all about the character choices that stand out. "Almost every character I've ever wanted out of maybe over 500 now, I've booked, because I had to make a bold enough choice to where everybody goes, 'That was hers. Give it to her.'"

The other end of the spectrum, then, is that if your show is written to sound like a nine-year-old wrote some of your dialogue, like in *I Think You Should Leave*, making your show look nice helps sell the absurdity of it even more. Adding the cinematic layer is just another opportunity of grounding something to reality so that the dialogue, situations, and the facial expressions of Tim Robinson can properly threaten to untether you. *Drunk History* is the sketch-adjacent version of the same concept; in this case, the cinema look oversells the historical importance of the story, as drunken blather comes out of sober faces in period wigs.

Sketch comedy is still cheap to produce, or production companies wouldn't be making it, but as networks are more apt to put money into reality shows on one end and prestige stuff on the other, sketch mostly gets lost in the shuffle. It continues to thrive online, and with short-short-form bits on TikTok serving as proto-sketches, you can see the potential for sketch to stick around as a form. It's not clear if networks have any interest in trying to compete with or copy the success of *SNL* anymore and, if you're talking about the progression of the concept of the sketch, a few well-written seasons from a tight-knit established group is the way to go anyway—those groups always have more to say. There's also still the potential to widen audiences, representation, and tastes, which increases the likelihood of more diverse sketch in the future (someone should give The 1491s their own show, for a start).

The person I spoke with for this book who might have been the most vocal in his love of sketch was Bob Odenkirk. "I'm super proud of all the different shows I got to work on, and I love sketch comedy," he says. Odenkirk worked on, in various capacities, five (and change) of the shows that I wrote chapters on, plus a few others that didn't make it in. "You know, some part of me wants to do it again. Like right now. You know, I'll just always love it . . . There's things that a feature film can do that a series can't do. There's things that a series can do that a feature film can't do. But I honestly think that to me sketch comedy gets to the heart of humanity, almost more than any other thing."

Not by rule, but by nature, sketch comedy is communal. You find a group, you make friends, and maybe you make a show together. The other community aspect comes from the level of obsession that almost every show I've written about has inspired. Even for some of these rarely-seen one-offs, there's a person or two who hasn't gotten this show out of their head since they first saw it and has been waiting for someone to digitize it. Among those are usually a few comedians, specifically the kind who use sketches to find like minds or to communicate with their fellow obsessives in the form of relentless quoting, which might eventually turn into creatively stealing from ones heroes, as it often does. Laughter is universal, but sketch inspires a very specific dialect of laugh, because it's not about the personality of the performers like stand up, and it's not about the depth of the story like a film or a play. Sketch comedy is a sublimely impatient expression of an idea, an unnecessary expansion on the tiniest thought, and so incredibly specific to someone else that we have no choice but to listen.

AUTHOR'S NOTES

The Shows That Aren't in Here

Decisions had to be made. As a lover of sketch comedy, some of these decisions were not ideal. There were instances where a show had the skill but not the impact. In some cases, not being able to interview the stars or primary writers from a show combined with having no contemporary sources to pull from. If those people reach out between this edition and the next, some of these could change, and some of "the rest" might be expanded upon.

A good chunk of my interviews on some of these shows could fill their own books, and the impact of most of them is obvious, as they tend to have engaged fan bases online, even still. Kids' shows are maybe the biggest problem in this whole proposed scenario of "let's talk about every sketch show," because most kids' shows are, by their nature, filled with self-contained bits that qualify as sketch. For that reason, I covered the ones I knew I could get people to talk about.

Here's a list of some of the shows and subjects I couldn't fit into the book, many worth digging into, at least for research purposes. I spoke with some folks about elements of these, but they just didn't make the cut.

Studio 59 (aka Into the Night)
Howie Mandel's Sunny Skies
Small Doses
Histeria
Townsend Television
The Chris Rock Show
The Apollo Comedy Hour
Sunday Comics

This Just In
Saturday Night Special
The Jenny McCarthy Show
Big Bag
Haywire
Tompkins Square
Morton and Hayes (a show about fictional sketch comics)

The Martin Short Show (a sitcom about a sketch actor that also featured actual sketches)
The Martin Short Show (a talk show with sketches)
You Can't Do That on Television
The Amanda Show
The Mickey Mouse Club
The Weird Al Show
Bill Nye the Science Guy
TV (yes, that was the name of it)

Madness on Our Tongues (a sketch pilot script by Sean Sullivan and Paul Feig)
The Guys Next Door
Random Acts of Comedy (a game show with improvised bits)
The ½ Hour Comedy Hour
Night after Night with Allan Havey
Red Green
The ACME Comedy Theatre
The Canadian Alt Comedy Scene

A Few More Things

- The one '90s sketch show I wanted to, but couldn't write about in this book (since it's a British one) was *A Bit of Fry & Laurie*, which is to me the perfect TV sketch show. It's Hugh Laurie and Stephen Fry at their best, and you should seek it out.

- I will not apologize for the reference to "MacArthur Park" earlier in this book.

- There's a non-existent *SNL* sketch that deserves discussion. It is talked about in Jordan Peele's *NOPE*, concerning the fictional sitcom "Gordy's Home," that ended in a chimpanzee massacring the cast. Steven Yeun plays Ricky 'Jupe' Park, telling the story of the time *SNL* turned the events into a sketch, with too much reverence for how good Chris Kattan is as the chimp, Gordy. It references a real 1997 episode, hosted by Scott Wolf (in which, incidentally, Jim Wise got a sketch on the air), and it's a wonderful scene inside a fantastic movie.

- I am not the person to be commenting on certain things in any depth, since any kind of race face can't affect me the way it affects people of color, but I wanted to address the fact that almost every show I covered has done it in some form. Intention doesn't excuse it, even if you explain it by saying you were being ironic (you're still perpetuating the stereotype, regardless). Just because your intentions *weren't bad* doesn't mean your intentions *were good*, either, or well thought out. *We're making fun of racists!* Is a convenient way to get around having to think through your ill-conceived idea, even if it comes from a genuine place. I've only ever heard one person from any sketch show thoughtfully address their own participation in such a scene: the brilliant Paul F. Tompkins, discussing *Mr. Show*'s "Five Voices" sketch, on his podcast, *Stay F. Homekins.*

"We're all playing these broad stereotype characters, and I am like a Japanese businessman. I'm in a suit, I have a briefcase on my lap, and I'm in a wig, and like, Asian makeup . . . and I did like an accent and stuff." These broad characters end up becoming the four voices that guide us all, according to a doctor, played by Cross. Another doctor, played by Odenkirk, has written his own treatise on the subject, wherein Cross is the fifth voice, the False Doctor Voice. Cross' doctor then calls Odenkirk's voice that of "Doctor Jealousy," the voice that tries to undermine the system. "Let me tell you something. I forgot that I did that. I forgot that that ever happened," Tompkins says.

"We were an all-White writers' room, pretty much all-White production staff. There was no one in that building who would have felt empowered to say, 'Hey, maybe get an Asian actor to play this Asian part.'" No one is lining up to justify these few bits in an otherwise stellar series of shows, but for his part, Tompkins makes a heartfelt apology on the podcast. "I will say this on the record: I'm sorry that I did that. I wish I hadn't done it. And I apologize to anyone who sees that now. Whether they're offended by it or not, I apologize. It's wild to me that there was no one there to check us. We didn't think twice about it."

- A LOT of these shows are hard to find in order to watch them. Most haven't been released on DVD, and the ones you'll find on major video sharing sites are usually of low quality. They're worth checking out for your own research, but don't discount archive. org as a repository of fewer, if higher-quality, copies of some of these shows (sometimes with fun old commercials).

- I interviewed around 150 people for this book, and a few of those people's stories did end up cut from the book for space and consideration of the overall theme of the book, so as not to distract from any narrative within their respective chapters. However, each and every interview did aid me in my research and in firming up each show's history.

- Mike Sweeney once roasted Dan Gomiller and me for wearing second-hand suits in the audience of *Late Night with Conan O'Brien* and it is one of our great shared memories. It was Andy's last regular show, with Scott Thompson as one of the guests, and we also got in trouble for holding up handmade signs.

- The following books are great primers on some of the shows discussed in this book:

  o *Almost Live!: The Show That Wouldn't Die* by Bryan Robert Johnston

  o *Mr. Show: What Happened?* by Naomi Odenkirk

  o *Hollywood Said No!* by Bob Odenkirk & David Cross with Brian Posehn

  o *The Kids in the Hall: One Dumb Guy* by Paul Myers

  o *Homey Don't Play That!: The Story of In Living Color and the Black Comedy Revolution* by David Peisner

  o *The Union of The State* by Corey Stulce

- There are two great comedy documentaries about two of these shows:

  o *Kids in the Hall: Comedy Punks*

  o *Too Funny to Fail: The Life & Death of The Dana Carvey Show*

ACKNOWLEDGMENTS

This book would have been impossible to complete without the help of some people I've known for a very long time, some folks I've only met recently, and some people who, for whatever reason, continue to do me favor upon favor with no request for reciprocation.

Thank you to Jen for her never-ending support and for editing everything else I write. Thank you to Daisy for being the best cat and for being my writing companion for this entire book.

Thanks to Brooke Williams for her immense research help and for turning me onto *Almost Live!* Geoffrey Golden mistakenly assumed I knew what a Bert Fershner was and blew my research wide open. To Patric Verrone, immense thanks for connecting me to the entire world of television writing. Thank you to Tavie Philips for her help in getting Bruce McCulloch to agree to an interview (Tavie's name rhymes with gravy).

Bermuda Schwartz suggested I speak with his publisher, and changed my life for the second time. Thank you to Matthew Chojnacki at 1984 Publishing for his constant support and willingness to check in with me and help me hone this idea. Adam Koford's amazing artwork adorns this book's cover, and that is an honor.

Thank you to Ren and Dan, my sister and brother, for making me worship comedy because they are unendingly funny, and for their support while I wrote this book. Thank you to the late Mike Shaver for making me obsessed with *Wayne's World*—I got to talk to WAYNE, Mike!

Thank you to Ari for her support, and for being an unfailing sounding board and benefit to the reading minds of Boise. Thank you to three dorks known as Thaddeus Scott, Lauren Weston and Thom Turner for their kind support; special thanks to Lauren for amazing sourdough bread.

Without Mike Worden, I couldn't have produced the first four years of *Comedy on Vinyl*, which means this book wouldn't have ever happened; without Dan Schlissel, the show never would've sounded good. Without Mike Preister, I wouldn't have been able to interview many of these folks in the first place.

Thank you to Joshua Bermont and Kelly Hager for their friendship and passwords, I mean research help. Allen Rueckert, as always, was an amazing sounding board and font of genuine enthusiasm, and a connection to the world of The Smothers Brothers. Thank you to Paul F. Tompkins and Janie Haddad-Tompkins for allowing the use of some words from their podcast *Stay F. Homekins.*

For their guidance and mentorship that continues to this day, great thanks to Barb Capozzola, Ron Perry, Mark Rathbun and all of Upward Bound in Hartwick, New York, as well as the late Mike Newell, Fielding Dawson, and Karen Rollins—the three people who made me realize I could write.

Dad, thank you for borrowing the camera from work so we could make sketches back in 1994, and thanks to you and Steph for the support as I wrote this book. Mom, hi.

Thank you to Will Harris, CK Mendax, Calli Nelson, Erica Canela, Betsy Sherman, Jude McCulley, Leslie Guenther, Jenn O'Chall, and Shelby Cies for their support over the years.

Hi again, mom, I just wanted to make you sweat. Thanks for introducing me to good comedy when I was young, much of it when I was far too young. You laughed way too hard at Dana Carvey's fake nipples.

To B.J. Defrane-Smith, you've helped more than you know, and I'll always be thankful for that.

Thanks to Hilary Swett, The Writers Guild Foundation, Aretha Sills, Dave Rath and Dan Gomiller for research materials.

Thank you to Matt Besser, Paul Bellini, Paul Chepikian, Joey Garfield, Josh Lewis, Ross Shafer, Peter Atencio, Sheila Lawrence, Tom Stern, Beverly Leech, Scott Dikkers, Derek Waters, Dick Chudnow, Steve Spishak and Laura Milligan for providing photos for use in this book. Thanks to Taylor Jessen for scanning some of these photos.

Thanks very much to Scott Dikkers for digitizing the two pilot episodes of *The Onion's Comedy Castaways* and putting them online.

Thank you to all of my interviewees for your massive contributions to this book and your fantastic conversations: Jamie Alcroft, Kevin Allison, Kent Alterman, Peter Atencio, Scott Aukerman, Chris Ballew, David Bar Katz, Dan Berrett, Matt Besser, Mary Birdsong, Wayne Brady, Julie Brown, Kevin "Dotcom" Brown, Carol Burnett, Blaine Capatch, Cindy Caponera, Pat Cashman, Paul Chepikian, Bill Chott, Dick Chudnow, Graham Clark, Rob Cohen, Janet Coleman, Tracey Conway, Bill Corbett, Stephanie Courtney, David Cross, Seán Cullen, Tommy Davidson, Scott Dikkers, Paul Dooley, Kevin Dorff, Brandon Dziengielewski, Rob Edwards, Meagen Fay, Diane Flacks, Jake Fogelnest, John Fortenberry, Rich Fulcher, Kurt Fuller, Joe Furey, Joey Garfield, Paul Germain, Mitchell Gold, Matt Gourley, Allan Graf, T. Faye Griffin, Joe Guppy, Nancy Guppy, Charna Halpern, Becky Hartman Edwards, Bill Hayes, Marc Hershon, Mark Hervey, Doug Herzog, Gregg Heschong, David Anthony Higgins, Will Hines, Jessica Holmes, Todd Holoubek, Ken Hudson Campbell, Saul Ilson, Anne-Marie Johnson, Keith Johnstone, Jeff Kahn, John Keister, Kerri Kenney-Silver, David Koechner, Jay Kogen, Jeremy Kushnier, Phil Lamarr, Sheila R Lawrence, Bruce Leddy, Beverly Leech, Marty Lester, Jay Levey, Debbie Liebling, John Lloyd, Allaudin Mathieu, Bruce McCulloch, George McGrath, Adam Mckay, Nick McKinney, Andy Merrill, Paul Miller, Troy Miller,

Laura Milligan, Jerry Minor, Andrew Moskos, Mike Myers, Paul Myers, Alan Myerson, Mick Napier, Kevin Nealon, Bob Nelson, Tracy Newman, Bill Odenkirk, Bob Odenkirk, Patton Oswalt, Rick Overton, Brett Paesel, Stuart Pankin, Nicole Parker, Chris Parnell, Brian Posehn, Dave Rath, Tamara Rawitt, Ian Roberts, Mike Rock, Alan Ruck, Tom Ruegger, Salli Saffioti, Don Scardino, Eban Schletter, Ross Shafer, Marc Shaiman, Jim Sharp, Rita Sheffield Hester, Brad Sherwood, Noah Shopsowitz, Brian Shortall, Aretha Sills, Robert Smigel, Penelope Spheeris, Steve Spishak, Brian Stack, Tom Stern, Sean Sullivan, Mark Sweeney, Mike Sweeney, Hilary Swett, Chris Tallman, Danny Tamberelli, Deborah Theaker, Dave Thomas, Scott Thompson, Skye Townsend, Patric Verrone, David Wain, Mary Walsh, Marsha Warfield, Derek Waters, Mark Waxman, Marlene Weisman, April Winchell, Alex Winter, Jim Wise, Steve Young and Paul Zaloom.

IMAGE CREDITS

Photo plate 12 (bottom) – Al Levine (photographer) / © NBC / Courtesy: Everett Collection

Photo plate 13 (all images) – © Paramount / Courtesy: Everett Collection

Photo plate 14 (top) – © NBC / Courtesy: Everett Collection

Photo plate 14 (bottom) – Stephen Danelian (photographer) / TV Guide / © NBC / Courtesy: Everett Collection

Photo plate 15 (top left and bottom) – © Fox / Courtesy: Everett Collection

Photo plate 15 (top right) – Michael Lavine (photographer) / © Fox Television / Courtesy: Everett Collection

Photo plate 16 (top and center) – © 20th Century Fox / Courtesy: Everett Collection

Photo plate 16 (bottom) – © Warner Bros. Television / Courtesy: Everett Collection

Photo plate 17 (top) – Bonnie Schiffman (photographer) / © HBO / Courtesy: Everett Collection

Photo plate 17 (center and bottom) – © Brillstein-Grey Entertainment / Courtesy: Everett Collection

Photo plate 18 (all images) – © Brillstein-Grey Entertainment / Courtesy: Everett Collection

Photo plate 19 (top) – Courtesy: Josh Lewis

Photo plate 19 (center) – Frank Micelotta (photographer) / © Comedy Central / Courtesy: Everett Collection

Photo plate 19 (bottom) – © Comedy Central / Courtesy: Everett Collection

Photo plates 20 and **21** (all images) – *Upright Citizens Brigade* is © Comedy Central / Courtesy: Matt Besser

Photo plate 22 (all images) – *The Idiot Box* is © MTV / Courtesy: Tom Stern

Photo plate 23 (top) – Courtesy: Paul Chepikian

Photo plate 23 (bottom) – Nickelodeon is © Paramount / Courtesy: Sheila R. Lawrence

Photo plate 24 (all images) – *Key & Peele* is © Comedy Central / Courtesy: Peter Atencio

ABOUT THE AUTHOR

J ason Klamm is a comedian, filmmaker and voice actor. He co-
hosts the *Dan and Jay's Comedy Hour* podcast and formerly hosted
the *Comedy on Vinyl* podcast; he also founded the StolenDress Podcast Network. He directed the feature documentary *Lords of Soaptown*,
the mockumentary *Looking Forward*, and one of the world's earliest
viral videos. He is a founding member of the worldwide hit stage
show "A Drinking Game," and has been making sketch comedy
with his best friend, Dan Gomiller, for thirty years as Dan and Jay's
Comedy Hour. Jason lives in the Metro Detroit area of Michigan with
his wife, Jen, and their cat, Daisy.

THIS PAGE UNINTENTIONALLY LEFT BLANK

We let Curt go because he failed to put something on this page.

We even gave him a blank pink slip to make a point.

But it wasn't hand-delivered, and it was an unclear gesture, at best.

So Curt just came in to work the next day with more questions.

We didn't have the guts to let him go in person.

My job is to fill these pages on the rare occasion Curt makes this mistake again.

— *Champlain Margiturd*